Batsford Chess Library

Tactics in the French

GENNADY NESIS with
Professor Igor Blekhtsin

Translated by Malcolm Gesthuysen

An Owl Book
Henry Holt and Company
New York

Henry Holt and Company, Inc.
Publishers since 1866
115 West 18th Street
New York, New York 10011

Henry Holt® is a registered
trademark of Henry Holt and Company, Inc.

First published in the United States in 1994 by
Henry Holt and Company, Inc.
Originally published in Great Britain in 1993 by
B. T. Batsford Ltd.

Library of Congress Catalog Card Number: 93-80836

ISBN 0-8050-3279-7 (An Owl Book: pbk.)

First American Edition—1994

Printed in the United Kingdom
All first editions are printed on acid-free paper. ∞

10 9 8 7 6 5 4 3 2 1

Adviser: R. D. Keene, GM, OBE
Technical Editor: Andrew Kinsman

Contents

Introduction 9

Part One – Tactical Features of the Main Variations of the French Defence 11
I Chigorin Variation and King's Indian Attack
II Exchange Variation
III Advance Variation
IV Rubinstein Variation
V Classical Variation
VI Winawer Variation
VII Tarrasch Variation

Part Two – Particular Tactical Methods 29
1 Enticement 29
Game No. 1 – **Yanovsky–Kindermann,** *Biel 1991*
Game No. 2 – **J. Polgar–L. B. Hansen,** *Vejstrup 1989*
Game No. 3 – **Reshevsky–Vaganian,** *Skopje 1976*
Game No. 4 – **Spasov–Imocha,** *Tunja 1989*
Game No. 5 – **Enders–Uhlmann,** *Gothenburg 1985*

2 Deflection 43
Game No. 6 – **Ivell–Beliavsky,** *London 1985*
Game No. 7 – **Smyslov–Ståhlberg,** *Zürich 1953*

Game No. 8 – **Chandler–Psakhis,** *Moscow 1990*
Game No. 9 – **Hazai–Uhlmann,** *Halle 1981*

3 Eliminating the Defence and Liquidating the Enemy King's Pawn Cover 55
Game No. 10 – **Karpov–Speelman,** *Reykjavik 1991*
Game No. 11 – **Nezhmetdinov–A. Chistyakov,** *Kharkov 1956*
Game No. 12 – **Kupreichik–Farago,** *Polanica Zdroj 1981*
Game No. 13 – **Kruppa–Komarov,** *Kherson 1991*
Game No. 14 – **Timman–Vaganian,** *Montpellier 1985*
Game No. 15 – **Godena–Bareev,** *Aosta 1989*

4 Clearing and Opening Lines or Squares 76
Game No. 16 – **Nimzowitsch–Salwe,** *Carlsbad 1911*
Game No. 17 – **Afek–Psakhis,** *Israel 1990*
Game No. 18 – **Boleslavsky–Ufimtsev,** *Moscow 1944*
Game No. 19 – **Spielmann–L'Hermet,** *Magdeburg 1927*
Game No. 20 – **Fischer–Kovacevic,** *Rovinj/Zagreb 1970*

5 The Positional Exchange Sacrifice 92
Game No. 21 – **Ljubojevic–Vaganian,** *Belgrade 1974*
Game No. 22 – **Frolov–Ulybin,** *Dimitrovgrad 1988*
Game No. 23 – **Armas–Komarov,** *Bad Mergentheim 1989*

6 Counter–Attack and Counterpunch 100

Game No. 24 – **Kir. Georgiev–Dolmatov,** *Moscow 1990*

Game No. 25 – **Lukin–Cherepkov,** *Leningrad 1983*

Game No. 26 – **Fischer–Tal,** *Leipzig Ol. 1960*

Game No. 27 – **Karpov–Korchnoi,** *12th match game, Moscow 1974*

Game No. 28 – **Kramnik–Ulybin,** *USSR Ch., Moscow 1991*

7 Interference and Isolation 115

Game No. 29 – **Euwe–Maróczy,** *6th match game, Bad Aussee 1921*

Game No. 30 – **Duras–Spielmann,** *Piestany 1912*

Game No. 31 – **Rachels–Penkalski,** *USA 1991*

8 Combinations of the Theme of the Pin 128

Game 32 – **Timman–Yusupov,** *4th match game, Tilburg 1986*

Game 33 – **G. Timoshenko–Styrenkov,** *Budapest 1991*

Game 34 – **R. Rodriguez–Yusupov,** *Thessaloniki Ol. 1988*

9 The Back Rank 139

Game No. 35 – **Capablanca–Alekhine,** *1st game, World Ch., Buenos Aires 1927*

Game No. 36 – **A. Sokolov–Yusupov,** *3rd match game, Riga 1986*

Game No. 37 – **Smyslov–Botvinnik,** *9th game, World Ch., Moscow 1954*

10 The Intermediate Move 149
Game No. 38 – **Fischer–R. Byrne,** *USA Ch., New York 1965*

11 Combining Tactical Methods 153
Game No. 39 – **Tischbierek–E. Vladimirov,** *Berlin 1989*
Game No. 40 – **Kotronias–Short,** *Novi Sad Ol. 1990*
Game No. 41 – **Zapata–E. Vladimirov,** *Salamanca 1991*
Game No. 42 – **Ermenkov–Kovacevic,** *Kavala 1990*
Game No. 43 – **Short–Bareev,** *Tilburg 1991*
Game No. 44 – **Barash–Monin,** *17th USSR corr. Ch. 1986/88*
Game No. 45 – **Psakhis–Vaganian,** *Moscow 1981*

Index of Variations 174

Introduction

This opening got its name after a win by a team of French chessplayers in a correspondence game played between London and Paris (1834–36).

The French Defence was not particularly popular during the last century. But in the present century it has been enriched with new strategic ideas and tactical subtleties and has gained widespread recognition.

Em. Lasker wrote: “This opening provides many a problem to gladden the heart of every genuine chess-lover”.

Significant contributions to the theory and practice of the French Defence have been made by Tarrasch, Steinitz, Rubinstein, Nimzowitsch, Alekhine, Euwe, Maróczy, Botvinnik, Petrosian and Bronstein. Today the French Defence is a favourite and dangerous weapon in the hands of Vaganian, Yusupov, Portisch, Korchnoi, Uhlmann, Short and Gulko, amongst others.

A characteristic feature of many variations of the French Defence is that complicated, non-standard positions, with irrational piece-placements and pawn structures, arise in the opening almost immediately.

One advantage of the French Defence is that Black, having consolidated his position and maintained the equilibrium in the centre, can undermine the centre at the first opportunity with the moves ... c7–c5 or ... f7–f6 and begin a counter-attack.

The main disadvantage of the French Defence is associated with Black’s difficulties in developing his light-squared bishop, as a result of which White frequently gains the initiative and obtains a spatial advantage in the complicated and sharp positions that arise. But Black’s resources are quite considerable and as a rule involve tactical possibilities which are so abundant in ‘French’ middlegame positions. As evidence of this we may take a recent game between two of today’s most brilliant representatives of the school of sharp combinative play.

Kasparov–Anand

Reggio Emilia 1991/92

1 e4 e6 2 d4 d5 3 ♘c3 ♗b4 4 e5 c5 5 a3 ♗xc3+ 6 bc ♘e7 7 h4 ♘bc6 8 h5 ♕a5 9 ♗d2 cd 10 cd ♕a4 11 ♘f3 ♘xd4 12 ♗d3 ♘ec6 13 ♔f1 ♘xf3 14 ♕xf3 b6 15 h6 ♗a6 16 hg ♖g8 17 ♗xa6 ♕xa6+ 18 ♔g1 ♖xg7 19 ♕f6 ♖g8 20 ♖xh7 ♕b7 21 ♗g5 ♘d4 22 c4 ♘e2+ 23 ♔h2 ♘c3 24 ♖h8

White's threats look very dangerous, but Black manages to exploit his counter-chances and save the game.

24 ... ♖xh8 25 ♕xh8+ ♔d7 26 ♕h7 ♖f8 27 ♗h6 ♖e8 28 ♕xf7+ ♖e7 29 ♕g6 ♕b8 30 cd ♘xd5 31 ♖d1 ♕xe5+ 32 f4 ♕h8 33 f5 ♕e5+ 34 ♔h1 Drawn.

PART ONE: TACTICAL FEATURES OF THE MAIN VARIATIONS OF THE FRENCH DEFENCE

I Chigorin Variation and King's Indian Attack
1 e4 e6 2 ♕e2/2 d3

This paradoxical queen manoeuvre was devised by and adopted in practice by the great Russian chessplayer Mikhail Chigorin. The immediate aim of this early move with the queen is to prevent the thrust ... d7–d5. This system was destined to become a distinctive predecessor of King's Indian set-ups for White.

White is clearly intent on an attack against the black king and is ready to make use of all attacking methods at his disposal, primarily a pawn storm followed by the loosening of Black's position, the opening of lines and the demolition of the pawns shielding the king.

Typical in this regard is the following game:

Chigorin–Zinkl
Berlin 1897

1 e4 e6 2 ♕e2 ♗e7 3 g3 d5 4 d3 ♘f6 5 ♗g2 0–0 6 ♘h3 c5 7 0–0 ♘c6 8 c3 de 9 de e5 10 ♘a3 h6 11 ♘c2 ♗e6 12 f3 ♕d7 13 ♘f2 ♖ad8 14 ♘e3 g5 15 ♔h1 ♔h7 16 ♕c2! ♔h8 17 ♘f5 ♗xf5 18 ef ♖g8 19 g4 ♔g7 20 ♖e1 a6 21 ♗f1! ♖ge8 22 ♗d3 ♕c7 23 h4! ♖h8 24 ♔g2 gh 25 ♗e4 ♘d5 26 ♗xd5! ♖xd5 27 ♘e4!

"Chigorin has built up an excellent attacking position, and with a number of stabbing blows he overwhelms his opponent", writes Tarrasch in his annotations to this game.

27 ... ♖hd8 28 ♖e2 ♕d7 *(1)*

White now concludes the game quite beautifully:

29 f6+! ♗xf6 30 ♗xh6+ ♔xh6 31 ♘xf6 Black resigned.

II Exchange Variation
1 e4 e6 2 d4 d5 3 ed

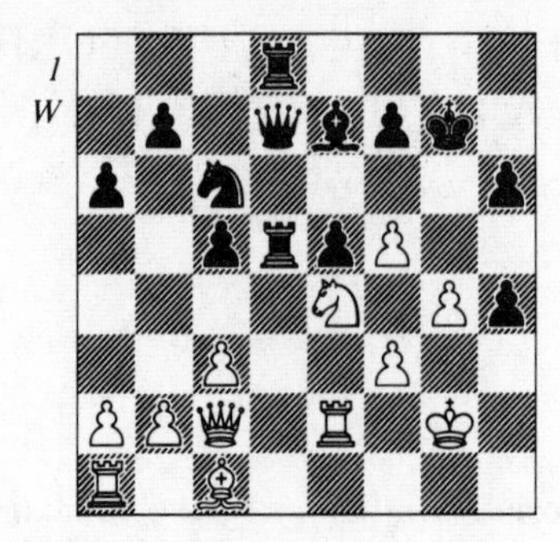

A continuation which is rarely adopted, resulting in equality. This whole variation has an entirely well-deserved reputation as a tame, drawish system, although it was readily adopted by such great players as Morphy and Capablanca.

In recent years the Exchange Variation has again become popular, Kasparov in particular having taken it into his repertoire.

Despite the outward simplicity of the positions arising in this variation, extremely precise and careful play is required from Black (as is also the case in other symmetrical positions). If Black lags behind in development, the open e-file may prove to be significant in enabling White to unleash an attack on the black king left stranded in the centre.

By way of example we shall quote an exemplary attack by White in a game played nearly 150 years ago.

Petrov–Szymansky
Warsaw 1847

1 e4 e6 2 d4 d5 3 ed ed 4 c4 ♗b4+ 5 ♘c3 ♘e7 6 ♘f3 ♗g4 7 ♗e2 dc 8 0–0 ♗xf3 9 ♗xf3 c6 10 ♕e2! ♕xd4?

This opens another file for White's attack. Black should have castled immediately, although even then after 11 ♕xc4 his position would have remained difficult.

Petrov exploits his opponent's loss of several tempi quite superbly in order to launch a vigorous attack on the king.

11 ♖d1 ♕f6 12 ♘e4 ♕e6 13 a3 ♗a5 14 ♗g4 ♕g2 *(2)*
15 ♗f5!!

A spectacular and stunning blow! The black queen has no retreat-squares, and if it captures the bishop it is enticed into a fork (15 ... ♕xf5 16 ♘d6+). The move 15 ♗h5 would also have

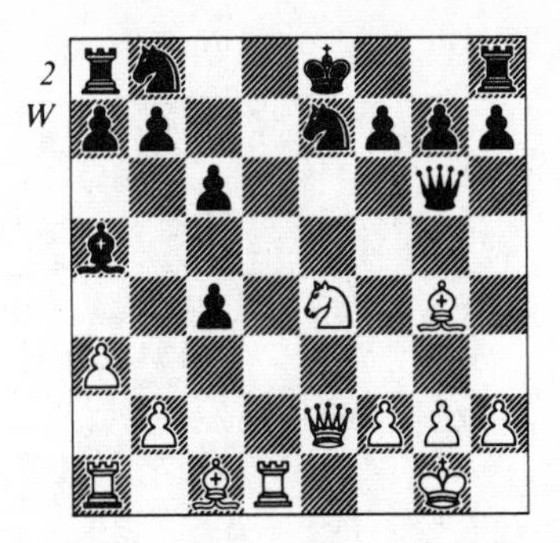

finished the game beautifully. After the only move — the retreat of the queen to e6 — there would have followed 16 ♗xf7+! — a double enticement into a fork (16 ... ♕xf7 17 ♘d6+, or 16 ... ♔xf7 17 ♘g5+).

15 ... ♘xf5 16 ♘f6++ Black resigned.

III Advance Variation
1 e4 e6 2 d4 d5 3 e5

This time-honoured system was willingly adopted by Paulsen and Steinitz. The system is based upon the central white pawn, which cramps Black's development. Black by no means always manages to establish counterplay and obtain equal chances. Here is a typical example:

Nimzowitsch–Håkansson
Kristianstad 1922

1 e4 e6 2 d4 d5 3 e5 c5 4 ♕g4 cd 5 ♘f3 ♘c6 6 ♗d3 f5 7 ♕g3 ♘ge7 8 0–0 ♘g6 9 h4 ♕c7 10 ♖e1 ♗d7

Black should have played 10 ... ♗c5 11 h5 ♘f8.

11 a3 0–0–0 12 b4 a6

Somewhat better was 12 ... ♔b8 13 c3! dc 14 ♘xc3 ♘xb4 15 ab ♕xc3 16 ♗e3 ♕xd3 17 ♗xa7+ ♔c8 18 ♖ec1+ ♗c6 19 b5 ♕xb5 20 ♘d4 with complications.

13 h5 ♘ge7 14 ♗d2 h6 15 a4 g5 16 b5 f4 17 ♕g4 ♘b8 18 c3 ♖e8 19 cd ♔d8 20 ♖c1 ♕b6 21 a5 ♕a7 22 b6 ♕a8

This sort of position for the queen is usually only encountered in problems.

23 ♖c7 ♘f5 24 ♘c3 ♗e7 25 ♘xd5 ♘xd4 26 ♘xd4 ed *(3)*

An exceptionally colourful position!

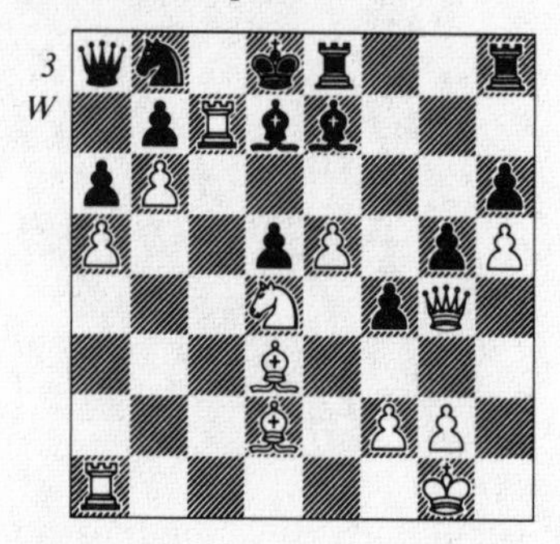

27 ♕xd7+! Black resigned.

Total suffocation is concluded with smothered mate: 27 … ♘xd7 28 ♘e6 mate.

Even today some players consider the system with 3 e5 to be the most fundamental response to the French Defence. One such player in particular is Grandmaster Sveshnikov. But, as many games have shown, Black has sufficient resources, which generally are associated with his possibilities for initiating tactical complications.

For example, in the following game a wing thrust set the scene for most interesting complications.

Sveshnikov–Chernin
USSR Ch., Riga 1985

1 e4 e6 2 d4 d5 3 e5 c5 4 c3 ♘c6 5 ♘f3 ♗d7 6 a3 ♖c8 7 ♗d3 cd 8 cd ♕b6 9 ♗c2 g5 10 h3 *(4)*

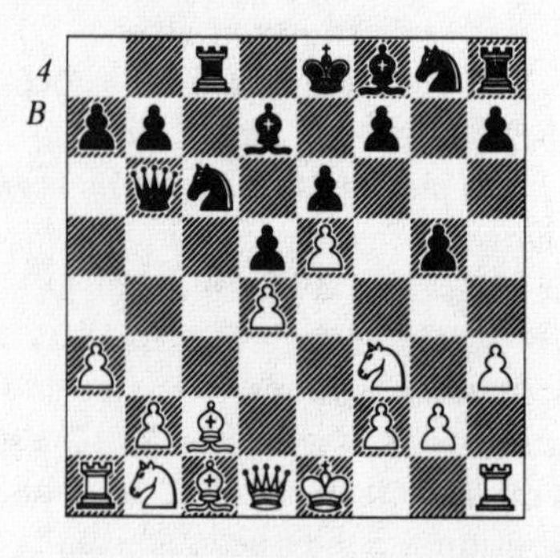

Now vast and crazy complications begin: Black opens lines at the cost of a piece.

10 … ♘xd4 11 ♘xd4 ♗c5 12 ♘e2 ♗xf2+ 13 ♔f1 f6 14 ♗a4 fe 15 ♗xd7+ ♔xd7 16 ♕a4+ ♖c6 17 g3 ♘e7 18 ♔g2 ♘f5 19 ♘bc3 *(5)*

White allows the sacrifice of another piece: stronger was 19 ♖f1.

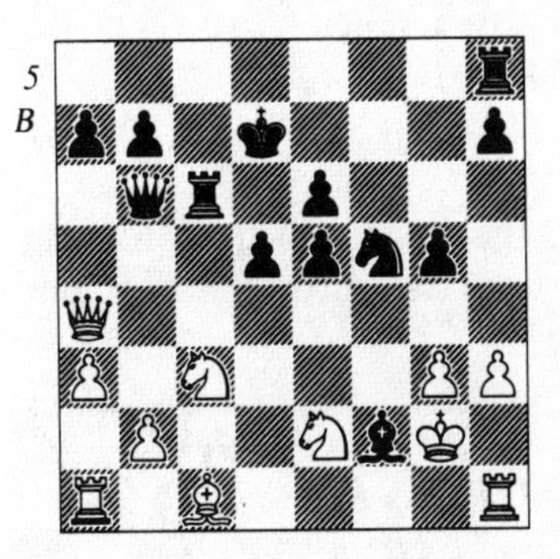

19 … ♗xg3! 20 ♘xg3 ♘h4+ 21 ♔f1 ♖f8+ 22 ♔e1 ♕f2+ 23 ♔d1 ♕xg3

Black would have obtained good winning chances with 23 … ♖f3, but now White obtains counterplay and Black forces a draw by perpetual check just before White forces perpetual check himself.

24 ♕xa7 ♕f3+ 25 ♔c2 ♕e4+ 26 ♔b3 ♕c4+ 27 ♔c2 ♕e4+ 28 ♔b3 Drawn.

IV Rubinstein's Variation
1 e4 e6 2 d4 d5 3 ♘c3 de

The idea behind exchanging pawns is that, while conceding the centre to White without a fight, Black intends in the near future to fianchetto his light-squared bishop (… b6 and … ♗b7).

All the same, the pawn configuration which arises is in White's favour (pawn on d4 against pawn on e6). This small advantage in the centre guarantees him lasting positional superiority.

White's spatial advantage and the favourable formation of his pieces in many cases provide the basis for carrying out successful tactical operations, primarily in those cases where Black lags behind in development and does not manage to evacuate his king from the centre.

In this connection the following short game deserves attention:

Kotov–Kalmanok

Moscow 1936

1 d4 e6 2 e4 d5 3 ♘c3 ♘f6 4 ♗g5 de 5 ♘xe4 ♗e7 6 ♗xf6 gf 7 ♘f3 ♘d7 8 ♗c4 c6 9 ♕d2 b6 10 ♕h6!

White has outstripped his opponent in development and proceeds to take decisive action.

The threat is 11 ♕g7 and 12 ♕xh7.

10 … ♗f8 11 ♕f4 ♗b7 12 0–0–0 h5 13 ♔b1 ♗e7 14 ♕g3 ♘f8 15 ♖he1 f5 *(6)*

This move was played in anticipation of the natural retreat of the white knight from its central position. But White's reply was totally unexpected.

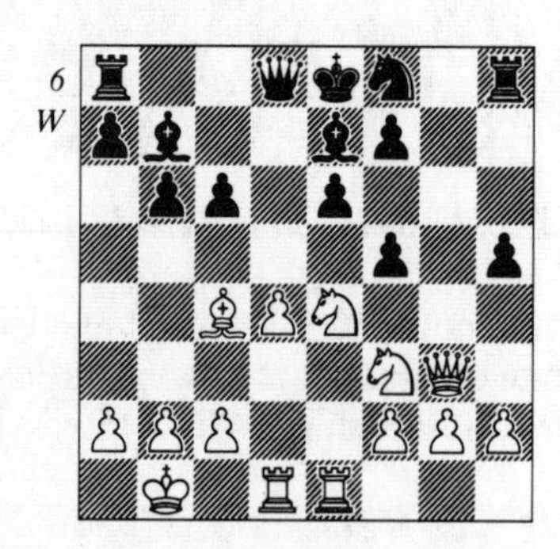

16 d5!!

A typical battering-ram attack in such positions, resulting in the centre being opened up. Black's position now falls apart.

16 … cd

Bad for Black were both 16 … fe 17 de, and 16 … ed 17 ♘f6 mate.

17 ♗b5+ ♘d7 18 ♘e5 ♕c7

The game would have ended beautifully in the event of 18 … ♗c8–19 ♕g7 ♖f8 20 ♖xd5! ed 21 ♘d6+! ♗xd6 22 ♘xd7+ and 23 ♕xf8 mate.

19 ♗xd7+ ♔d8 20 ♕g7 ♖f8 21 ♘g5 ♕c5 22 ♗xe6 Black resigned.

V Classical Variation

1 e4 e6 2 d4 d5 3 ♘c3 ♘f6

This move with Black's king's knight, characterising the Classical

System, leads to the most varied situations in which tactical subtleties abound.

For instance, after the usual 4 ♗g5 ♗e7 5 e5 ♘fd7 White has the gambit continuation 6 h4!, commonly known as the Alekhine-Chatard Attack, and introduced into tournament practice by Alekhine. In the event of Black accepting the pawn sacrifice White obtains substantial compensation, as can be seen from the following game, as a result of which this variation achieved respectability.

Alekhine–Fahrni
Mannheim 1914

1 e4 e6 2 d4 d5 3 ♘c3 ♘f6 4 ♗g5 ♗e7 5 e5 ♘fd7 6 h4 ♗xg5 7 hg ♕xg5 8 ♘h3 ♕e7 9 ♘f4 ♘f8

For his sacrificed pawn White has obtained a lead in development, the open h-file and good chances of a kingside attack.

10 ♕g4 f5 11 ef gf 12 0–0–0 c6 13 ♖e1 ♔d8 14 ♖h6 e5 15 ♕h4 ♘bd7 16 ♗d3 e4 17 ♕g3 ♕f7 *(7)*

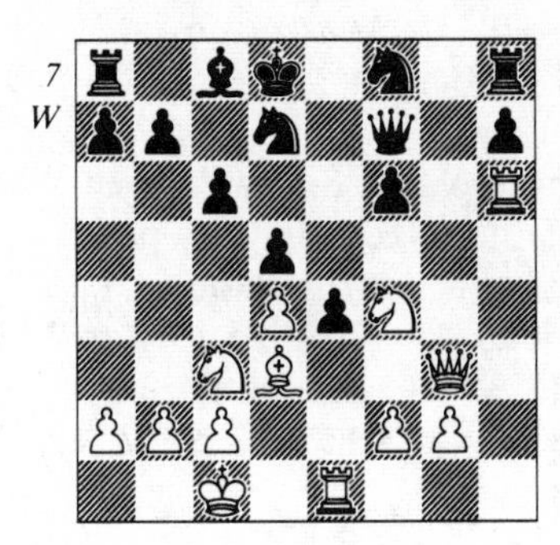

18 ♗xe4!

White breaks through his opponent's defences. The bishop offers itself up in order to clear a path for White's other pieces.

18 ... de 19 ♘xe4 ♖g8

It would have been bad to play 19 ... ♕xa2, because of 20 ♘xf6 ♘xf6 21 ♕g7!.

20 ♕a3! ♕g7 21 ♘d6! ♘b6 *(8)*

The rook cannot be taken because of 22 ♘f7+, but now comes a decisive blow.

22 ♘e8!

Now any retreat by the queen loses: 22 ... ♕xh6 23 ♕e7 mate;

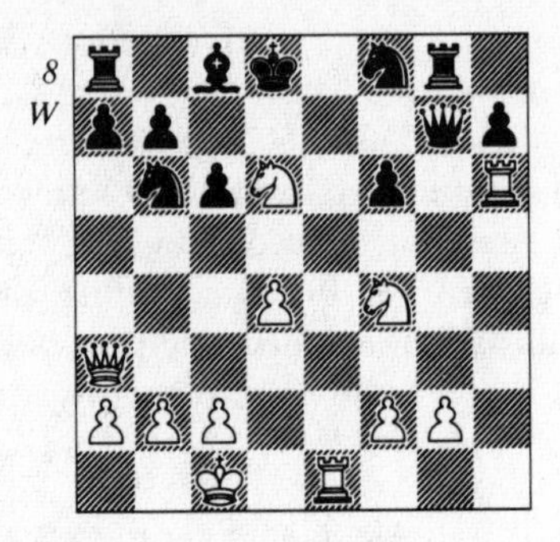

22 ... ♕d7 23 ♘xf6. On 22 ... ♘c4 White decides the issue with 23 ♕c5 ♕f7 24 ♖xf6.

22 ... ♕f7 23 ♕d6+ Black resigned.

Black defended in a different way in the following game, declining the gambit pawn, but here too he was unable to avoid trouble.

Lyuboshits–Shagalovich
Minsk 1956

1 e4 e6 2 d4 d5 3 ♘c3 ♘f6 4 ♗g5 ♗e7 5 e5 ♘fd7 6 h4 c5 7 ♘b5 f6 8 ♗d3 ♕a5+

Black should have played 8 ... a6!, when White evidently has nothing better than to force a draw by perpetual check: 9 ♕h5+ ♔f8 10 ♖h3 ab 11 ♗h6! gh 12 ♕xh6+. If 11 ... ♕a5+ then 12 ♗d2 ♕c7 13 ♖g3! cd 14 ♘f3 ♘xe5 15 ♖xg7! h6 16 ♗h7! ♔xg7 17 ♕xh6+ ♔f7 18 ♕h5+, also with a draw.

9 ♗d2 ♕b6 10 ♕h5+ ♔f8 11 ♖h3 cd 12 ♖g3 fe *(9)*

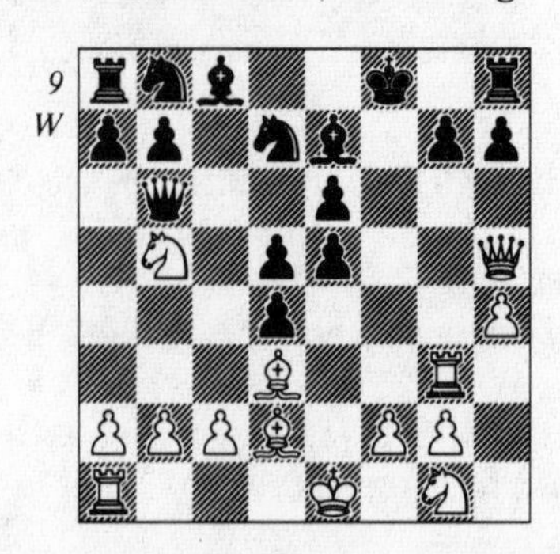

White's superiority on the kingside is certainly considerable, but it is hard to believe that Black only managed to make two more moves in this game.

13 ♖xg7!! ♔xg7 14 ♗h6+ ♔g8 15 ♗g6!! Black resigned.

A brilliant final blow. The threat of 16 ♗f7 mate is unstoppable.

Another interesting game which opened with the Alekhine–Chatard Variation is the following, in which there were some quite astonishing adventures.

Panov–Yudovich

USSR Ch., Tbilisi 1937

1 e4 e6 2 d4 d5 3 ♘c3 ♘f6 4 ♗g5 ♗e7 5 e5 ♘fd7 6 h4 f6 7 ♗d3?!

Correct is 7 ♕h5+ g6 8 ef! ♘xf6 (8 ... gh? 9 fe!) 9 ♕e2 c5 10 dc ♘c6 11 0–0–0 with advantage to White.

7 ... c5 8 ♕h5+ ♔f8 9 ♘xd5 fg

It would be bad to play 9 ... ed because of 10 e6.

10 ♖h3 g4! 11 ♘f4 ♘xe5 12 de gh 13 ♗xh7?

White has fallen into an extremely cunning trap.

Better chances were offered by 13 0–0–0 or 13 ♘gxh3, although also in these variations Black repels the attack.

13 ... ♖xh7! 14 ♕xh7 *(10)*

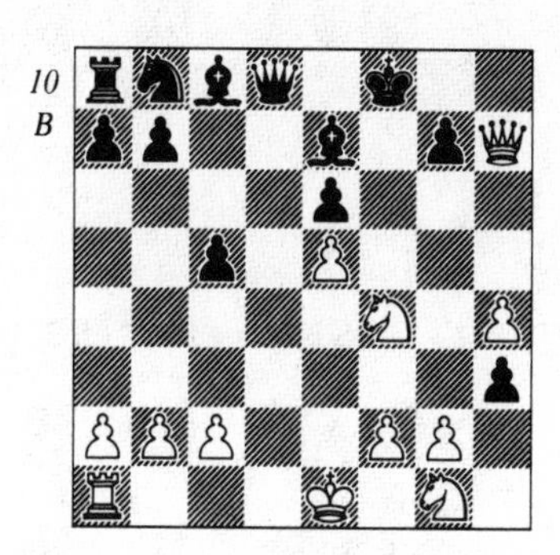

14 ... h2!!

This move borders on the unreal! With plenty of pieces still on the board the black pawn that started out on f7 manages to queen. The rest of the game requires no comment.

15 ♔e2 h1(♕) 16 ♘g6+ ♔f7 17 ♘h8+ ♕xh8! 18 ♕xh8 ♘c6 19 ♕h5+ ♔g8 20 ♘h3 ♕xg2 21 ♕e8+ ♗f8 and Black won.

Another extremely rare tactical idea could have been carried out in the following game, in which the MacCutcheon Variation was played.

Grigoriev–Alekhine
Moscow 1915

1 e4 e6 2 d4 d5 3 ♘c3 ♘f6 4 ♗g5 ♗b4 5 e5 h6 6 ef hg 7 fg ♖g8 8 h4 gh 9 ♕g4 ♗e7

Black gets an excellent game after 9 … ♕f6.

10 g3 c5

The game continued 11 0–0–0 ♘c6 12 dc ♕a5! and White eventually lost. Alekhine's analysis runs as follows:

11 gh cd 12 h5! dc 13 h6 cb 14 ♖b1 ♕a5+ 15 ♔e2 ♕xa2 16 h7 ♕xb1 17 hg(♕)+ ♔d7 18 ♕xf7 ♕xd2+ 19 ♔f3 *(11)*

The white king escapes from the checks, but Black's resources are not quite exhausted.

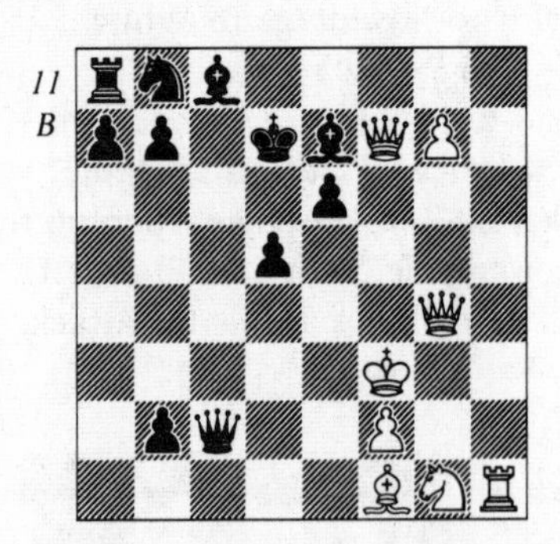

19 … ♘c6!

Defending both bishops at the same time and threatening a knight fork on e5.

20 ♕xe6+ ♔c7 21 ♕f4+ ♔b6 22 ♕ee3+ ♗c5 23 g8(♕) b1(♕) *(12)*

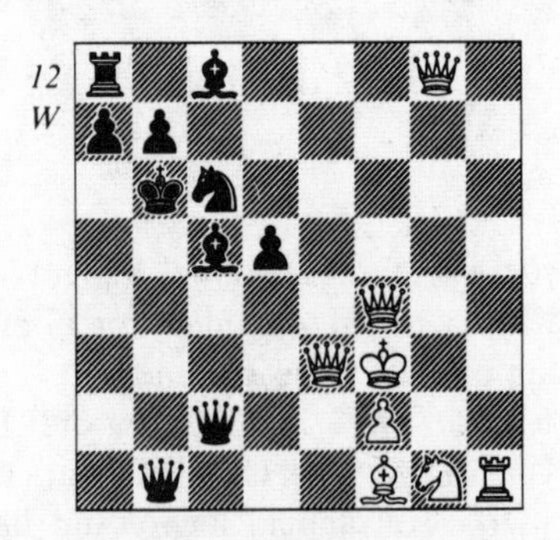

"This position is certainly unique of its kind!" (Alekhine).

In fact, these improbable adventures have resulted in there being five (!!) queens on the board, and moreover in a position where White's kingside pieces have still not made a single move.

In this position White has an elegant way to win: 24 ♖h6!! (with the threat of 25 ♕d8 mate) 24 ... ♕xf1 25 ♕b4+! (making use of two pins at once) 25 ... ♕b5 26 ♕d8+ ♔a6 27 ♕ea3+, with mate.

VI Winawer Variation
1 e4 e6 2 d4 d5 3 ♘c3 ♗b4

The advantage of the move 3 ... ♗b4 over 3 ... ♘f6 is substantial – White has a reduced choice of continuations to defend the pawn on e4. True, he will subsequently obtain the advantage of the two bishops (eventually Black is generally forced to exchange off his bishop on c3) and he frequently also has prospects of an attack on the kingside or on the dark squares. Black, however, will aim to exploit the weaknesses in his opponent's queenside pawn structure and to get counterplay in the centre.

Characteristic of this system is the tactical destruction of the flanks even before the opening phase is over. This occurs when, right from the opening, White begins a forceful piece attack on the kingside. The most energetic plan in response is a counter-attack in the centre and on the queenside.

A good demonstration of this is, for example, the 'irrational' play arising in one of the topical variations of this system:
1 e4 e6 2 d4 d5 3 ♘c3 ♗b4 4 e5 c5 5 a3 ♗xc3+ 6 bc ♘e7 7 ♕g4 cd!? 8 ♕xg7 ♖g8 9 ♕xh7 ♕c7 10 ♘e2 ♘bc6 11 f4 ♗d7 12 ♕d3 dc *(13)*

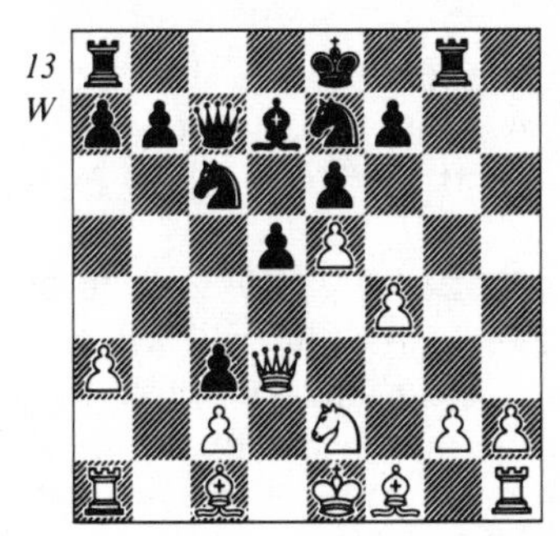

13
W

Here Black's kingside pawn cover has been demolished and

White's pawn position on the queenside has been disrupted. In such positions the plan for White is a pawn offensive on the kingside, combined with play on the dark squares. In turn, Black intends to begin counter-operations in the centre and on the queenside, frequently combined with threats to the white king, which usually remains in the centre for some time.

Characteristic in this regard is the following game, in which, after the opening moves given above, White came to grief as a result of his kingside pawns becoming excessively frisky.

Bronstein–Uhlmann

Tallinn 1977

13 h4?! 0–0–0 14 h5 ♘f5 15 h6 ♖g6 16 ♖h3 d4 17 h7 ♖h8 18 ♖b1 ♗e8 19 ♕f3 ♕d8 20 g4 ♘h4 21 ♕h1 ♖xg4 22 ♘g3 ♖xh7 23 ♘e4 *(14)*

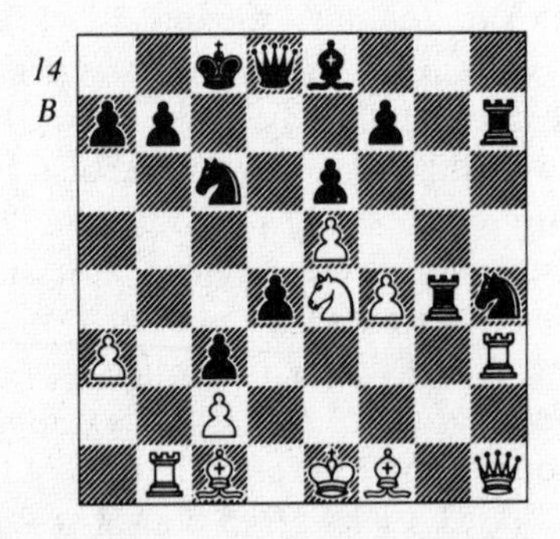

At first sight White has obtained an excellent attack, but the opening of lines, in conjunction with a pin, enabled Black to create irresistible threats.

23 ... ♘xe5! 24 fe ♗c6 25 ♗d3

It would not have been good to play 25 ♘d6+, because of 25 ... ♕xd6! 26 ed ♗xh1 27 ♖xh1 ♘f3+ 28 ♔f2 ♖xh1 29 ♔xf3 ♖gg1.

25 ... ♔c7 26 ♔f2 ♖h5 27 ♖f3 ♕g8 28 ♗f4 ♘xf3 29 ♕xh5 ♖xf4 30 ♕h6 ♘g5+ and White resigned.

The move 7 ♕g4 is perhaps the sharpest plan. Play in this line may become very complex and frequently results in enormous tactical complications. A most interesting contest develops when Black replies 7 ... 0–0. This decision looks paradoxical – Black boldly moves his king to precisely the area of the board where the main offensive will be directed, and therefore he needs to play with extreme precision. Otherwise the following might happen:

Khalifman–Pr. Nikolic
Moscow 1990

1 e4 e6 2 d4 d5 3 ♘c3 ♗b4 4 e5 c5 5 a3 ♗xc3+ 6 bc ♘e7 7 ♕g4 0–0 8 ♗d3 ♘bc6 9 ♕h5 ♘f5 10 ♘f3 f6

10 ... c4 11 g4! cd 12 gf f6 13 ♖g1 transposes to the game.

11 g4 c4 12 gf! cd 13 ♖g1 ef

Black's position is already rather difficult. After 13 ... ♔h8 quite troublesome is 14 ♘h4! ♕e8 15 ♘g6+ ♔g8 16 ♗h6!, with a very strong attack. The move 13 .. ♘e7 was brilliantly refuted in the game Kruppa–Komarov (see Game 13).

14 ♗h6 ♖f7 15 ♔d2!

White allows his queen's rook to join in the attack. Now on 15 ... ♕e7 there would follow 16 ♗xg7! ♖xg7 17 ♖xg7+ ♔xg7 (17 ... ♕xg7 18 ♕e8+) 18 ♖g1+ ♔h8 (no better is 18 ... ♔f8 19 ♕h6+ ♔e8 20 ♖g8+ ♔c7 21 ♖g7) 19 ♘h4.

15 ... ♗e6 *(15)*

This move also fails to save Black from a rout.

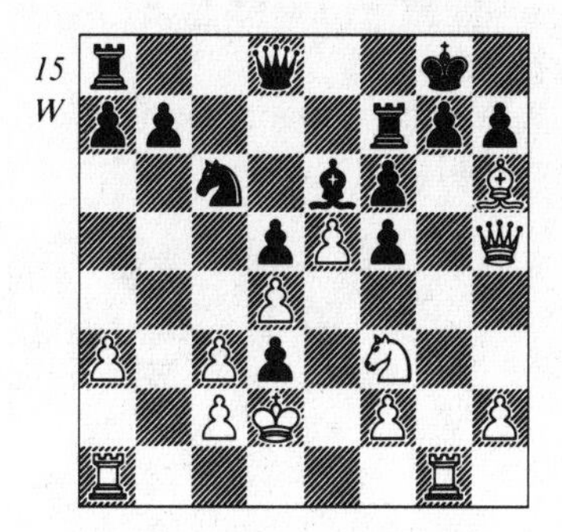

16 ♗xg7! ♖xg7 17 ♖xg7+ ♔xg7 18 ♖g1+

Now on 18 ... ♔h8 there follows 19 ♘h4 ♘e7 20 ef; more stubborn would be 18 ... ♔f8 19 ♕xh7 ♗f7 (no help either is 19 ... ♘e7, because of 20 ef ♘g8 21 ♖xg8+ ♗xg8 22 ♕g7+ ♔e8 23 ♘e5) 20 ♖g7 ♕e8, but here too after 21 ♘h4 ♔e7 22 ♘xf5+ ♔e6 23 ♘d6 Black cannot avoid loss of material, so Black resigned.

Castling on opposite sides is rather widespread in practice, with the black king seeking shelter on the queenside. Play in such cases, when the position is closed and there are blocked pawn chains on both sides, is rather complicated. Sometimes Black succeeds in carrying out an attack on the kingside (see Game 9: Hazai–Uhlmann).

In other cases White manages to exert decisive pressure by making use of the dark squares.

Fischer–Darga

West Berlin 1960

1 e4 e6 2 d4 d5 3 ♘c3 ♗b4 4 e5 c5 5 a3 ♗xc3+ 6 bc ♘e7 7 a4 ♕c7 8 ♘f3 b6 9 ♗b5+ ♗d7 10 ♗d3 ♘bc6 11 0–0 c4 12 ♗e2 f6 13 ♗a3!?

An interesting pawn sacrifice. In this way White keeps Black's king in the centre and obtains a dangerous initiative.

13 ... fe 14 de ♘xe5 15 ♖e1 ♘7c6

As Fischer pointed out, in the event of 15 ... ♘5g6 16 h4! ♘c6 17 ♘g5, or 15 ... ♘5c6 16 ♘g5! 0–0 17 ♗g4 ♕f4 18 ♗xe6+! ♗xe6 19 ♘xe6 ♕xf2+ 20 ♔h1 ♖f5 21 ♖e2! ♕h4 22 ♘d4! White's attack is very strong.

16 ♘xe5 ♘xe5 17 f4 ♘c6 18 ♗g4 0–0–0 19 ♗xe6 ♗xe6 20 ♖xe6 ♖d7 21 f5 ♘d8 22 ♖e3 ♕f4 23 ♖f3 ♕e4 24 a5! ♘c6 25 ab ab 26 ♕b1! ♔c7 *(16)*

Now, thanks to an effective manoeuvre with his dark-squared bishop, White concludes the game by force.

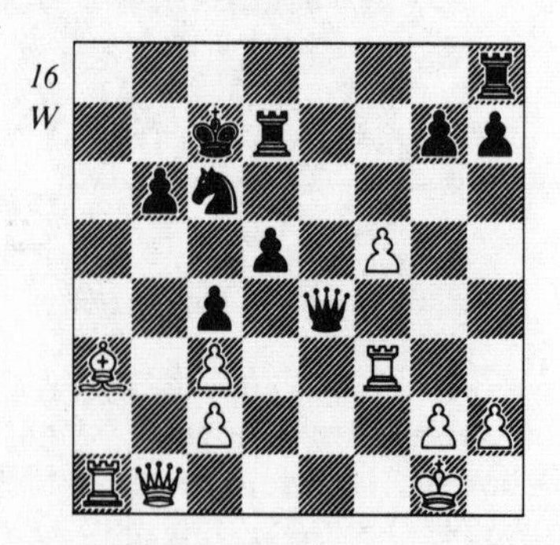

27 ♗c1! ♕e1+ 28 ♖f1 ♕xc3 29 ♗f4+ ♔b7 30 ♕b5! and Black resigned.

Black is unable to avoid mate without losing material.

Let us examine one more game, in which a sharp but not entirely correct variation was played.

Bonsdorf–Liipola
Helsinki 1957

1 e4 e6 2 d4 d5 3 ♘c3 ♗b4 4 ♕g4?!

Theory considers this move to be unfavourable for White, since Black rapidly succeeds in getting a counter-attack in the centre.

4 ... ♘f6 5 ♕xg7 ♖g8 6 ♕h6 ♘xe4?

A stronger continuation is that suggested by Alekhine: 6 ... ♖g6 7 ♕e3 c5!

7 ♕xh7 ♖g6 8 ♕h8+ ♔d7 9 ♕xd8+ ♔xd8 10 ♗d2 ♘xd2 11 ♔xd2 c5 12 a3 cd 13 ab dc+ 14 bc ♘c6 15 ♘f3 e5?

With this move Black went for a forced variation, but he had overestimated its consequences as far as he was concerned.

16 b5! e4 17 bc ef 18 cb fg 19 ba(♕) hg(♕) *(17)*

This is the sharp position Black had been aiming for, considering that he had a certain draw.

But there was an unexpected denouement ...

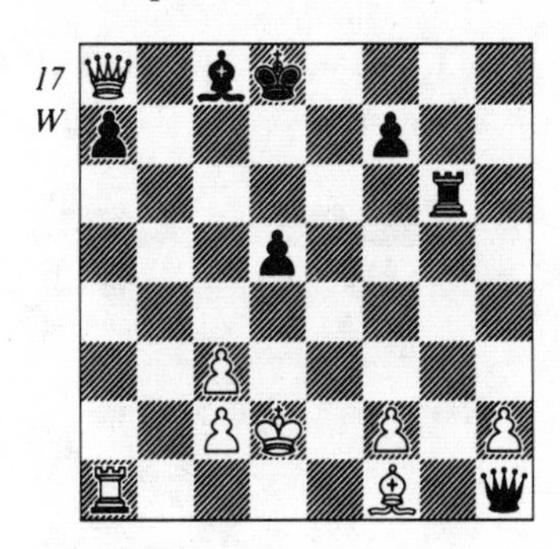
17
W

20 ♕xc8+! ♔xc8 21 ♗h3+ Black resigned.

VII Tarrasch Variation
1 e4 e6 2 d4 d5 3 ♘d2

This system is characterised by the move 3 ♘d2, which Tarrasch introduced into practice in a game against von Scheve (Manchester 1890).

The idea of the move 3 ♘d2 is that Black is deprived of the opportunity to attack the e4-square with the move ... ♗b4, and in addition White always has the move c2–c3, reinforcing his pawn chain.

On the other hand, the knight is much more passive on d2 than it is on c3, since it prevents the queen and bishop from moving out. In a number of variations this results in White's falling slightly behind in development and it provides additional possibilities for Black.

After the move 3 ♘d2 Black is faced with a choice: either to provoke White into playing e4–e5, or to initiate active play in the centre at once with ... c7–c5, not being afraid of getting left with an isolated pawn.

In the first case White's tactical possibilities are associated with an attack in the centre and on the kingside. Therefore Black usually undermines the centre (... c7–c5 and ... f7–f6) and then attempts to demolish it with tactics, particularly at the stage when White solves the problem of hiding his king away.

We shall quote a recent example:

Ljubojevic–M. Gurevich
Linares 1991

1 e4 e6 2 d4 d5 3 ♘d2 ♘f6 4 e5 ♘fd7 5 f4 c5 6 c3 ♘c6 7 ♘df3 ♕b6 8 h4 cd 9 cd ♗b4+ 10 ♔f2 f6 11 ♔g3 0–0 12 ♗d3 *(18)*

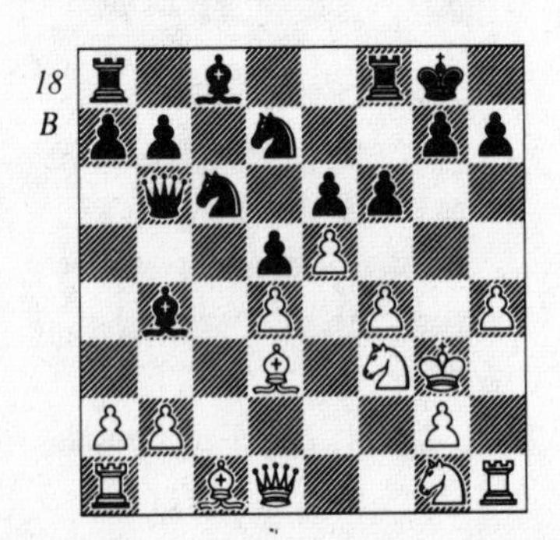
18
B

White has succeeded in obtaining a considerable spatial advantage and in preparing for an attack on the black king, but the drawbacks of his position are obvious (in particular, the unfortunate position of his king) and Black exploits them vigorously, opening up some very important lines with the aid of a piece sacrifice:

12 ... ♘xd4! 13 ♘xd4 fe

Of course, not 13 ... ♕xd4??, because of 14 ♗xh7+.

14 fe ♘xe5 15 ♗c2 ♘g6! 16 ♗xg6 hg

Now the threat is 17 ... ♗d6+ 18 ♔h3 e5+. After 17 ♗f4

unpleasant for White is 17 ... ♖xf4 18 ♔xf4 e5+!, since he cannot play 19 ♔xe5? because of 19 ... ♕d6 mate.

17 ♘de2 ♕f2+ 18 ♔h3 ♗d6 19 ♕b3 e5+ 20 ♔h2 ♕xh4+ 21 ♘h3 ♗xh3

In view of 22 ♕xh3 e4+ 23 g3 ♖f2+, White resigned.

However, in those cases where Black plays passively, retribution for indecisiveness may follow very quickly.

Shashin–Dashkevich
Riga 1955

1 e4 e6 2 d4 d5 3 ♘d2 ♘f6 4 e5 ♘fd7 5 ♗d3 c5 6 c3 ♘c6 7 ♘e2 ♗e7?

This sort of sluggishness is inadvisable. Black can maintain the tension by playing 7 ... ♕b6 or 7 ... f6.

8 0–0 ♕b6 9 ♘f3 0–0 10 ♘f4 cd 11 cd a5 12 ♗b1 ♘d8 13 ♕d3 f5?

Better was 13 ... g6, though also in this case Black's position is not easy.

14 ef ♘xf6 15 ♘g5 ♖e8 *(19)*

If now 15 ... g6 then 16 ♘xg6. With his move in the game Black allows White to land a knock-out punch.

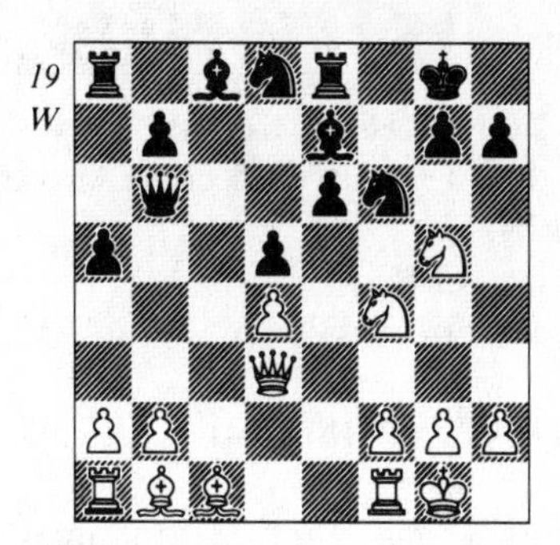
19
W

16 ♕xh7+! Black resigned.

Mate is unavoidable: 16 ... ♘xh7 17 ♗xh7+ and 18 ♘g6 mate.

After 3 ♘d2 c5 Black usually gets excellent play for his pieces by way of compensation for his isolated d-pawn (see Game 27: Karpov–Korchnoi). But lively play may arise not just in positions with an isolated pawn. Interesting in this respect is the following game, in which a great advocate and connoisseur of the French Defence — the German Grandmaster, Wolfgang Uhlmann —

played the opening too riskily and his king left stranded in the centre was exposed to a devastating attack.

Tal–Uhlmann
Moscow 1971

1 e4 e6 2 d4 d5 3 ♘d2 c5 4 ♘gf3 ♘c6 5 ♗b5 de 6 ♘xe4 ♗d7 7 ♗g5 ♕a5+ 8 ♘c3 cd 9 ♘xd4 ♗b4?

The start of an incorrect plan which, although gaining a pawn, also results in a considerable weakening of the dark squares and a lack of development. Black should have played 9 … ♗e7 10 ♗e3 ♕c7, with an equal position.

10 0–0 ♗xc3 11 bc ♕xc3 *(20)*

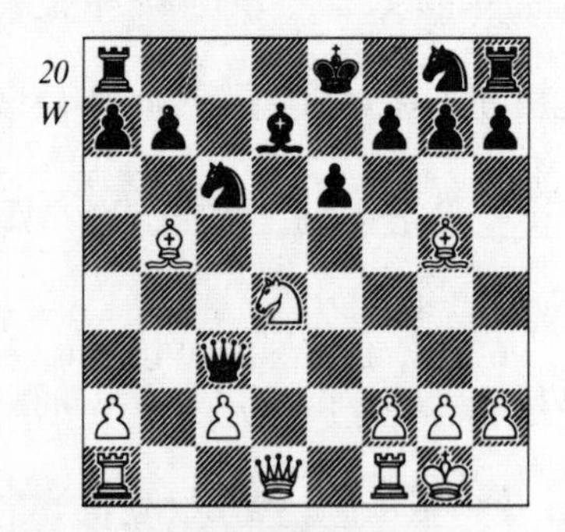

12 ♘f5!! ef 13 ♖e1+ ♗e6 14 ♕d6 a6

If 14 … ♘f6 then 15 ♖ad1 is decisive, in view of the threat of 16 ♗d2 and ♗b4.

15 ♗d2! ♕xc2 16 ♗b4!

But not 16 ♖ac1?, in view of 16 … ♕xc1! 17 ♖xc1 ab 18 ♖xc6 ♖d8!.

16 … ab 17 ♕f8+ ♔d7 18 ♖ed1+ ♔c7 19 ♕xa8 and Black resigned.

White threatens 20 ♖ac1 and 21 ♕d8 mate. On 19 … ♕a4 a possible continuation is 20 ♗d6+ ♔b6 21 ♕f8 ♕g4 22 ♗c5+ ♔c7 23 ♕d6+ ♔c8 24 ♗b6.

PART TWO: PARTICULAR TACTICAL METHODS

1 Enticement

Enticement is an extremely common tactical device. By means of enticement an opposing piece is compelled to occupy an unfavourable position.

One variety of this tactical device is the extraction of the enemy king, whereby the king is forced to abandon its shelter and face the enemy head-on. This usually leads to a mating situation or to substantial loss of material by the defending side.

To illustrate the idea of enticement we shall quote a typical example.

Chistyakov–V. Kogan
Moscow 1933

1 d4 e6 2 e4 d5 3 ♘c3 ♗b4 4 e5 c5 5 ♕g4 ♘e7 6 ♘f3 ♘bc6 7 ♗d3 cd 8 ♘xd4 ♘xe5 9 ♗b5+ ♗d7 10 ♕xg7 ♘5g6 11 ♕f6 e5! 12 ♗xd7+ ♕xd7 13 ♘e2 d4 14 a3 ♗xc3+ 15 bc d3 16 cd ♕xd3 17 ♖a2 ♘d5 18 ♕d6 ♖d8 19 ♕c5, resulting in the following position *(21)*:

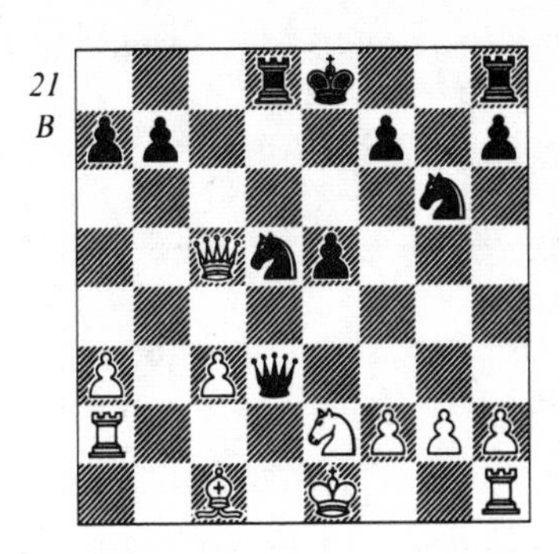

19 ... ♕d1+!!

A variation on a classical theme. The white king is enticed into a double check. Moreover, after 20 ♔xd1 ♘e3++ his retreat is restricted, since Black takes control of the c2-square. After the only move, 21 ♔e1, the follow-up is 21 … ♖d1 mate.

Game No. 1
Yanovsky–Kindermann
Biel 1991

1	**e4**	**e6**
2	**d4**	**d5**
3	**e5**	**c5**
4	**c3**	**♘c6**
5	**♘f3**	**♗d7**
6	**♗e2**	**♘ge7**
7	**0–0**	

One of the foremost authorities on this system, Evgeny Sveshnikov, often plays 7 ♘a3 cd 8 cd ♘f5 9 ♘c2 ♘b4 10 0–0 ♘xc2 11 ♕xc2 ♕b6 12 ♕d2, when there may follow: 12 … a6 13 ♗d2 h5 14 a4 a5 15 ♖fd1 ♗e7 16 h3 ♖e8 17 ♗c3 h4 18 ♕d2 (Sveshnikov–Zlotnik, Moscow 1991), or 12 … ♗e7 13 a4 0–0 14 a5 ♕c7 15 ♗d2 a6 16 ♖fc1 ♗d6 17 ♕b3 (Sveshnikov–Nikolaev, Sibenik 1990); in both these games White had the advantage.

7 … ♖c8!?

Also playable is 7 … ♘g6 8 g3 ♗e7 9 h4 cd 10 cd 0–0 11 h5 (Hjartarson–Korchnoi, Amsterdam 1991).

8	**♘a3**	**cd**
9	**cd**	**♘f5**
10	**♘c2**	**♕b6**
11	**♕d3?!**	

A move of dubious quality. After the natural 11 ♗d3 ♘b4 (11 … ♘fxd4? leads to the loss of a piece: 12 ♘fxd4 ♘xd4 13 ♗e3 ♗c5 14 b4!) 12 ♗xf5 ef 13 ♘xb4 ♗xb4 the position is approximately equal.

11 … a6

Black does not hurry to play 11 … ♗e7, in view of 12 g4.

12	**g4**	**♘fe7**
13	**a4?!**	

Worth considering was 13 b4!?, when Black cannot play 13 … ♘xb4 because of 14 ♕b3 ♘ec6 15 a3.

13 … ♘a5

14	**b4**	**♘c4**
15	**♕b3**	**♘c6**
16	**♖b1**	**♗e7**
17	**♖d1**	**0–0**
18	**♗e3**	**♕d8**
19	**h3**	**b5**
20	**ab**	**ab**
21	**♖a1**	

One gets the impression that White has achieved a definite measure of success by taking possession of the open a-file, but this is just a superficial perception of the position; in fact, the weaknesses on White's kingside and the passive position of his pieces ensure a real advantage for Black.

21	**...**	**f6!**
22	**ef**	**♖xf6**
23	**♘fe1**	

White would have lost after 23 ♗g5? ♖xf3!.

23 ... ♘xe3!

At first sight this is a peculiar exchange of a strong knight for a bad bishop, but this move is in fact the prelude to a spectacular combination.

24 fe?

White should have bought himself out of trouble at the cost of a pawn: 24 ♕xe3 ♘xb4 25 ♘xb4 ♗xb4 26 ♘d3.

24	**...**	**♕c7**
25	**e4** *(22)*	

25 ♔g2 would have led to a mating finish after 25 ... ♖f2+! 26 ♔xf2 ♕h2+ 27 ♘g2 ♗h4+.

22
B

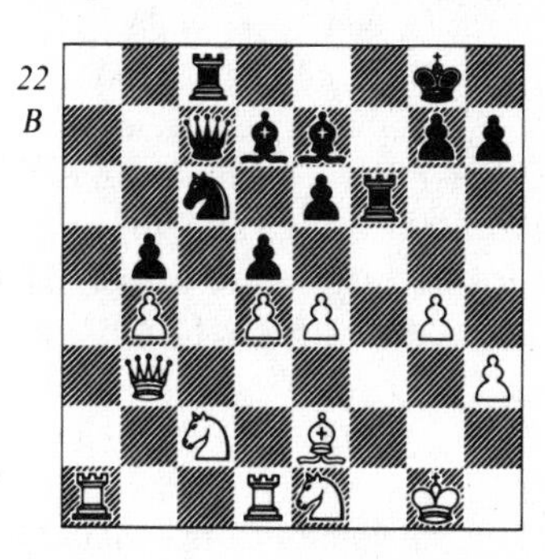

25 ... ♖f2!!

At the cost of a rook Black entices the white king into the middle of the board, where it is exposed to a crushing attack.

26 ♔xf2 ♛h2+
27 ♔e3

White would have been mated after 27 ♔f1 ♝h4 28 ♕e3 ♛h1+ 29 ♕g1 ♜f8+ 30 ♗f3 ♜xf3+; also bad was 27 ♘g2 ♝h4+ 28 ♔e3 ♛xg2.

27 ... ♝g5+
28 ♔d3 *(23)*

23
B

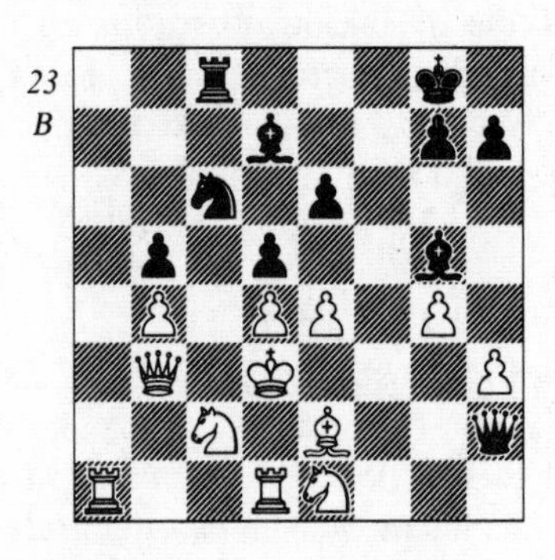

28 ... ♞xb4+!

White resigned, not waiting for the mate: 29 ♕xb4 de+ 30 ♔xe4 ♛xe2.

Game No. 2

J. Polgar–L. B. Hansen

Vejstrup 1989

1 e4 e6
2 d4 d5
3 ♘c3 ♝b4
4 e5 ♞e7

This is one of the moves which enable Black to avoid the variations arising from the 4 e5 c5 system, which have been worked out in great detail. It is justified to a considerable degree in the event of 5 ♕g4 ♞f5 6 ♗d3 h5 7 ♕f4 ♛h4, or 5 ... c5 6 a3 ♛a5 7 ♗d2 cd.

5 a3 ♝xc3+
6 bc b6

After 6 ... c5 play transposes to the main line.

7 ♕g4 ♚f8

At the cost of losing the right to castle Black avoids weakening his position; another possibility is 7 ... ♘g6, but this continuation also leads to some advantage for White after 8 h4 h5 9 ♕g3 ♗a6 10 ♗xa6 ♘xa6 11 ♗g5 ♕d7 12 ♘e2.

8 ♘f3 ♗a6

9 ♗d3 c5

10 dc

Worth considering was 10 ♘g5.

10 ... ♗xd3

11 cd bc

12 0–0 ♘d7

13 a4!

White is going to place her dark-squared bishop on the a3–f8 diagonal.

13 ... ♘c6

14 ♗a3 h6

15 c4

Apparently even stronger was 14 ♖fe1, reinforcing the e5–square.

15 ... ♘cxe5

16 ♘xe5 ♘xe5

17 ♕g3

17 ♕d4 would have caused Black more trouble; after 17 ... ♘d7 18 cd ♔g8 19 ♗xc5 ♘xc5 20 ♕xc5 ed 21 ♖fe1 Black's prospects would have been bleak.

17 ... ♘c6

18 ♗xc5+ ♔g8

19 ♖ab1 ♔h7

20 ♖b7 ♕f6

21 cd ed

22 ♕g4

On 22 ♕c7 there would have followed 22 ... ♖ac8! 23 ♕xf7 ♕xf7 24 ♖xf7 ♘d8!, when White loses her bishop.

22 ... ♖hd8

23 h3 ♔g8

24 d4 ♖de8

25 ♕h5 ♖ad8

Black wrongly rejects the natural capture of a central pawn: after 25 ... ♘xd4 26 ♗xd4 ♕xd4 27 ♕xf7+ ♔h7 he would have maintained the equilibrium.

26 ♖fd1 ♖e4

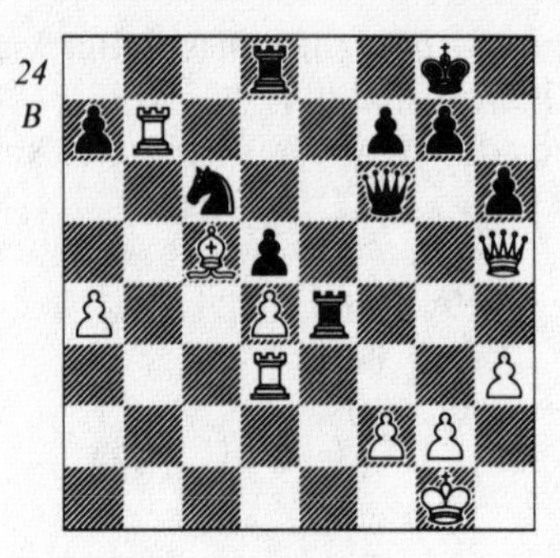

27 ♖d3?! *(24)*

White is unable to come to terms with the loss of her advantage and attempts to wrest it back by forceful means, taking a definite risk in the process.

27 ... ♖e1+
28 ♔h2 ♕xf2
29 ♖df3 ♕g1+
30 ♔g3 g6
31 ♕xh6

The spectacular 31 ♖fxf7 leads to mate in three in the event of acceptance of the queen sacrifice, but after the simple 31 ... ♖e3+ it is Black who wins.

31 ... ♖e2
32 ♔h4!?

A cunning trap, into which Black falls.

32 ... ♕xg2? *(25)*

This natural move gives White the opportunity to conclude the game brilliantly. Correct was 32 ... ♕e1+ 33 g3 ♖e4+ 34 ♖f4 ♘e7! 35 ♗xe7 ♖xe7, when it is White who has to think about equalising.

33 ♕g7+!! Black resigned.

Magnificent! At the cost of sacrificing a whole queen White entices the enemy king onto g7, the square where mate is finally delivered: 33 ... ♔xg7 34 ♖fxf7+ ♔g8 35 ♖g7+ ♔h8 36 ♖h7+ ♔g8 37 ♖bg7 mate.

Game No. 3
Reshevsky–Vaganian
Skopje 1976

1 e4 e6

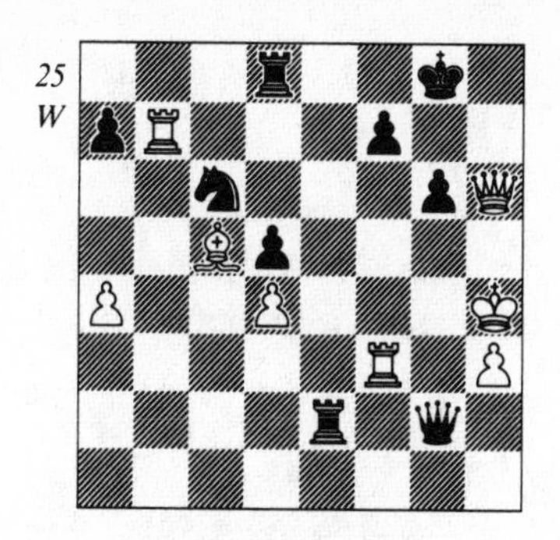

25
W

2	**d4**	**d5**
3	**♘d2**	**♘f6**
4	**e5**	**♘fd7**
5	**f4**	

This move became popular after the game Gufeld–Khasin, USSR Ch., Moscow 1961, which continued as follows: 5 ... c5 6 c3 ♘c6 7 ♘df3 (precisely this, in order to maintain the pawn on d4) 7 ... ♕b6 8 g3! (preparing a shelter for the king) 8 ... cd 9 cd ♗b4+ 10 ♔f2 f6 11 ♔g2 0–0 12 ♗d3 ♔h8 (better was 12 ... ♗e7 and then ... f6–f5) 13 ♘e2 fe 14 de ♗e7 15 h4 ♘c5 16 ♘g5 ♘xe5? (better was 16 ... h6, although Black's position would have remained difficult) 17 fe ♘xd3 18 ♕xd3 ♗xg5 19 ♗xg5 ♕xb2 20 ♗f4 and Black resigned.

5	**...**	**c5**
6	**c3**	**♘c6**
7	**♘df3**	**♕a5**

This thrust with the queen, preventing the bishop from being developed to d3 (8 ♗d3? cd), promises Black good chances of equality.

8 ♔f2

Worth considering is 8 ♗e3; after the unsuccessful reply 8 ... b5?! White can get a big advantage with 9 dc b4 10 ♘d4 ♗b7 11 a3! (Tseshkovsky–Vaganian, Vilnius 1975).

8	**...**	**♗e7**
9	**♗d3**	**♕b6**
10	**♘e2**	**f6**

Now Black threatens to win a pawn after exchanging on d4 and e5.

11	**ef**	**♗xf6**
12	**♔g3**	**cd**
13	**cd**	**0–0**
14	**♖e1** *(26)*	

It was essential to play 14 h3, opening a path so that the king can retreat. But now comes a brilliant combination.

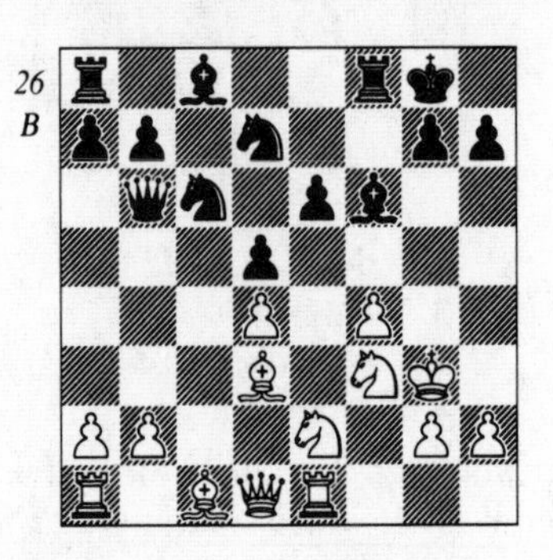

14 ... e5!!

Not worrying about loss of material, Black literally tears the centre apart and opens up all the files and diagonals.

15 fe ♘dxe5

The same move would have followed upon 15 de.

16 de *(27)*

Of course, not 16 ♘xe5? because of 16 ... ♗xe5+ 17 de ♕f2 mate.

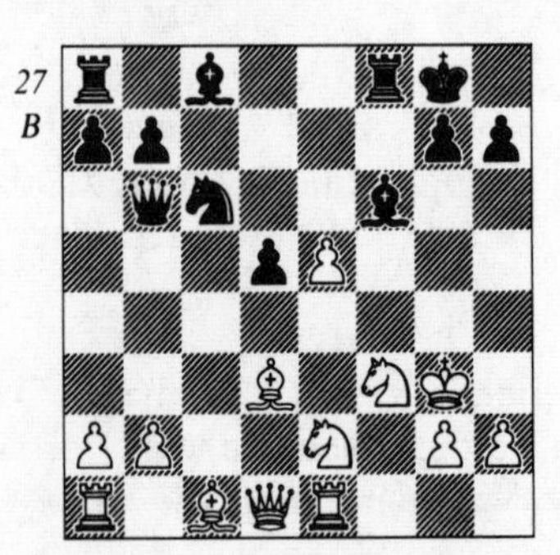

16 ... ♗h4+!!

A very spectacular and unexpected sacrifice of a second piece. White's king is enticed onto the fourth rank (he cannot play 17 ♘xh4 because of 17 ... ♕f2 mate), where it is exposed to a very strong attack.

17 ♔xh4 ♖xf3!

Another tremendous move, eliminating an important defender. In the event of 18 gf ♕f2+ White is mated: 19 ♔g5 h6+ 20 ♔g6 (20 ♔f4 g5 mate) 20 ... ♘e7+ 21 ♔h5 ♕xh2 mate, or 19 ♘g3 ♕xh2+ 20 ♔g5 ♕h6 mate.

18 ♖f1 ♕b4+!
19 ♗f4 ♕e7+
20 ♗g5 ♕e6
21 ♗f5

There does not appear to be any other possibility. On 21 h3? there follows 21 ... ♖xh3+ 22 gh ♕xh3 mate.

21 ... ♖xf5
22 ♘f4 ♕xe5

As a result of all these complications Black has won a pawn and he retains a very strong attack.

23 ♕g4 ♖f7
24 ♕h5 ♘e7
25 g4

Defending against the threat of 25 ... ♘f5+. White is also unable to save the game with 25 ♗xe7 ♖xf4+ 26 ♖xf4 ♕xf4+ 27 g4 ♕xh2+ 28 ♔g5 h6+ 29 ♔g6 ♕c2+. Nor was it of any use to play 25 ♕xf7+ ♔xf7 26 ♘d3+, because of 26 ... ♘f5+!.

25 ... ♘g6+
26 ♔g3

If 26 ♘xg6 then 26 ... ♕xh2 mate.

26 ... ♗d7
27 ♖ae1 ♕d6
28 ♗h6 ♖af8

In this hopeless position White lost on time.

Game No. 4
Spasov–Imocha
World Jun. Ch., Tunja (Colombia) 1989

1 e4 e6
2 d4 d5
3 ♘d2 ♘f6
4 ♗d3 c5
5 e5 ♘fd7
6 c3 ♘c6

7 ♘e2 ♕b6

This traditional queen manoeuvre has been adopted less frequently in recent years. A more fashionable continuation is 7 ... cd 8 cd f6.

8 ♘df3

If 8 0–0 cd 9 cd ♘xd4 10 ♘xd4 ♕xd4 11 ♘f3 ♕b6 12 ♕a4 then 12 ... ♕b4! 13 ♕c2 g6.

8 ... cd

9 cd f6

After 9 ... ♗b4+ White can either transpose to a rather favourable endgame with 10 ♗d2 ♗xd2+ 11 ♕xd2 ♕b4 12 ♖c1 ♕xd2+ 13 ♔xd2, or he can go for double-edged complications after 10 ♔f1 f6!? 11 ♘f4!? fe 12 ♘xe6 e4 13 ♗f4.

10 ef ♘xf6

11 0–0 ♗d6

12 ♘c3

White gets less chance of an opening advantage with either 12 ♗f4 ♗xf4 13 ♘xf4 ♕xb2 14 ♖e1 0–0 15 ♘xe6 ♗xe6 16 ♖xe6 ♖ae8, or 12 ♘f4 0–0 13 ♖e1 ♗d7 14 ♘xe6 ♖fe8 15 ♗f5 ♘a5 16 ♗g5 ♗xe6 17 ♗xe6+ ♖xe6 18 ♖xe6 ♗xh2+. White also gets nowhere after 12 b3 0–0 13 ♗b2 (13 ♗f4 ♘xd4!) 13 ... ♗d7 14 ♘g3 ♘e7 15 a4 a5 16 ♘e5 ♗e8 (Bosman–I. Farago, Dieren 1990).

12 ... ♗d7

12 ... 0–0 13 ♗e3 ♕d8 14 ♖e1 ♕e8 15 ♘e5 ♗xe5 16 de ♘xe5 17 ♗c5 ♘xd3 18 ♕xd3 leads to some advantage for White (Tal–Diez del Corral, Malaga 1981).

13 ♗e3 0–0

14 ♖e1

Also not bad is 14 a3, and now after 14 ... ♕d8 15 ♖c1 ♗e8 16 h3 ♘h5? 17 ♘g5 ♗b8 18 f4 White obtains a big advantage (Svidler–Djurhuus, Gausdal 1991).

14 ... ♖ae8

15 ♘e5! ♗xe5?!

Too risky, though otherwise Black might have fallen into an annoying positional bind.

16 de ♕xb2 *(28)*

17 ♗d2!

The most accurate continuation. White achieves nothing after 17 ef ♕xc3 18 fg ♕xg7 19 ♕h5 ♖f7.

17 ... ♘e4

28
W

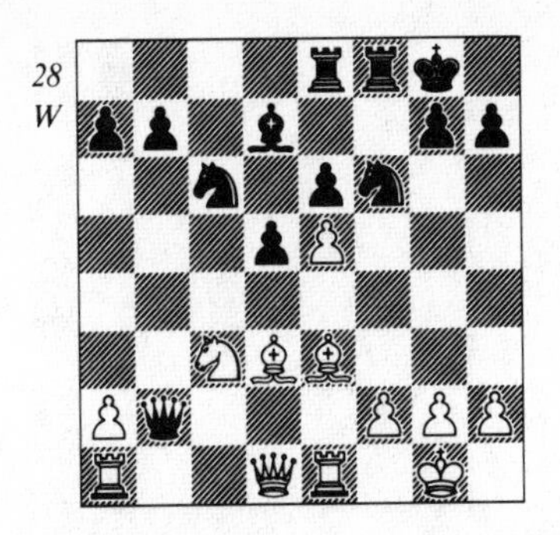

18	**Nxe4**	**de**
19	**Rxe4**	**Nxe5**

Stronger was 19 ... Qb6 20 Be3 Qd8.

20	**Rb1**	**Qa3**
21	**Rb3**	**Qc5**
22	**Be3**	**Qa5**
23	**Rxb7**	**Bc6**
24	**Rxa7**	**Qd5**
25	**Bd4**	

As a result of this forced variation White has not only won a pawn, he has also maintained his attack.

25	**...**	**Rf5**
26	**Rg4!**	**g6**

Not very attractive for Black was 26 ... Nxg4 27 Rxg7+ Kf8 28 Qxg4.

27	**Be4**	**Qd6**
28	**Rh4**	**Rg5**
29	**f3**	

On 29 Bxc6 Black would have played 29 ... Qxc6, with the threat of mate on g2, and White does not have the move 30 f3 because of 30 ... Nxf3+.

29	**...**	**Rd8**

Apparently 29 ... h5 would have put up more resistance.

30	**Raxh7**	**Rh5**
31	**R4xh5**	**gh**
32	**Rxh5**	**Bxe4** *(29)*

Now on 33 de an unpleasant reply is 33 ... Ng6, but White had prepared a stunning blow.

33	**Rh8+!!**	

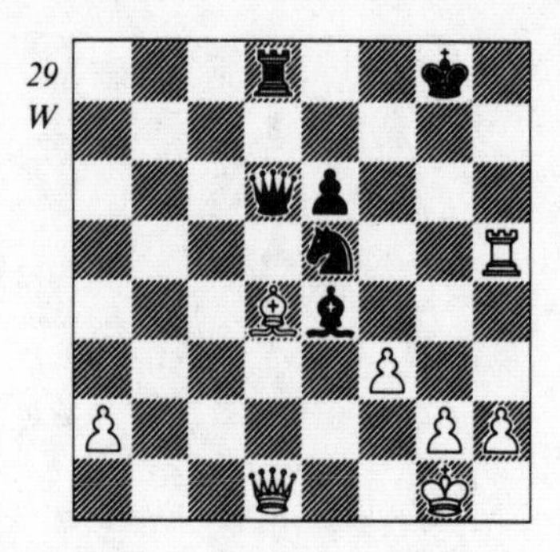

The black king is enticed into a check.

33 ... ♔xh8

Or 33 ... ♔f7 34 ♖xd8 ♕xd8 35 fe, with three extra pawns.

34 ♗xe5+ ♕xe5
35 ♕xd8+ ♔g7
36 fe

And White won.

Game No. 5
Enders–Uhlmann
Gothenburg 1985

1 e4 e6
2 d3 d5
3 ♘d2 ♘f6
4 ♘gf3 b6

A good alternative here is 4 ... ♘c6 (see Game 21: Ljubojevic–Vaganian).

5 e5

A premature advance of the pawn, and not a logical continuation in this position. Better is 5 c3 or 5 ♕e2.

5 ... ♘fd7
6 g3

The natural 6 d4 leads after 6 ... c5 7 c3 f6 8 ef ♕xf6 9 ♘b3 ♗b7 10 ♗g5 ♕f7 11 ♗b5 ♗c6 to a position with chances for both sides (Vasiukov–Bagirov, USSR Ch., Kharkov 1967).

6 ... c5
7 c3 ♘c6
8 d4 f6!
9 ef

Interesting complications may unfold in the event of the bishop manoeuvre 9 ♗h3 cd 10 cd fe 11 ♗xe6 ♘c5! 12 ♗xc8 ♘d3+ 13 ♔f1 (or 13 ♔e2? ♕xc8! 14 ♔xd3 ♘b4+ 15 ♔e2 ♕a6+ 16 ♔e1 ♖c8) 13 ... ♕xc8 14 ♘xe5 ♕h3+ 15 ♔e2 ♘dxe5 16 de ♗c5! 17 ♘f3 ♕g4 with advantage to Black (analysis by Uhlmann).

9 ... ♕xf6
10 ♗h3 cd
11 0–0

A forced pawn sacrifice, since 11 cd ♗a6 12 ♕a4 ♘b4 13 ♘e5 b5! 14 ♘xd7 ba 15 ♘xf6+ gf would have led to a clear advantage for Black.

11 ... dc
12 bc ♘c5!

An important manoeuvre, thanks to which Black takes control of the central squares and defends the pawn on e6.

13 ♗a3 ♗e7
14 c4 0–0
15 ♕e2 dc
16 ♗g2 ♗a6

With accurate play Black cuts across all his opponent's attempts to begin active operations.

17 ♗xc5 ♗xc5
18 ♘e4 ♕e7
19 ♘fg5

19 ♘xc5 ♕xc5 20 ♕xe6+ ♔h8 would promise White nothing.

19 ... ♘d4
20 ♕g4 ♖ae8
21 ♖fd1 *(30)*

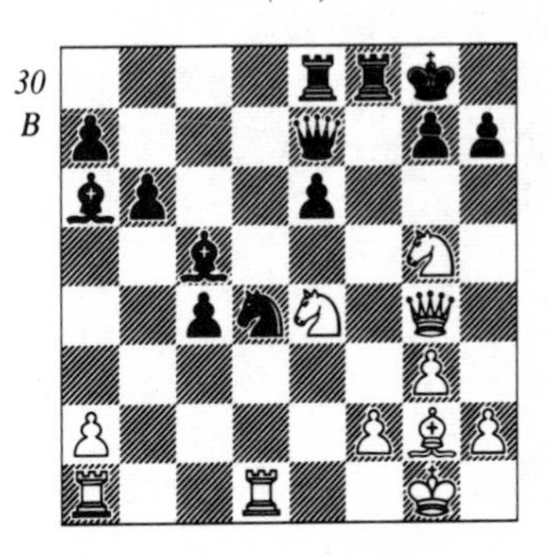
30
B

21 ... c3

22 ♘xc3 ♖xf2!!

The white king is lured out into the centre of the board and enticed into a very strong attack.

23 ♔xf2 ♘c2+
24 ♔f3 ♖f8+
25 ♔e4 ♕b7+
26 ♔e5 ♕c7+
27 ♔e4 *(31)*

27 ♔xe6 leads to mate: 27 ... ♖e8+ 28 ♔f5 ♘e3 mate.

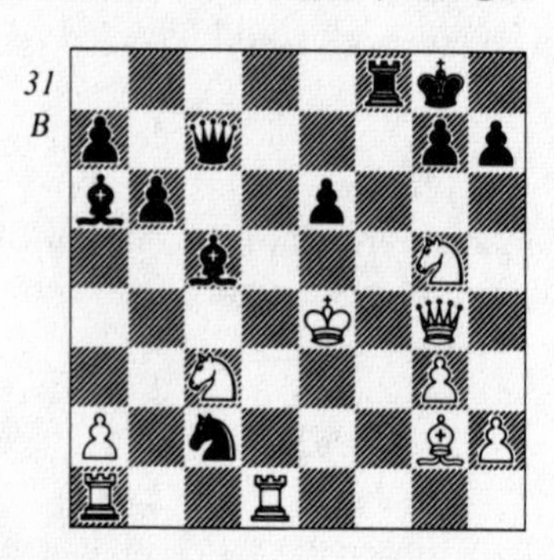
31
B

27 ... ♖f5!

Also quite good was 27 ... ♗b7+.

28 ♖d5

White cannot save the game by playing 28 ♕xf5 ef+ 29 ♔xf5, in view of 29 ... ♘e3+.

28 ... ed+
29 ♔xf5 g6+
White resigned.

In 30 ♔f6 then 30 ... ♕e7 mate.

2 Deflection

The essence of this tactical device is that an opposing piece is deflected away from defending a key square by means of a sacrifice.

An interesting example is the following game:

Koshtenko–Lerner
USSR 1962

1 e4 e6 2 d4 d5 3 ♘c3 ♗b4 4 ♘e2 de 5 a3 ♗xc3+ 6 ♘xc3 ♘f6 7 ♗g5 ♘c6 8 ♗b5 0–0 9 ♗xc6 bc 10 ♘xe4 ♕d5 11 ♘xf6+ gf 12 ♗xf6 ♕xg2 *(32)*

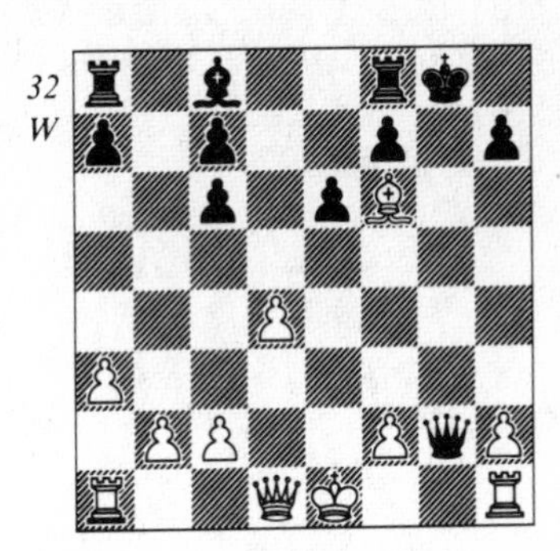

It would appear that White is in quite a lot of trouble. 13 ♖f1 loses to 13 … ♗a6. White loses a bishop after 13 ♔e2 ♕e4+ 14 ♔d2 ♕f4. But suddenly White replied with a quite stunning move.

13 ♕f3!!

In the event of the white queen being captured, the black queen is deflected away from the g-file and White plays 14 ♖g1+ with mate. On 13 … ♕g6 there follows 14 0–0–0 ♕h6+ 15 ♔b1. Black resigned.

Game No. 6
Ivell–Beliavsky
London 1985

1	**e4**	**e6**
2	**d4**	**d5**
3	**e5**	**c5**
4	**c3**	**♕b6**
5	**♘f3**	**♗d7**
6	**♗e2**	

An equal game results after 6 ♘a3 cd 7 cd ♗b4+ 8 ♗d2 ♘c6 9 ♘c2! a5 10 ♗d3 ♗xd2+ 11 ♕xd2 ♘b4 12 ♘xb4 ♕xb4 13 ♕xb4 ab (Kupreichik–Zlotnik, Chelyabinsk 1975).

6	**...**	**♗b5**

The preliminary exchange 6 ... cd 7 cd, and only then 7 ... ♗b5, is good for White: 8 ♘c3 ♗b4 9 0–0 ♗xe2 10 ♘xe2 (Hübner–Debarnot, Las Palmas 1976).

7	**c4!?**	

Zaitsev's move, which leads to a sharp fight. White gets a small advantage after either 7 0–0 ♗xe2 8 ♕xe2 ♕a6 9 ♕d1 ♘d7 10 dc! ♘xc5 11 b4 ♘d3 12 ♗e2 ♘b2 13 ♕b3 ♘c4 14 ♘bd2! ♘xe3 15 fe ♘h6 16 e4 (Kaidanov–Zlotnik, Moscow 1979), or 7 dc ♗xc5 8 0–0 a5 9 ♗xb5 ♕xb5 10 ♘a3 ♗xa3 11 ba ♘e7 12 a4 ♕c4 13 ♖b1 (Gulko–Vitolins, Tbilisi 1979).

7	**...**	**♗xc4**
8	**♗xc4**	**♕b4+!**
9	**♘bd2**	**dc**
10	**a3**	**♕b5**

Worth considering is 10 ... ♕a5 11 0–0 ♘c6 12 ♘xc4 ♕a6.

11	**♕e2**	**cd**
12	**♘xd4**	**♕d5**
13	**♘2f3**	

It is possible that 13 ♘4f3 is somewhat stronger.

13	**...**	**♗c5**
14	**♗e3**	**♗xd4**
15	**♗xd4**	**♘c6**
16	**0–0–0**	**♘ge7**
17	**h4**	

White could have regained his pawn by playing 17 ♗xa7, but rather than lose time he decided to launch an attack against the kingside fortress of the enemy king.

17 ... 0–0
18 ♗c3 ♕b5
19 ♘g5 h6?!

An inaccuracy, and the principal reason for Black's subsequent difficulties; after the correct reply 19 ... ♘d5 Black would have succeeded in repelling the attack and seizing the initiative. For example: 20 ♕e4 g6 21 ♘xh7 ♘xc3! (worse is 21 ... ♔h7 22 h5 ♔g7 23 hg fg 24 ♖xd5 ♕xd5 25 ♕h4 with a very strong attack) 22 bc (or 22 ♘f6+ ♔g7 23 bc ♕xe5) 22 ... ♔xh7 23 h5 ♕xe5 24 hg+ ♔g8 25 ♕h4 ♕xc3+ 26 ♔b1 ♕g7 (analysis by Beliavsky).

20 ♘e4 ♖ad8

In the event of 20 ... ♘d5 21 ♘f6+! gf 22 ef ♔h7 23 ♕c2+ ♔h8 24 ♕d2 White has a certain draw.

21 ♘d6 ♕b6 *(33)*

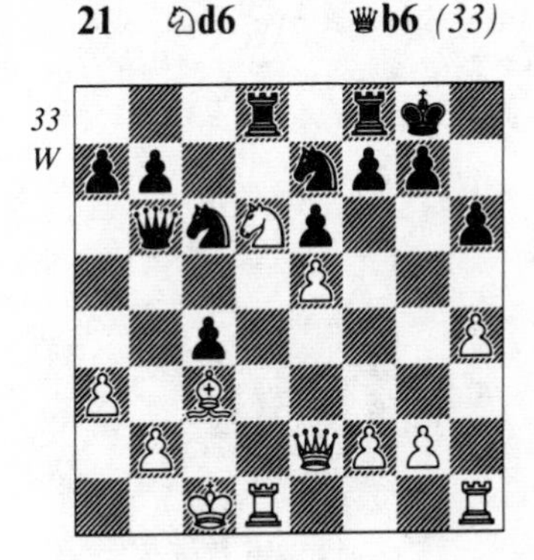

33
W

22 h5!

Consistent. White is not diverted by regaining the pawn on c4 and instead prepares to storm the black king.

22 ... ♘f5

After 22 ... ♘d5 23 ♖xd5 ed 24 ♘f5! White gets an irresistible attack.

23 ♘xf5 ef
24 e6 ♕c5
25 ef+

It looked even better, as Beliavsky notes, for White to play 25 ♖d7 ♖xd7 26 ed, when the passed pawn on d7 establishes a big advantage.

25 ... ♔xf7
26 ♕f3 ♔g8
27 ♕f4!

This move takes control of the central squares and deprives Black of any active play.

27	**...**	**♖xd1+**
28	**♖xd1**	**♖f7**
29	**♖e1**	**♖d7**
30	**g4**	**♘d4**
31	**♕b8+**	

Instead of forcing events White should apparently have preferred the quiet 31 ♔b1.

31	**...**	**♔h7**
32	**♕e8**	**♕c6!**
33	**gf**	

It would appear that Black's game is rather bad: the threat is 34 ♕g6 with mate; in the event of 33 ... ♘xf5 a decisive continuation is 34 ♖e6 ♕h1+ 35 ♗e1. But, even so, Black has a resource which saves the game.

33	**...**	**♘b3+**
34	**♔c2** *(34)*	

Of course, not 34 ♔b1?? ♖d1+ 35 ♖xd1 ♕xe8.

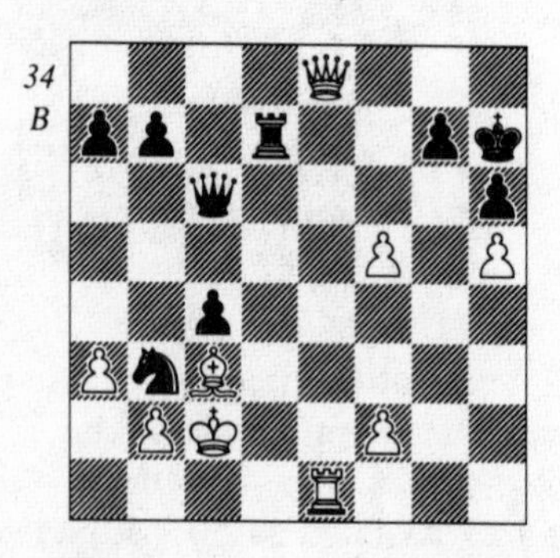

34	**...**	**♘a1+!!**

An unexpected check from the corner! The knight cannot be captured: if 35 ♖xa1 then 35 ... ♕a4+ with mate. Neither can White play 35 ♔b1, because of 35 ... ♖d1+! (deflection of the rook on e1 from its defence of the queen on e8) 36 ♔a2 ♕xe8 37 ♖xe8 ♘b3 38 ♖e1 ♖xe1 39 ♗xe1 ♘d4 with an excellent endgame for Black.

35	**♔c1**	**♘b3+**
36	**♔c2**	**♘a1+**
	Drawn.	

A most peculiar finish.

Game No. 7
Smyslov–Ståhlberg
Zürich 1953

1	**e4**	**e6**
2	**d4**	**d5**
3	**♘c3**	**♘f6**
4	**♗g5**	**de**
5	**♘xe4**	**♗e7**
6	**♗xf6**	**♗xf6**

On 6 … gf White usually plays 7 ♘f3 b6 8 ♗c4 ♗b7 9 ♕e2 and then 10 0–0–0. Weaker is 7 g3, since after 7 … f5 8 ♘c3 ♗f6 9 ♘ge2 Petrosian's move 9 … ♘c6, which he adopted in the third game of his match against Fischer (Buenos Aires 1971), casts doubt on White's opening plan. In that game there followed: 10 d5 ed 11 ♘xd5 ♗xb2 12 ♗g2 0–0 13 0–0 ♗h8, and Black, having rejected a risky line to win the exchange, retained his extra pawn in a good position.

7	**♘f3**	**♘d7**

The more natural 7 … 0–0 is considered in the next game: Chandler–Psakhis.

8	**♗c4**	**0–0**
9	**♕e2**	**♘b6**
10	**♗b3**	**♗d7**
11	**0–0**	**♕e7**

In the game Smyslov–Ståhlberg, Budapest 1950, Black had continued 11 … ♗a4, but it turned out that after 12 ♘xf6+ it is not good to play 12 … ♕xf6, because of 13 ♗xa4 ♘xa4 14 ♕c4 ♘b6 15 ♕xc7, when White wins a pawn. In this game Ståhlberg exchanges light-squared bishops two moves later, but he does not obtain any substantial improvement in his position.

12	**♖fe1**	**♖ad8**
13	**♖ad1**	**♗a4**

Black has found himself in a cramped position and so tries to ease his defence by means of exchanges.

14	**♗xa4**	**♘xa4**

But now after 15 ♘xf6+ ♕xf6 it is not possible for White to play 16 ♕c4, because of 16 … ♘xb2 with a 'fork'.

15	**♕b5**	**♘b6**
16	**c4**	**c6**
17	**♕b3**	**♕c7**

White threatened 18 ♘xf6+, forcing 18 … gf, since on 18 … ♕xf6 White would have played 19 c5, winning the pawn on b7. But the move 17 … ♕c7 does not repel this threat. Better was 17 … ♖d7, although also in this case White has a spatial advantage and could have continued with 18 a4, increasing the pressure.

18 ♘xf6+ gf

19 ♕e3

The start of an attack. Now after 19 … ♘xc4 there would have followed 20 ♕h6 ♕e7 21 ♖d3. Here, as Smyslov notes, if 21 … ♔h8 then a decisive continuation is 22 ♘h4, with the threat of 23 ♘f5, and the move 22 … ♖d5 does not help, because of 23 ♘f5! ♖xf5 24 ♖h3.

On 21 … ♖d5 there follows 22 ♘e5 ♘xe5 23 ♖xe5, when mate is unavoidable. After 21 … ♘d6 the attack is concluded with 22 ♘h4 ♔h8 23 ♖h3.

19 … ♔g7 *(35)*

If Black had played 19 … ♔h8 there would have followed 20 ♕h6 ♕e7 21 ♘h4, with the threat of 22 ♘f5. After the move in the game it is essential for White to transfer his knight to g4 in order to continue his attack, but how can this be achieved?

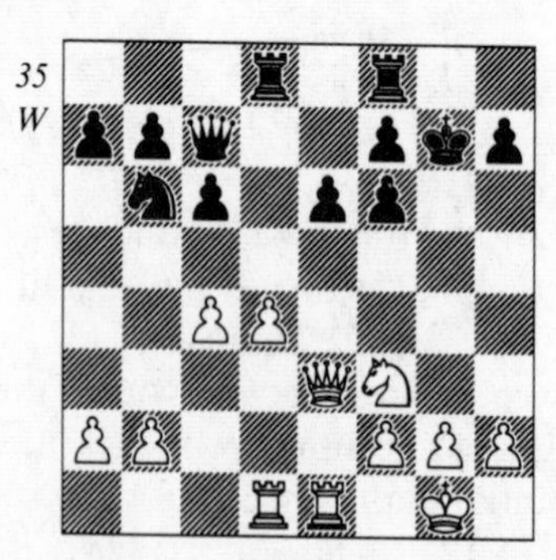
35
W

20 ♘e5!

"An excellent move, with a charmingly simple idea", writes Bronstein. The knight cannot be captured: after 20 … fe a decisive continuation is 21 ♕g5+ ♔h8 22 ♕f6+ ♔g8 23 ♖d3 ♖fe8 24 ♕h6! ed 25 f4! ♔h8 26 ♖g3, when mate is inevitable.

20 … ♕e7

The threat was 21 ♕g3+ ♔h8 22 ♘g6+.

21 ♘g4 ♖g8

No use either was 21 … ♔h8. After 22 d5 cd 23 ♕h6 ♘d7 24

♖xd5 ♖g8 25 ♖xd7 26 ♘xf6 White has a technically won position.

22 ♘h6!

A complicated crowning manoeuvre: the rook cannot move away, in view of the threat of 23 ♘f5+.

22 ... ♕c7
23 ♘xg8 ♖xg8
24 b3

The exchange ahead, White had no trouble in converting his advantage into a win.

24 ... ♔h8
25 ♕h6 ♖g6
26 ♕h4 ♔d7 → KNIGHT TO D7
27 ♖e3 ♕a5
28 ♖h3 ♘f8
29 ♖g3 ♕xa2
30 ♖xg6 ♘xg6
31 ♕xf6+ ♔g8
32 ♕f3 ♕c2
33 ♕d3 Black resigned.

Game No. 8
Chandler–Psakhis
Moscow 1990

1 e4 e6
2 d4 d5
3 ♘c3 ♘f6
4 ♗g5 de
5 ♘xe4 ♗e7
6 ♗xf6 ♗xf6
7 ♘f3 0–0

The system with 7 ... ♘d7 is passive (see Game 7: Smyslov–Ståhlberg).

8 ♕d2 b6
9 ♘xf6+!?

Kosten–Bareev, Hastings 1990/91, continued 9 0–0–0 ♗e7 10 ♗d3 ♗b7 11 h4 ♘d7 12 ♘fg5 h6 13 ♔b1 ♘f6 with sharp play.

9 ... ♕xf6
10 ♗d3 ♗b7

On 10 ... h6 unpleasant is 11 ♗e4 c6 12 ♘e5.

11 ♘g5 h6!?

This exchange sacrifice has become quite a common continuation. But is it necessary? In our opinion, after 11 .. g6 12 h4 h6 13 ♗e4 ♘c6 Black has an entirely acceptable position.

12 ♘h7 ♕xd4

13 ♘xf8 *(36)*

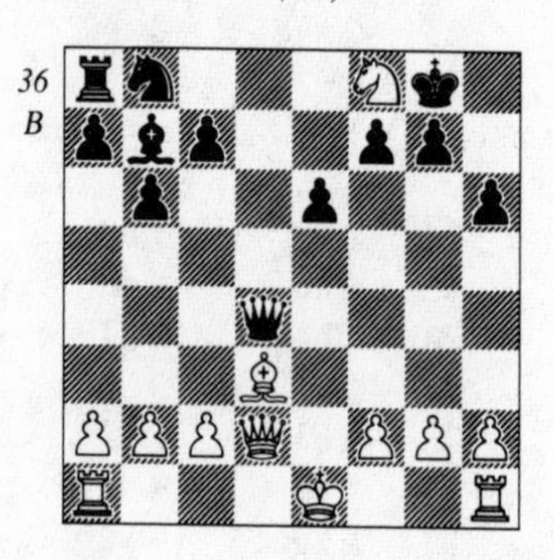

13 ... ♔xf8

Worth considering is 13 ... ♕xb2!?, and now after 14 ♗h7+! ♔h8 (but not 14 ... ♔xf8?? 15 ♕d8 mate) 15 0–0 ♘a6! 16 ♘xe6 ♔xh7 17 ♘f4 ♔f6, or 14 0–0 ♔xf8 15 ♗e4 ♘c6, chances are roughly equal.

14 c3!

Weaker are both 14 0–0–0 ♗xg2 15 ♖hg1 ♗c6, and 14 0–0 ♗xg2 15 ♔xg2 ♕g4+ 16 ♔h1 ♕f3+ with perpetual check.

14 ... ♕h4

Worse for Black is 14 ... ♕e5+ 15 ♗e2 ♘c6 16 ♖d1 ♖d8 17 ♕e8.

15 0-0-0

In Chandler–Prasad, Novi Sad Ol. 1990, Chandler chose a different line: 15 g3 ♕f6 16 ♖f1 ♘d7 17 f4 ♘c5 18 0–0–0 a5 19 ♗c2 ♗c6 20 ♕e3 and obtained a small advantage.

15 ... ♗xg2

16 ♖hg1 ♗c6

17 f4!

White would have achieved nothing with 17 ♖g3 ♘d7 18 ♖dg1 ♘e5 19 ♗e2 g5!.

17 ... ♘d7

18 ♕e3 ♖e8

More precise was 18 ... ♘f6 19 ♕e5 ♘e8 20 ♗e4 ♗xe4 21 ♕xe4 ♖d8.

19	**♗e4!**	**♗d5**
20	**c4**	**♗xe4**

Any attempt by Black to get counterplay can be easily parried: 20 ... ♘f6? 21 cd ed 22 ♕a3+, or 20 ... ♘c5?! 21 ♗c2!.

21	**♖xd7**	**♗g6**
22	**♕e5**	

In the event of 22 ♖xc7 Black activates his pieces by playing 22 ... ♖d8!.

22	**...**	**♖d8?** *(37)*

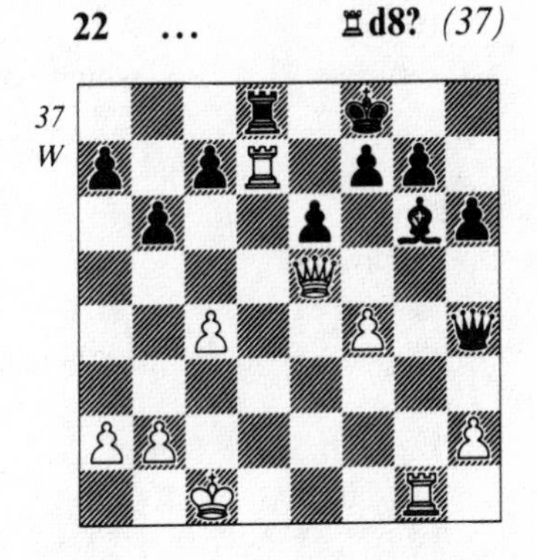

It was essential to play 22 ... ♖e7! 23 ♖d8+ ♖e8 24 ♖xe8+ ♔xe8 25 ♕xc7 ♕xh2, when Black's game is quite in order.

23	**♖g4!**	

White inflicts a typical deflecting blow and the fate of the game is decided.

23	**...**	**♕xg4**
24	**♖xd8+**	**♔e7**
25	**♕xc7+**	**♔f6**
26	**♕e5+**	**♔e7**
27	**♕d6+**	**♔f6**
28	**♕d4+**	**♔e7**
29	**♖b8**	Black resigned.

Game No. 9

Hazai–Uhlmann

Halle 1981

1	**e4**	**e6**
2	**d4**	**d5**
3	**♘c3**	**♗b4**
4	**e5**	**♘e7**

5 a3 ♗xc3+
6 bc c5
7 ♘f3 ♗d7

Another common plan for Black is 7 ... b6, followed by exchanging light-squared bishops (see Game 36: A. Sokolov–Yusupov).

8 a4 ♕a5
9 ♗d2 ♘c6
10 ♗b5

White provokes the move 10 ... a6, which would weaken the b6-square.

10 ... c4

Now the only prospect for White's light-squared bishop is to be exchanged on the square c6.

11 ♕c1 f6

Forcing White to exchange on f6, which results in the g-file being opened up.

12 ef gf
13 0–0 ♖g8
14 ♖e1 ♔f7!

Here the king is not only secure, it also protects the pawn on e6; and thanks to this move the rook on a8 can come into play.

15 ♔f1

The tempting 15 ♗f4 was no good, because of 15 ... ♕xc3, and on 16 ♗d2? Black plays 16 ... ♕xf3.

15 ... ♘f5
16 ♗f4 h5
17 h3 ♖g6
18 ♕a3 h4!

Black does not hurry to play ... ♖ag8, seeking first to fix the white pawn on g2.

19 ♘h2 ♖ag8
20 ♘g4 *(38)*
20 ... ♖xg4!

Otherwise Black's attack would have come to a dead end.

21 hg ♖xg4
22 ♗h2 ♕d8!
23 f3 ♖g6
24 ♕c1 ♕g8
25 ♕d2 ♘g3+

38
B

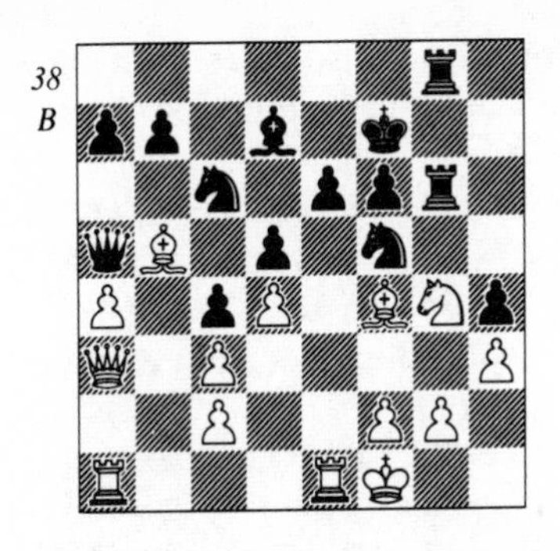

26 ♗xg3

The only move: on 26 ♔g1 Black would have played 26 ... h3; and not 26 ♔f2 because of 26 ... ♘e4+! and 27 ... ♖xg2+.

26 ... ♖xg3
27 ♗xc6 bc

The bishop remains on d7 to defend the pawn on e6.

28 ♖e2 h3
29 ♖b1 h2
30 ♕h6 ♖xf3+
31 ♖f2 *(39)*

39
B

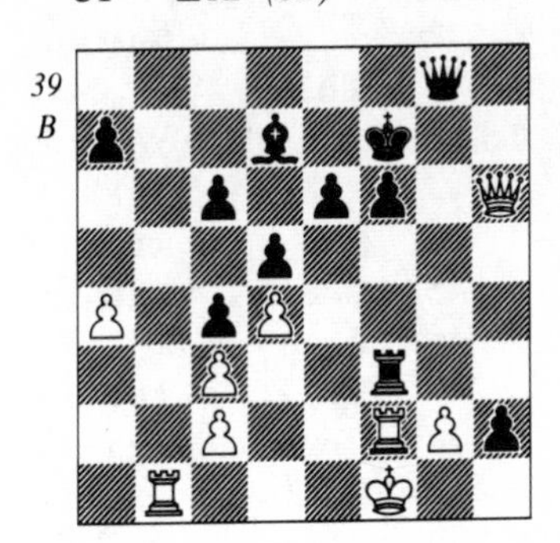

Of course, White cannot play 31 gf?? because of 31 ... ♕g1 mate, but worth considering was 31 ♔e1!, when a possible variation was 31 ... ♖xc3 32 ♕xh2 ♔e7 33 ♖b7 a5 34 ♕c7 ♕g3+ 35 ♕xg3 ♖xg3 36 ♖a7 ♔d6 37 ♖xa5 e5 with sharp play (analysis by Uhlmann). But now comes a quite stunning move, one which is strikingly counter-intuitive.

31 ... ♕g6!!

With this move Black not only deflects the white queen away

from the pawn on h2 but also takes control of the c2-square. On 32 ♕xh2 there would have followed 32 ... ♖xf2+ 33 ♔xf2 ♕xc2+.

32 ♕xg6+ ♔xg6
33 ♔e2 ♖xc3
34 ♔d2 ♖g3!

White would have had greater chances after 34 ... ♖a3 35 ♖f3! ♖xa4 36 ♖h3.

35 ♖h1 c3+
36 ♔c1 ♖g4
37 ♖xh2 ♖xd4
38 ♖f3!

A cunning trap: after the natural 38 ... ♖xa4 there follows 39 ♖g3+ ♔f7 (39 ... ♔f5 40 ♖h5+ ♔f4 41 ♖h4+ ♔xg3 42 ♖xa4 ♔xg2 43 ♖xa7 ♗e8 44 ♖e7) 40 ♖h7+ ♔f8 41 ♔d1.

38 ... e5
39 ♖xc3 ♖xa4
40 ♖g3+ ♗g4
41 ♖c3 e4!
42 ♖h8

White would lose at once after 42 ♖xc6, in view of 42 ... e3!.

42 ... ♖a1+
43 ♔b2

After 43 ♔d2 ♖d1+ 44 ♔e3 d4+ White loses a rook.

43 ... ♖g1
44 g3 ♗f3
45 ♖d8 ♖d1
46 ♖xc6 e3
47 ♖f8 ♗e4!
48 ♖cxf6+ ♔g5
49 ♖6f7 ♔g4
50 ♖f4+ ♔h3!
51 ♖h4+ ♔g2
52 ♖hf4 ♖d2

White resigned.

After 53 ♖f1 the decisive continuation is 53 ... ♖xc2+ 54 ♔b3 ♖f2.

3 Eliminating the Defence and Liquidating the Enemy King's Pawn Cover

In combinations on the theme of eliminating the defence, enemy pieces or pawns performing an important defensive function are eliminated with the aid of a sacrifice.

Frequently the pawn cover of the enemy king is demolished by means of a sacrifice (or sacrifices), after which either the king is left alone to face the oncoming forces or the defending side suffers considerable loss of material.

Let us examine a game which opened with the comparatively rare Anderssen Attack (Classical System). A future grandmaster played the opening very unsuccessfully as Black. His pieces found themselves a long way from the kingside at the moment when his opponent took aim against his king.

Richter–Darga

Berlin 1950

1 e4 e6 2 d4 d5 3 ♘c3 ♘f6 4 ♗g5 ♗e7 5 ♗xf6 ♗xf6 6 e5 ♗e7 7 ♕g4 0–0 8 ♗d3 c5 9 dc ♘d7 10 ♘f3 ♘xc5 11 0–0–0 ♕a5? *(40)* (it was essential to eliminate the dangerous bishop by playing 11 ... ♘xd3+).

A typical sacrifice followed:

12 ♗xh7+ ♔xh7 13 ♕h5+ ♔g8 14 h4!

This threatens the standard 15 ♘g5, with the opening-up of the h-file. This same move would also have followed after 14 ... f6.

14 ... ♖e8 15 ♘g5 ♗xg5 16 hg ♔f8

Deprived of defenders, the king has to flee.

17 g6! fg

If 17 ... ♕c7 then 18 ♕h8+ ♔e7 19 ♕xg7 ♖f8 20 ♕f6+ ♔e8

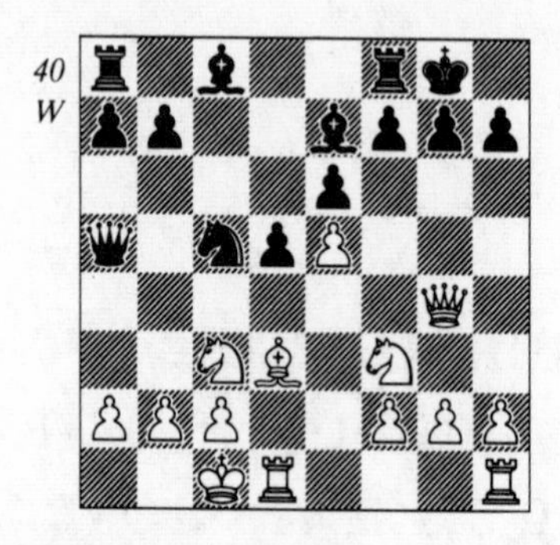

21 g7 ♖g8 22 ♖h8; no use either is 17 … ♔e7, in view of 18 ♕g5+ ♔d7 19 gf ♖f8 20 ♕xg7 ♔e7 (20 … ♕d8 21 ♘xd5!) 21 ♕f6+ ♔d7 22 ♘xd5!.

18 ♕xg6 ♗d7 (the threat was 19 ♖h8+) **19 ♖h7** resigns.

Black can only defend the g7-square with the move 19 … ♖e7, but then White has 20 ♖h8 mate. And the king is unable to hide: on 19 … ♔e7 White brings it back with a check from the square g5.

Consequently mate is unavoidable.

Game No. 10

Karpov–Speelman

Reykjavik 1991

1	**e4**	**e6**
2	**d4**	**d5**
3	**♘d2**	**de**
4	**♘xe4**	**♘d7**
5	**♘f3**	**♘gf6**
6	**♘xf6+**	

White gets no advantage after 6 ♗d3 ♘xe4 7 ♗xe4 ♘f6 8 ♗g5 ♕d6! 9 ♗xf6 gf 10 0–0 f5 11 ♗d3 ♗g7 12 ♕e2 0–0 13 ♖ad1 c5 14 c3 b6 15 ♗a6 ♗xa6 16 ♕xa6 ♖fd8 (Anand–Speelman, Linares 1991).

6	**…**	**♘xf6**
7	**♗d3**	**c5**

The passive 7 … h6 is considered in Game 19: Spielmann–L'Hermet.

8	**dc**	**♗xc5**
9	**♕e2**	**0–0?!**

Stronger is 9 ... ♕c7 10 ♗d2 ♗d7 11 0–0 ♗d6 (Nunn–Korchnoi, Amsterdam 1990). Also possible is 9 ... a6 10 ♗g5 ♕a5+ 11 c3 ♕c7 12 0–0 (Jansa–J. Fries Nielsen, Rimavská Sobota 1991).

10	**♗g5**	**♕a5++**
11	**c3**	**♗e7**
12	**♘e5**	**h6**

It is not good to play 12 ... b6, because of 13 ♗b5! a6 14 ♗c6 ♖a7 15 b4 ♕a3 16 ♕c2 with a considerable advantage to White (Tal–Rogers, San Francisco 1991).

13	**♗h4**	**♖d8**
14	**0–0**	**♕c7**
15	**♖ad1**	**b6**
16	**♖fe1**	**♗b7** *(41)*

Black's position is already quite difficult, but he goes for complications. Relatively best was 16 ... ♘d5.

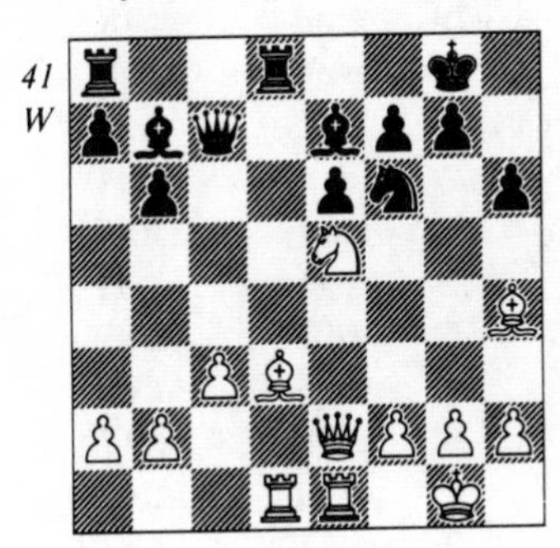

17	**♘xf7!**	**♕c6**

Altogether bad would be 17 ... ♔xf7 18 ♕xe6+ ♔f8 19 ♗c4.

18	**♗e4**	**♕xe4**
19	**♕xe4**	

On 19 ♖xd8+ Black would play 19 ... ♔xf7.

19	**...**	**♖xd1**
20	**♘xh6+!** *(42)*	
20	**...**	**♔f8!**

Black dare not allow the white queen to capture the pawn on e6 with check.

21	**♕xe6**	**♖xe1+**
22	**♕xe1**	**gh**
23	**♗xf6!**	**♗xf6**

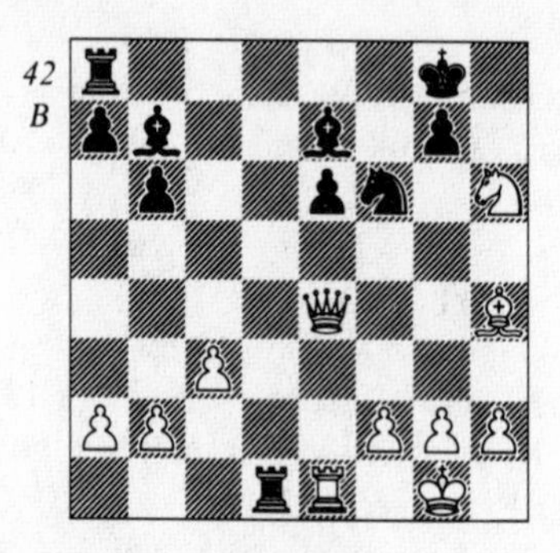

24 ♕e6

Black has quite a lot of material for his queen, but his pieces lack coordination and the white queen is totally dominant.

24	**...**	**♗g7**
25	**♕d6+**	**♔e8**
26	**♕g6+**	**♔f8**
27	**♕d6+**	**♔e8**
28	**♕c7**	**♖d8**
29	**f3**	**♖d1+**
30	**♔f2**	**♖d2+**
31	**♔g1**	**♖d1+**
32	**♔f2**	**♖d2+**
33	**♔e3**	**♖d7**
34	**♕b8+**	**♔f7**
35	**♕xa7**	**♖e7+**
36	**♔f2**	**♗xf3**
37	**♕xb6**	**♗d5**
38	**♕a5**	**♖e5**
39	**g3**	**♗f6**
40	**h4**	**♗e6**
41	**♕c7+**	**♔g6**
42	**a4**	

The passed a-pawn decides the outcome.

42	**...**	**♗g4**
43	**♕c4**	**h5**
44	**♕a6**	**♖f5+**
45	**♔e1**	**♖d5**
46	**♕b7**	**♖d7**
47	**♕b5**	**♗d8**

48	**a5**	**♗c7**
49	**♔f2**	**♖f7+**
50	**♔e3**	**♖e7+**
51	**♔d2**	**♗xg3**
52	**♕d3+**	Black resigned.

Game No. 11

Nezhmetdinov–A. Chistyakov

Kharkov 1956

1	**e4**	**e6**
2	**d4**	**d5**
3	**♘c3**	**♘f6**
4	**♗g5**	**♗b4**
5	**e5**	**h6**
6	**♗d2**	

The main line of the MacCutcheon counter-attack, introduced into practice by Emanuel Lasker.

6 … ♘fd7

A move recommended by Tartakower as long ago as the 1920s, but even so it does not have a good reputation. More common is 6 … ♗xc3 as in Game 29: Euwe–Maróczy.

7 ♕g4

Also worth considering is 7 ♘ce2 — in the event of the exchange 7 … ♗xd2+ 8 ♕xd2 Black is left with a bad light-squared bishop. But also after 7 … ♗e7 (or 7 … ♗f8) 8 ♘f4 White has quite good prospects.

7 … ♗f8

In the event of 7 … ♔f8 8 f4 c5 9 a3 ♗xc3 10 bc ♘c6 11 ♕d1! White has a strong initiative (Réti–Vukovic, Vienna 1922).

8 ♘f3

More forceful than 8 f4 c5 9 ♗d3 (or 9 ♘f3 ♘c6 10 0–0–0 a6 with counterplay for Black) 9 … ♘c6! 10 ♘f3 c4 11 ♗g6 ♘b6 12 f5 ♕d7 13 0–0 fg 14 fg ♘e7 15 ♕h5 ♖g8 and Black successfully repelled his opponent's onslaught (Vasiukov–Chistyakov, Moscow 1956).

8 … c5

In Nezhmetdinov's opinion this move is inaccurate. By allowing the knight to come to b5, Black gives his opponent the opportunity to begin an attack in the centre immediately, which is extremely dangerous for Black in view of the insecure position of his king.

Better was 8 … a6, although here also White gets a dangerous initiative: 9 b4! b6 10 ♘a4 c5 11 bc bc 12 ♘xc5 ♘xc5 13 dc ♕c7 14 ♗e2 ♗d7 15 0–0 g6 16 c4! (Nikitin–Chistyakov, USSR 1957).

9 ♘b5 g6?

This move merits severe criticism, since rather than developing his queenside Black weakens the dark squares on his kingside without there being any particular need. It was essential to capture on d4, after which White had intended to sacrifice a pawn: 9 … cd 10 c3! dc 11 ♗xc3 with sufficient compensation.

10 ♗d3 ♖g8 *(43)*

White threatened a sacrifice on g6. If 10 … h5 then 11 ♕xe6+!! fe 12 ♗xg6+ ♔e7 13 ♗g5+ ♘f6 14 ef+! ♔d7 15 ♘e5 mate.

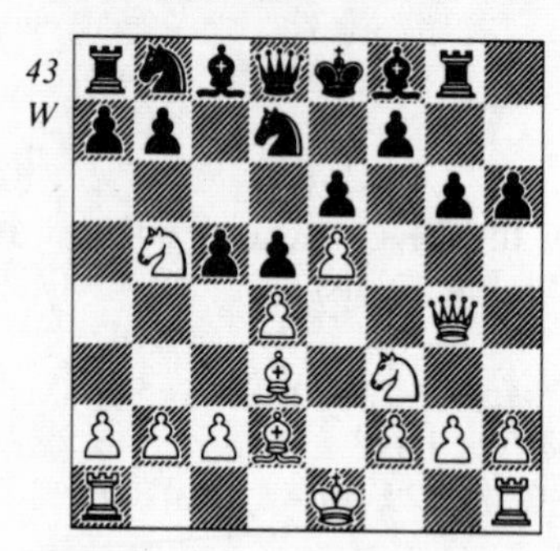

11 c4!

Exploiting his big lead in development, White undermines the centre.

11 … cd

The nature of the game is unchanged after 11 … dc 12 ♗xc4 a6 13 ♘d6+! ♗xd6 14 ed ♕b6 15 0–0 ♕xd6 16 dc ♘xc5 17 ♗xh6, with a position which is very hard for Black to defend.

12 cd ♘c5

If 12 … ed then 13 e6! ♘c5 (on 13 … ♘f6 there follows 14 ef+ ♔xf7 15 ♘e5+, with a rout) 14 ef+ ♔xf7 15 ♘e5+ ♔e7 16 ♘xg6+ and Black's position is bad.

In the event of 12 … a6 a decisive continuation is 13 de! ab 14 ef+! ♔xf7 15 e6+ ♔f6 (15 … ♔e7 16 ♗b4+; 15 … ♔e8 16 ♗xg6+) 16 ♕f4+ ♔xe6 17 ♘xd4+ ♔e7 18 ♗b4+ ♘c5 19 ♗xc5+ ♔e8 20 ♗xg6+! (analysis by Nezhmetdinov).

13 ♕xd4 ed *(44)*

Black overlooked the possibility of an interesting tactical trick: 13 … ♘c6!, when White achieves nothing with 14 dc ♘xd3+ 15

♔e2, in view of the intermediate move 15 … bc!. Nevertheless the simple 14 ♕e3! would have retained an advantage for White.

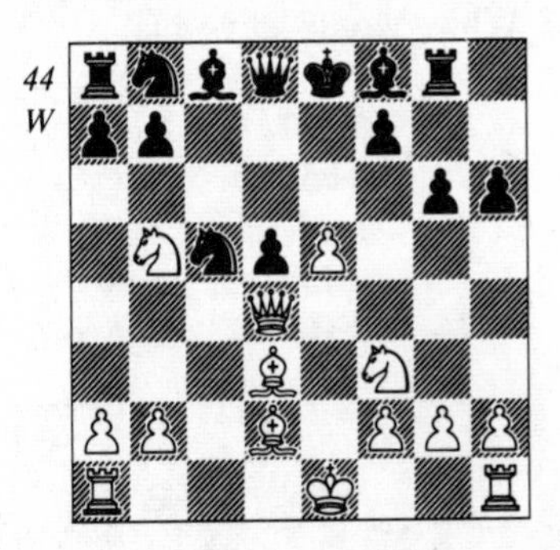
44
W

14 ♘d6+

Thanks to the sacrifice of a pawn White opens up lines for an attack on the black king stranded in the centre.

14 … ♗xd6
15 ed ♕xd6
16 0–0 ♘xd3

Black attempts to weaken the offensive by depriving White of the advantage of the two bishops.

17 ♕xd3 ♘c6
18 ♖fe1+ ♗e6
19 ♘d4!

Without wasting time in regaining the pawn, White brings his knight into the attack, reckoning that in the event of an exchange of knights his attack on the dark squares will be practically irresistible.

Now 19 … 0–0–0 is very risky, in view of 20 ♘b5 ♕b8 (20 … ♕d7 21 ♖ac1 ♔b8 22 ♗f4+ ♔a8 23 ♘c7+) 21 ♖ac1 ♔d7 22 ♕f3 ♘e5 23 ♕g3 ♘c4 24 ♗f4.

19 … g5
20 ♖ac1 ♔d7

20 … ♖g6 results in the loss of a piece: 21 ♕xg6; and on 20 … 0–0–0 there follows 21 ♗a5 ♖df8 (21 … ♖d7 22 ♕b5) 22 ♖xc6 bc 23 ♕a6+ ♔d7 24 ♕b7+ ♔e8 25 ♘f5 with mate.

21 ♘f5!

Forcing Black to disconnect his rooks.

It would be bad to play either 21 … ♕c7 22 b4 a6 23 a4, or 21 … ♗xf5 22 ♕xf5+ ♔c7 23 ♕xf7+ ♕d7 24 ♖e7.

21	**...**	**♕f8**
22	**♕b5!**	**♖c8**

On 22 ... ♖b8 White would have played 23 ♖e5, threatening 24 ♖xd5+.

23	**♕xb7+**	**♖c7**
24	**♕b5**	**a6**

24 ... ♕b8 would not help, because of 25 ♕c5.

25	**♕d3**	**♕b8**
26	**♘xh6**	**♖g6** *(45)*

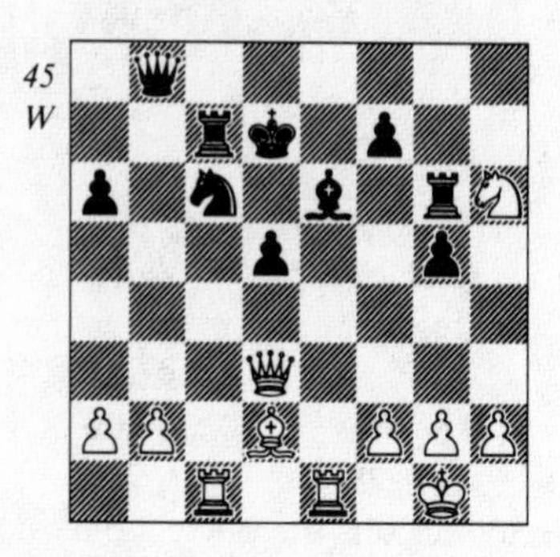

27 ♘xf7!

The last fortifications separating White from the enemy king are demolished.

27	**...**	**♗xf7**
28	**♕f5+**	**♔d8**

Another losing move is 28 ... ♔d6, because of 29 ♗xg5 ♖xg5 30 ♕xg5 ♕xb2 31 ♕f4+ ♘e5 32 ♖xc7.

29	**♖xc6!**	**♖cxc6**
30	**♗a5+**	**♕c7**
31	**♕xf7**	Black resigned.

Game No. 12

Kupreichik–Farago

Polanica Zdroj 1981

1	**e4**	**e6**
2	**d4**	**d5**
3	**♘c3**	**♗b4**
4	**e5**	**♘e7**
5	**♗d2**	

Not a bad move, but one which is rarely encountered in practice.

It demands extremely accurate play from Black; for example, White gets an advantage after 5 ... b6 6 ♘b5 (White achieves nothing after 6 ♘f3 ♕d7 7 a3 ♗xc3 8 ♗xc3 a5 9 a4 ♘f5 10 ♗d3 ♗a6 11 0–0 ♗xd3 12 ♕xd3 h5) 6 .. ♗xd2+ 7 ♕xd2 a6 (7 ... ♗a6?!) 8 ♘c3 a5 9 ♘b5 0–0 10 ♘f3 (Ljubojevic–Seirawan, Mar del Plata 1981).

5 ... c5

6 ♘b5

Other continuations lead to equality: 6 dc ♗xc5 7 ♕g4 ♘f5 8 ♗d3 ♕h4 9 ♕xh4 ♘xh4 10 g3 ♘g6 11 f4 ♗d7, or 6 a3 ♗xc3 7 ♗xc3 b6 (also quite good is 7 ... ♘bc6!? 8 ♘f3 cd 9 ♘xd4 ♘xe5! 10 ♘xe6 ♗xe6 11 ♗xe5 0–0 12 ♗d3 ♘c6 13 ♗g3 ♕f6 Obukhovsky–Khasin, Moscow 1957) 8 b4 ♕c7 9 ♘f3 ♘d7 10 ♗e2 ♘c6 11 bc bc 12 0–0 0–0 13 dc ♘xc5 14 ♗d3 ♘e4! 15 ♕e1 ♗b7 (analysis by Tal).

6 ... ♗xd2+

7 ♕xd2 0–0

8 f4?!

More precise is 8 c3 cd 9 cd ♘bc6 10 ♘f3, with a small positional advantage for White.

8 ... a6

9 ♘c3 cd

10 ♘ce2

The fourth move with the queen's knight in the opening. Generally speaking, no good can come of this.

10 ... ♘bc6

11 ♘f3 ♘f5

12 0–0–0

The attempt to regain the pawn would have led to the loss of the right to castle: 12 ♘exd4 ♘cxd4 13 ♘xd4 ♕h4+, since 14 g3 is no good in view of 14 ... ♘xg3 15 ♕f2 ♘f5.

12 ... ♘e3

13 ♖e1 ♘c4!

Black gets a strong attack against the enemy king.

14 ♕d3 ♕a5

15 ♔b1 ♕b4

16 b3

White has to weaken his castled position. He cannot play 16 ♕b3 because of 16 ... ♕xe1+! 17 ♘xe1 ♘d2+ and 18 ... ♘xb3+.

16 ... ♘a3+

17 ♔a1 ♕a5

With the threat of ... ♘c6–b4.

18 c3 dc

19 ♘g5

The only chance for counterplay.

19 ... g6

20 ♕h3 h5

21 ♖c1 d4?!

In such positions it is essential not to waste time, since this results in losing the initiative. Stronger was 21 ... ♘b4!. If 22 ♖xc3 then 22 ... ♘b5, winning the exchange, and on 22 ♘xc3 unpleasant for White would be 22 .. ♘b5 23 ♗xb5 ab.

22 ♘g3! f5 *(46)*

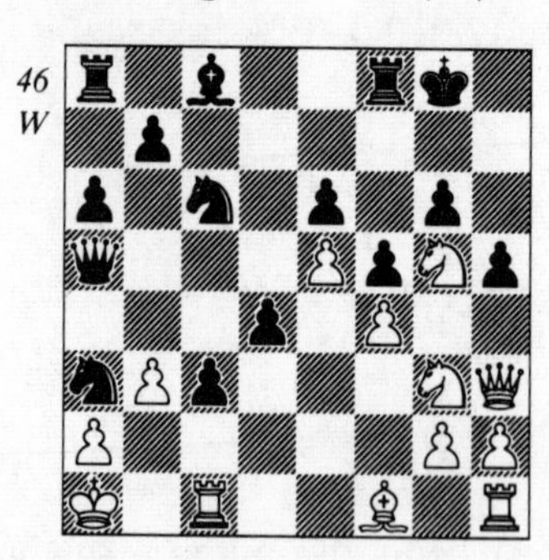

23 ♘xh5!

With its sixth move the queen's knight sacrifices itself, demolishing the black king's screen of pawns in the process.

23 ... gh

24 ♕xh5 ♕c7

Black has to go onto the defensive.

25 h4 ♘b4

26 ♖h3 ♘bc2+

27 ♖xc2 ♘xc2+

28 ♔b1 ♘b4 *(47)*

An astonishing position. Black has an extra rook and two menacing passed pawns in the centre; but the exposed position of the black king enables White to build up a decisive attack.

29 ♗c4

Defending against 29 ... c2+ and 30 ... ♘xa2+ and creating irresistible threats at the same time.

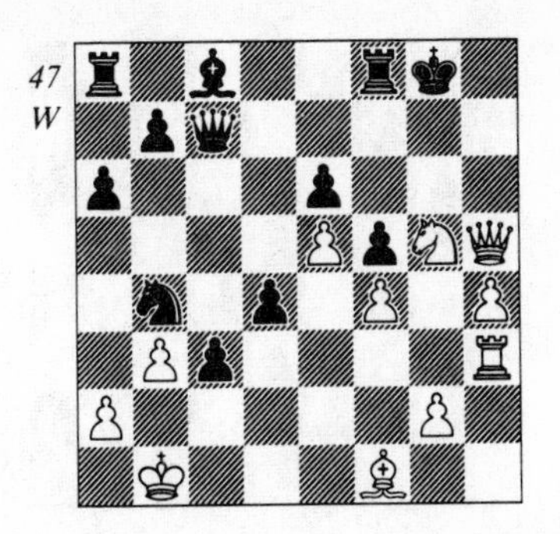

29	**...**	**c2+**
30	**♔b2**	**d3**
31	**♖g3?!**	

A simpler winning line was 31 ♘xe6 c1(♕)+ 32 ♔xc1 ♗xe6 33 ♖g3+ ♕g7 34 ♗xe6+ ♖f7 35 ♕xf7+.

31	**...**	**♕g7**
32	**♘e4?**	

Again White misses an immediate win: 32 ♘xe6!! ♕xg3 33 ♘g5+.

32	**...**	**fe**
33	**♖xg7**	**♔xg7**
34	**♕g5+**	**♔f7**

Stronger was 34 ... ♔h7, and now not 35 ♕e7+ ♔g8 36 ♕xb4 because of 36 ... b5.

35	**f5!**	

The advance of the menacing pawns is halted, and at the same time the threat of ♕g6+ appears.

35	**...**	**♘d5**
36	**♕g6+**	**♔e7**
37	**♗xd5**	**ed** *(48)*

A position from the realms of fantasy!

White's queen and four passed pawns are up against Black's two rooks, bishop and four passed pawns. White does have a draw (38 ♕d6+ ♔e8 39 ♕g6+). But is it possible to achieve more?

38	**♕d6+**	**♔e8**
39	**♕g6+**	**♔e7**
40	**♕d6+**	

Repetition to gain time.

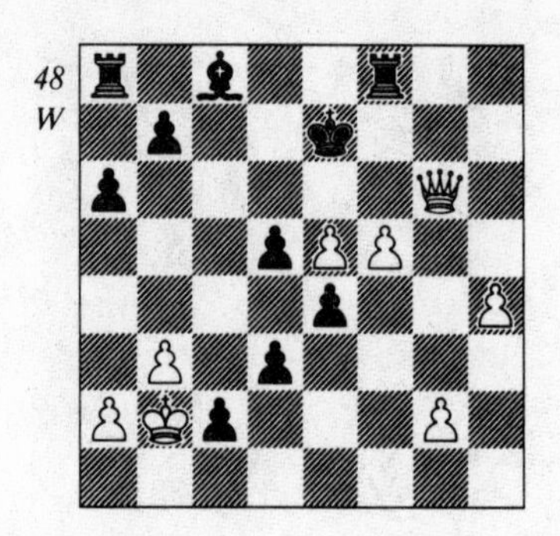

40	**...**	**♔e8**
41	**g4**	**♗d7?**

Here, as Kupreichik pointed out, Black could still have obtained a draw: 41 ... ♗xf5! 42 gf ♖c8!. The threat of the appearance of a new black queen (... c1(♕)+) would have obliged White to force perpetual check.

42	**f6**	**♖f7**

The only defence against 43 ♕e7 mate.

43	**e6**	**♗xe6**

Greater chances were offered by 43 ... ♖xf6 44 ed+ ♔f7 45 ♕xd5+ ♔g7.

44	**♕xe6+**	**♔f8**
45	**g5!**	

Now in the event of 45 ... ♖e8 White wins with 46 ♕d6+ ♔g8 47 g6 e3 48 ♕xd5.

45	**...**	**e3**
46	**g6**	

Now the outcome is clear.

46	**...**	**c1(♕)+**
47	**♔xc1**	**♖c7+**
48	**♔d1**	Black resigned.

48 ... e2+ 49 ♔d2 e1(♕) 50 ♕xe1.

Game No. 13

Kruppa–Komarov

Kherson 1991

1	**e4**	**e6**
2	**d4**	**d5**
3	**♘c3**	**♗b4**

4	**e5**	**♘e7**
5	**a3**	**♗xc3+**
6	**bc**	**c5**
7	**♕g4**	**0–0**

Frequently encountered is the sharp continuation 7 ... ♕c7 8 ♕xg7 ♖g8 9 ♕xh7 cd 10 ♘e2 dc 11 f4. With 7 ... 0–0 Black keeps his kingside intact at the risk of 'castling into it'.

Another possibility is a transition to an ending which is quite acceptable for Black: 7 ... ♘f5 8 ♗d3 h5 9 ♕f4 cd 10 cd ♕h4 11 ♕xh4 ♘xh4 12 ♗g5 ♘f5 13 ♘e2 ♘c6.

Black fails to equalise with 7 ... ♔f8 8 a4 b6 9 ♘f3 ♗a6 10 ♗d3 ♗xd3 11 cd ♘d7 12 ♗a3 ♔g8 13 0–0 h6 (Smirin–Eingorn, USSR Ch., Leningrad 1990). Here White should have played 14 c4 ♔h7 15 dc.

8	**♗d3**	**♘bc6**

Black is promised substantial counter-attacking resources by continuing with the more precise 8 ... f5 9 ef ♖xf6 (see Game 39: Tischbierek–E. Vladimirov).

9	**♕h5**	**♘f5?!** *(49)*

Possibly stronger is 9 ... ♘g6 10 ♘f3 ♘ce7 11 dc! ♕c7 12 0–0 ♘f5!? (Vasiukov–Naumkin, Voskresensk 1990).

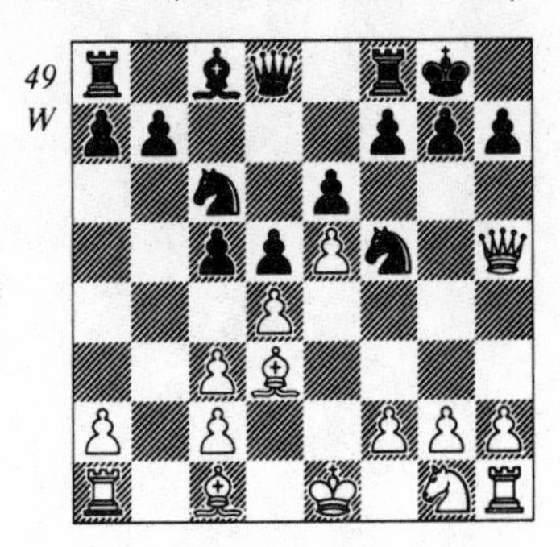

10	**♘f3**	

10 g4 leads to equality after 10 ... ♕h4 11 ♕xh4 ♘xh4 12 ♗g5 ♘g6 13 ♘f3 f6 14 ef gf 15 ♗h6 ♖f7 16 dc e5 (analysis by S. Ivanov).

10	**...**	**f6**
11	**g4**	**c4**

It is not good to play 11 ... g6, because of 12 ♕h3 ♘g7 13 ♕h6!.

12	**gf**	**cd**

13 ♖g1 ♘e7

For 13 … ef, see the game Khalifman–Pr. Nikolic, Moscow 1990, which was quoted in Part One.

14 ef ♖xf6 *(50)*

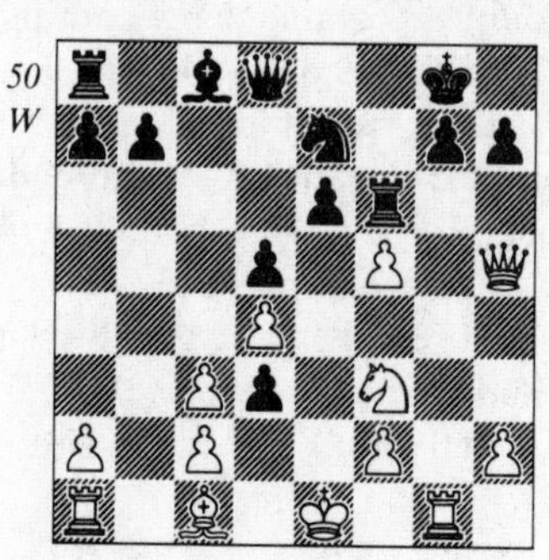

15 ♖xg7+!!

An unexpected demolition sacrifice in a position where White has still not completed his development.

15 … ♔xg7

16 ♕g5+ ♘g6

On 16 … ♔f7 White wins with 17 ♘e5+.

17 fg hg

The only move: Black loses after 17 … ♕e7? 18 ♕h6+ ♔g8 19 ♗g5 hg 20 ♕h4 ♔g7 21 ♘e5, followed by 22 ♘g4.

18 ♗f4 ♗d7

18 … ♕a5 19 ♗e5 ♕xc3+ 20 ♔f1 ♕xa1+ 21 ♔g2 ♔f7 22 ♕xf6+ ♔e8 23 ♗d6 ♔d7 24 ♘e5+ ♔xd6 25 ♕d8+, with mate to follow.

19 ♗e5 dc

It does not help to play 19 … ♖c8 20 cd ♖xc3 21 ♔d2 ♖c8, because of 22 ♖g1 ♗e8 23 ♖g4.

20 h4!

White has to play very precisely; for instance, the tempting 20 ♔d2?! leads after 20 … ♕e7 21 ♖g1 c1(♕)+! 22 ♔xc1 ♕xa3+ 23 ♔d2 ♕b2+ 24 ♔e1 ♕a1+ to perpetual check.

20 … ♗e8

No better is 20 … ♗a4 21 h5 ♔f7 22 ♗xf6 ♕xf6 23 ♘e5+ ♔e7 24 ♘xg6+ ♔f7 25 ♘e5+ ♔e7 26, f4, or 20 … ♕e7 21 h5 ♖af8 22 ♕xg6+ ♔h8 23 ♘h2.

21 ♘h2 ♔f7

22 ♕h6 ♔e7

In the event of 22 ... g5 there follows 23 ♕h7+ ♔f8 24 ♕h8+ ♔f7 25 ♘g4 ♖g6 26 h5.

23 ♗xf6+ ♔xf6
24 ♕f8+ ♗f7
25 ♘g4+ ♔f5
26 ♕xf7+ ♔xg4
27 ♔e2! *(51)* Black resigned.

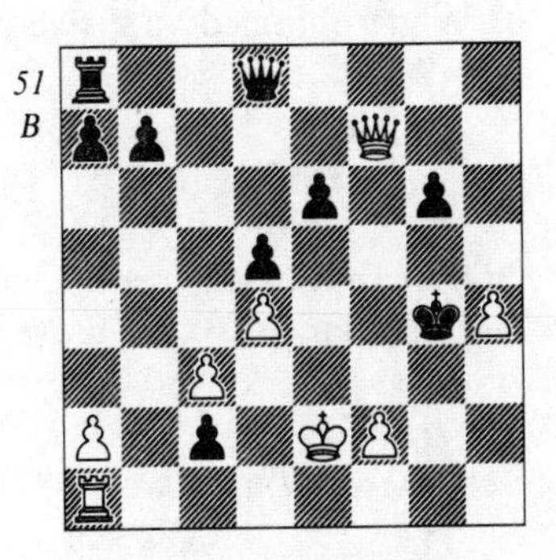
51
B

Mate is unavoidable: 27 ... ♕f8 28 ♕xg6+ ♔f4 29 ♕g5+ ♔e4 30 ♕g4+ ♕f4 31 f3 mate.

Game No. 14
Timman–Vaganian
Montpellier 1985

1 e4 e6
2 d4 d5
3 ♘c3 ♗b4
4 e5 c5
5 a3 ♗a5
6 b4!

This move was first recommended by Alekhine; weaker is 6 ♕g4?! ♘e7 7 dc ♗xc3+ 8 bc ♕a5 9 ♗d2 ♘g6 10 h4 h5 11 ♕g5 ♘d7 12 c4 ♕xc5 13 ♘f3 dc 14 ♗b4 ♕d5 with advantage to Black (Kruppa–Lputian, USSR Ch., Moscow 1991).

6 ... cd

In the event of 6 ... cb 7 ♘b5! ba+ 8 c3 ♗c7 9 ♗xa3, or 7 ... ♘c6 8 ab ♗xb4+ 9 c3 ♗e7 10 ♗a3!, White's attack more than compensates for the sacrificed pawn.

7 ♕g4!

Nezhmetdinov's bold thrust, which leads to sharp positions with better chances for White. In the game Nezhmetdinov–Aramanovich, Tbilisi 1949, there followed: 7 ... ♘e7 8 ♘b5 ♗c7 9 ♕xg7 ♖g8 10 ♕xh7 ♗xe5 11 ♘f3! ♖h8 12 ♕d3 ♗f6 13 ♗f4. If 10 ... a6 then 11 ♘xc7+ ♕xc7 12 ♘e2 ♕xe5 13 ♗b2 ♘bc6 14 0–0–0.

The continuation 7 ♘b5 ♗c7 8 f4 ♘e7 9 ♘f3 leads to a quiet manoeuvring game. In the third game of the World Championship match Smyslov–Botvinnik, Moscow 1954, after 9 ... ♗d7 10 ♘bxd4 ♘bc6 11 c3 White obtained an active position.

7 ... ♘e7
8 ba dc
9 ♕xg7 ♖g8
10 ♕xh7 ♘bc6

In the ninth game of the match mentioned above Botvinnik continued 10 ... ♘d7 (see Game 37). The move in the game leaves Black with more options.

11 f4

In Game 26: Fischer–Tal, White played 11 ♘f3.

11 ... ♕xa5
12 ♖b1 ♗d7

Worth considering was the immediate 12 ... ♘d4.

13 ♖xb7 ♘d4
14 ♕d3 ♘ef5
15 ♘f3

On 15 ♘e2 an unpleasant reply is 15 ... ♗b5.

15 ... ♘xf3+
16 ♕xf3 ♖c8

More accurate is 16 ... ♗c6, since now White does not have the move 17 ♖b3? because of 17 ... ♘d4 18 ♕xc3 ♘xb3.

17 ♗d3 ♗c6? *(52)*

Black has underestimated his opponent's attacking opportunities.

18 ♖xf7!

The only possible move. If the rook had retreated along the b-file then 18 ... d4 would have been very dangerous for White. On the other hand, Black's position now quickly falls apart.

18 ... ♔xf7
19 ♕h5+ ♔e7
20 ♗xf5 ♖cf8

The white bishop cannot be taken: on 20 ... ef there follows 21

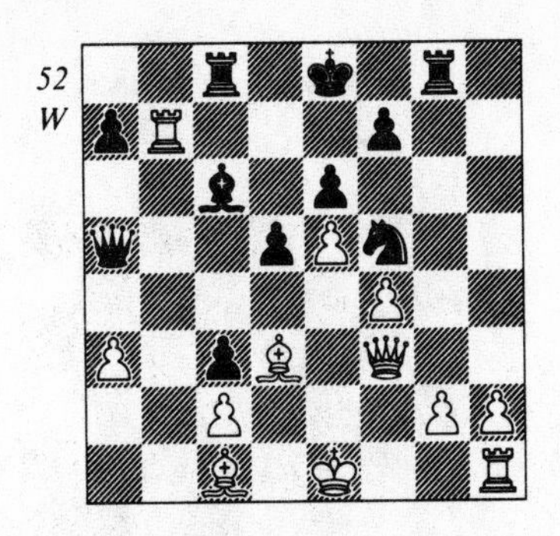
52
W

♕h7+ ♔e6 22 ♕h6+ ♔d7 23 ♕d6+ ♔e8 24 ♕e6+, capturing one of the black rooks with check. But here too White's attack is very dangerous.

21 ♕h4+ ♔e8 *(53)*

On 21 ... ♔d7 unpleasant was 22 ♗xe6+ ♔xe6 23 ♕h6+ ♔d7 24 ♕d6+.

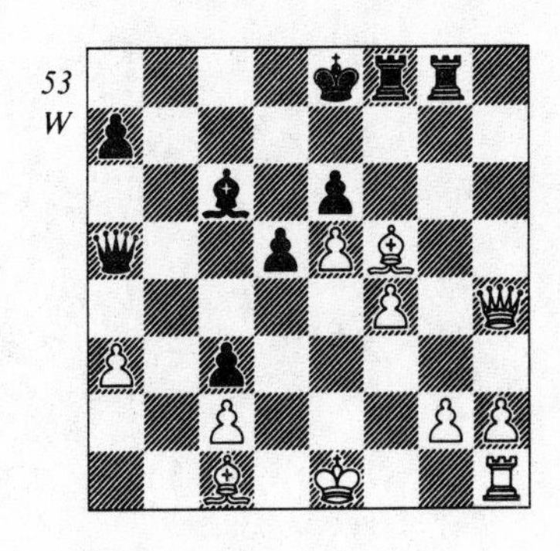
53
W

22 ♕h6!

Play is unclear after 22 ♗xe6 ♖xg2.

22 ... ♕c7

White has an irresistible attack after 22 ... ef 23 ♕xc6+ ♔d8 24 ♗e3!.

23 ♕xe6+ ♔d8
24 ♗h3 d4
25 0–0 d3
26 cd ♕b6+
27 ♖f2!

Avoiding a trap: 27 ♔h1?? ♗xg2+!. Also unclear is 27 d4 ♕xd4+ 28 ♔h1 ♗d7.

27	**...**	**♔c7**
28	**♕c4**	**♖h8**
29	**d4**	**♕b1** *(54)*

54
W

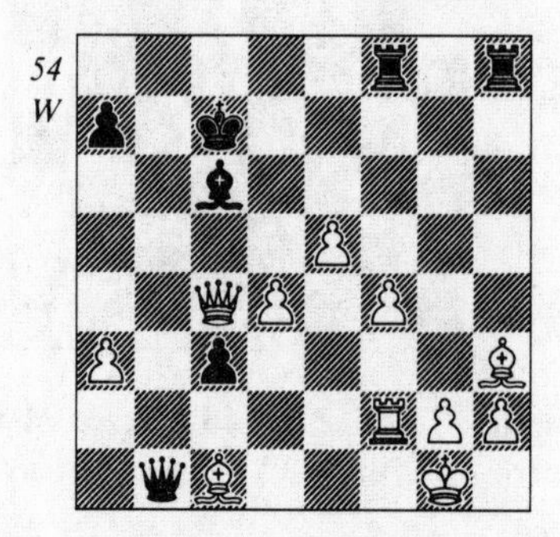

Black sets another trap: after the natural 30 ♕xc3 an annoying reply is 30 ... ♖xh3! 31 gh ♕e4. White's next move effectively ends the game.

30	**d5!**	**♕xc1+**
31	**♖f1**	**♕e3+**
32	**♔h1**	**♔b8**

No use either was 32 ... ♕b6, in view of 33 f5 (but not 33 ♕xc3? ♖xf4!).

33	**dc**	**♔c7**
34	**♕b4**	Black resigned.

34 ... ♔xc6 35 ♕d6+ and 36 ♖b1+ leads to mate.

Game No. 15
Godena–Bareev
Aosta 1989

1	**e4**	**e6**
2	**d4**	**d5**
3	**♘d2**	**c5**
4	**ed**	**ed**
5	**♘gf3**	**♘f6**

An unusual choice. Far more common is 5 ... ♘c6 (see Game 27: Karpov–Korchnoi and Game 45: Psakhis–Vaganian).

6 ♗b5+

More rarely encountered is 6 ♗e2!? — for example: 6 ... ♘c6 7 0–0 cd 8 ♘b3 ♗e7 9 ♘fxd4 0–0 10 ♗f4 ♘e4 11 c3 ♗f6 12 ♗f3 ♕b6 with equality (Wahls–Khalifman, Germany 1990).

6	**...**	**♗d7**
7	**♗xd7+**	**♘bxd7**
8	**0–0**	**♗e7**
9	**dc**	**♘xc5**
10	**♘d4**	**♕d7**
11	**♘2b3**	**♘ce4**
12	**♕f3**	**0–0**
13	**♘f5**	**♗d8**
14	**♗e3**	**g6**
15	**♘g3**	**♖e8**
16	**♖fd1**	**♕c8!**

A subtle move. The black queen gets out of the pin along the file and attacks the pawn on c2.

17	**c3**	**a5**
18	**a4**	**♖a6!**
19	**♘xe4?!**	

As a result of this exchange Black gets rid of his isolated pawn. More circumspect was 19 ♗d4.

19	**...**	**de**
20	**♕e2**	**♗c7**

The black bishop is transferred to the h2–b8 diagonal.

21	**h3**	**♗b8**
22	**♖d4**	**♕e6**
23	**♕b5** *(55)*	

23 ♘c5 would lose to 23 ... ♕e5 24 ♘xa6 ♕h2+.

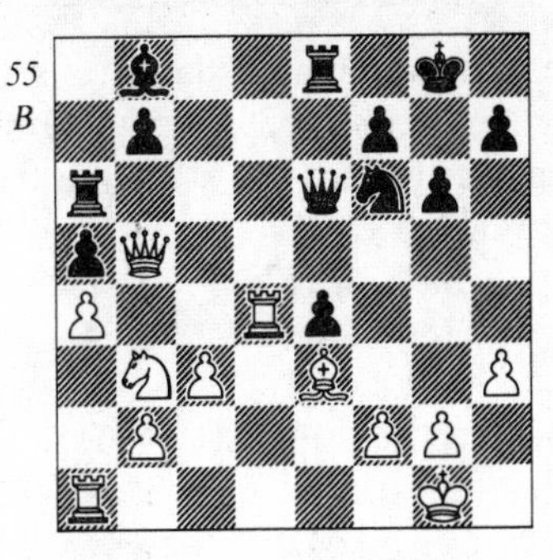
55
B

23	**...**	**♖b6!**

Forcing White to accept the pawn sacrifice.

24	**♖xe4**	**♘xe4**
25	**♕xb6**	

On 25 ♗xb6? Black has the ingenious reply 25 ... ♘d6!, when after the queen moves away White loses his knight on b3, and in the event of 26 ♘d4 ♘xb5 27 ♘xe6 ♖xe6 28 ab the bishop on b6 is undefended.

25 ... ♕e5
26 ♖d1

Not 26 ♕xa5? ♕h2+ 27 ♔f1 ♘d2+! or 26 g3? ♘xg3 27 f4 ♕d5 with a strong attack.

26 ... ♗c7
27 ♕xb7?

Better was 27 ♕b5 ♕h2+ 28 ♔f1 ♘g3+ 29 ♔e1 ♕g1+ 30 ♔d2 ♖d8+ 31 ♘d4 ♕xg2 32 ♔c1, when play is double-edged.

27 ... ♕h2+
28 ♔f1 ♕h1+
29 ♔e2 ♕xg2 *(56)*

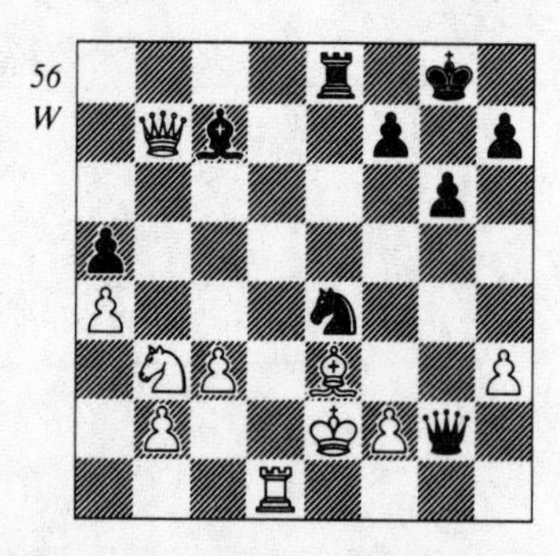

56
W

The black pieces have created dangerous threats against the white king. After the tempting 30 ♘c5 there would follow: 30 ... ♕xf2+!! (a queen sacrifice for the sake of a discovered check) 31 ♗xf2 ♘xc5+ and 32 ... ♘xb7.

30 ♕xc7 ♘xf2
31 ♖d8 ♘g4+
32 ♔d3

But not 32 ♔e1? ♕f2+! 33 ♔d1 ♘xe3+.

32 ... ♕e4+
33 ♔d2 ♕xe3+
34 ♔c2 ♕e4+
35 ♔c1

35 ♔d2 loses to 35 ... ♕e1+ 36 ♔c2 ♘e3+ 37 ♔d3 ♕f1+ 38 ♔d4 ♕f6+.

35	**...**	**♕e1+**
36	**♖d1**	**♕e3+**
37	**♔b1?**	

White should have played 37 ♘d2, retaining practical chances.

37	**...**	**♕e4+**
38	**♔c1**	

White does not have the move 38 ♔a2, because of 38 ... ♕xa4+.

38	**...**	**♘e3**

The threat is mate on c2, and on 39 ♖d2 Black plays 39 ... ♕h1+.

39	**♘d4**	**♘xd1**
40	**♔xd1**	**♕d3+**

White resigned.

Mate is unavoidable.

4 Clearing and Opening Lines or Squares

The expression 'clearing a line' (or 'vacating a square') refers to a move which frees a line (or a square) of a piece of one's own which is preventing a tactical operation or favourable manoeuvre from being carried out.

As for 'opening lines', this should be understood to mean an operation in which lines are freed of 'enemy' pieces or pawns.

In the game Mikh. Tseitlin–Osipov, corr. 1970, which began with the Rubinstein Variation of the French, the following position arose after Black's 22nd move *(57)*:

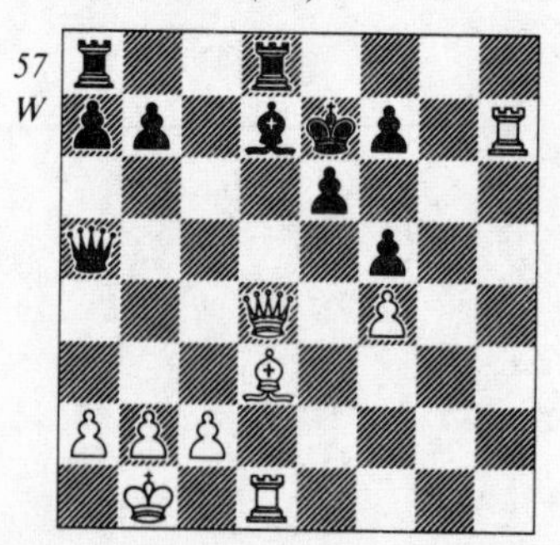
57
W

23 ♗b5!!

This spectacular combinational thrust decided the outcome of the game immediately. The white bishop, which had hindered the interaction of White's major pieces, was offered up as a sacrifice, thereby vacating the d-file and impeding the activity of the black pieces.

Now Black can play neither 23 ... ♕xb5 24 ♕d6+ ♔f6 25 ♖h6+ ♔g7 26 ♕e7, nor 23 ... ♗xb5 24 ♕c5+ ♔f6 25 ♖h6+ ♔g7 26 ♕g1+ ♔f8 27 ♖h8+ and 28 ♕g5+. Black is also unable to save the game with 23 ... ♕c7, in view of 24 ♕g7 ♗e8 25 ♕g5+.

Black resigned.

Typical tactical methods for opening lines can be seen in the following example *(58)*:

Ostrovsky–Shestoperov
Liepaja 1971

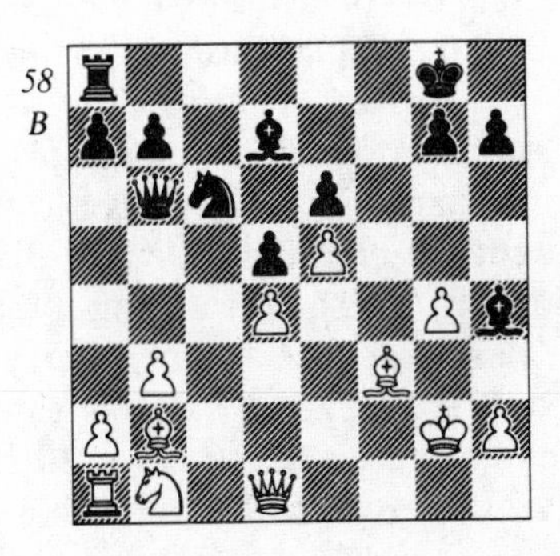

A typical position arising from the Advance Variation. Black has outstripped his opponent in development, he has deployed his pieces successfully, and he now proceeded to take decisive action:
18 ... ♘xe5!

The knight cannot be captured, since this would open up the diagonal: after 19 de Black plays 19 ... ♕f2+ and 20 ... ♕xb2.
19 ♘d2 ♘d3 20 ♗c3 ♖c8 21 ♘b1 ♖xc3! 22 ♘xc3 ♕xd4 23 ♕c2 ♘b4! 24 ♕b2 ♗f6
White resigned.

If 25 ♖c1 then 25 ... ♘d3.

Game No. 16
Nimzowitsch–Salwe
Carlsbad 1911

1	**e4**	**e6**
2	**d4**	**d5**
3	**e5**	**c5**
4	**c3**	**♘c6**
5	**♘f3**	**♕b6**

Black exerts pressure on the pawn at d4. Nimzowitsch called such a plan “the strategy of rapid pressure”.

6 ♗d3

A frequent continuation is 6 a3 (see Game 17: Afek–Psakhis). As for 6 ♗e2, this move leads to a comfortable game for Black: 6 ... cd (but not 6 ... ♘ge7? 7 dc ♕c7 8 ♘d4!, when 8 ... ♘xe5 loses to 9 ♘b5 ♕xc5 10 ♕d4! as in Euwe–Kramer, Zaandam 1946) 7 cd ♘h6 8 ♘c3 (8 ♘a3? ♗xa3 9 ba ♘f5 with advantage to Black) 8 ... ♘f5 9 ♘a4 ♕a5+ 10 ♗d2 ♗b4 11 ♗c3 b5 12 a3 ♗xc3+ 13 ♘xc3 b4 14 ab ♕xb4 15 ♗b5 ♗d7 16 ♗xc6 ♗xc6 17 ♕d2 0–0 18 0–0 ♖fb8 (Epshtein–Saunina, Tbilisi 1976).

6 ... ♗d7?!

Seemingly a natural move: Black intends first to play ... ♖c8 and only then to exchange on d4. But as a consequence of this game this move went out of fashion. Usually Black plays 6 ... cd 7 cd and only now 7 ... ♗d7, threatening to capture on d4. In the event of the pawn sacrifice (Milner–Barry Gambit) 8 0–0 ♘xd4 9 ♘xd4 ♕xd4 10 ♘c3, Black has no great problems; in fact it is even possible to capture another pawn: 10 ... ♕xe5!? 11 ♖e1 ♕b8! 12 ♘xd5 ♗d6 13 ♕g4 ♔f8 14 ♗d2 h5! 15 ♕h3 ♗c6.

7 dc!

A revolutionary move at the time when this game was played. White gives up his pawn centre in return for the possibility of controlling the centre with his pieces.

7 ... ♗xc5
8 0–0

The game Hort–Andersson, Reykjavik 1972, continued: 8 ♕e2 a5! 9 ♘bd2 a4 10 b4 ab 11 ♘xb3 ♗a3 12 0–0 ♘ge7 13 ♗d2 ♘g6 14 ♘bd4 ♗e7 15 ♖fe1 with some initiative for White.

8 ... f6?!

Black intends to eliminate yet another of his opponent's central pawns. But, as Nimzowitsch writes, this would be good only if by such means he could ensure the mobility of his own centre; White opposes this vigorously. More precise is 8 ... a5.

9 b4!

This move makes it possible for White to keep control of e5 for some considerable time. Less effective is 9 ♕e2, because of 9 ... fe 10 ♘xe5 ♘xe5 11 ♕xe5 ♘f6, after which it would not be difficult for Black to oust the blockading queen.

9 ... ♗e7
10 ♗f4 fe
11 ♘xe5 ♘xe5
12 ♗xe5 ♘f6

An attempt by Black to neutralise the bishop on e5 with his own bishop would have come to grief as a result of a queen check on h5: 12 … ♗f6 13 ♕h5+ g6? 14 ♗xg6+ hg 15 ♕xg6+ ♔e7 16 ♗xf6+ ♘xf6 17 ♕g7+.

13	**♘d2**	**0–0**
14	**♘f3!**	

Otherwise the blockade may be totally destroyed — for example: 14 ♕c2 ♘g4! 15 ♗xh7+ ♔h8 16 ♗d4 ♕c7 17 g3 e5. With this knight move White reinforces the blockade and prevents his opponent from playing 14 … ♗b5, since this would have been met by 15 ♗d4 ♕a6 16 ♗xb5 ♕xb5 17 ♘g5 ♕c6 18 ♖e1, when the pawn on e6 falls.

Black could now have tried to break through the blockade with 14 … ♘g4, but after 15 ♗g3 (if 15 ♗d4 then 15 … ♕c7, with the threat of 16 … ♖xf3) 15 … ♗f6 (15 … ♗d6? 16 ♗xh7+ and 17 ♘g5+) 16 h3 ♘h6 17 ♗e5 ♘f7 18 ♗xf6 gf 19 c4! and White has a significant advantage (19 … d4? 20 ♘xd4; 19 … dc 20 ♗xc4; or 19 … ♕xb4 20 cd ed 21 ♖b1 with a dangerous attack).

14	**…**	**♗d6**
15	**♕e2!** *(59)*	

Nimzowitsch preferred this move to the more obvious 15 ♗d4 (in order on 15 … ♕c7 to play 16 ♕e2 and then 17 ♘e5), since in this line he feared (and not without reason!) 16 … ♘g4 17 h3 (White gets nowhere with 17 ♗xh7+ ♔xh7 18 ♘g5+ ♔g6 19 ♕xg4 ♖f4! 20 ♕h3 ♔xg5 21 ♗xg7 ♔g6 22 ♕h6+ ♔f7 23 ♕h7 ♔e8) 17 … e5!.

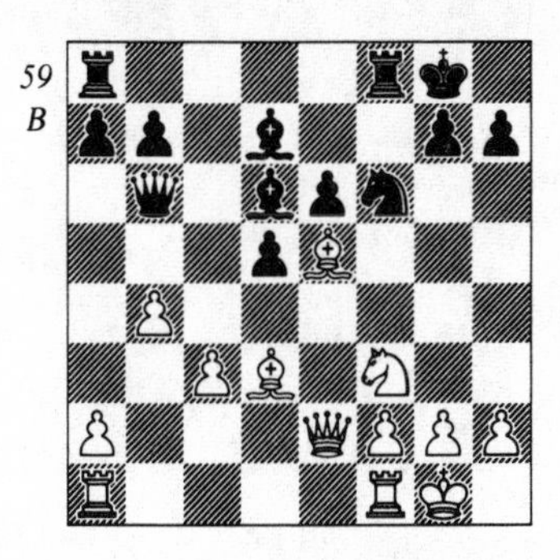

15	**…**	**♖ac8**
16	**♗d4**	**♕c7**

17	**♘e5**	**♗e8**
18	**♖ae1**	

Total suffocation!

18	**...**	**♗xe5**
19	**♗xe5**	

Now this bishop dominates the dark squares.

19	**...**	**♕c6**
20	**♗d4!**	

In order to compel the bishop on e8, which incidentally commands the h5-square, to take up a definite position.

20	**...**	**♗d7**
21	**♕c2!**	

With this move White frees a path for his rook and at the same time creates a decisive piece formation aimed at the h7-square.

21	**...**	**♖f7**
22	**♖e3**	**b6**
23	**♖g3**	**♔h8** *(60)*

60
W

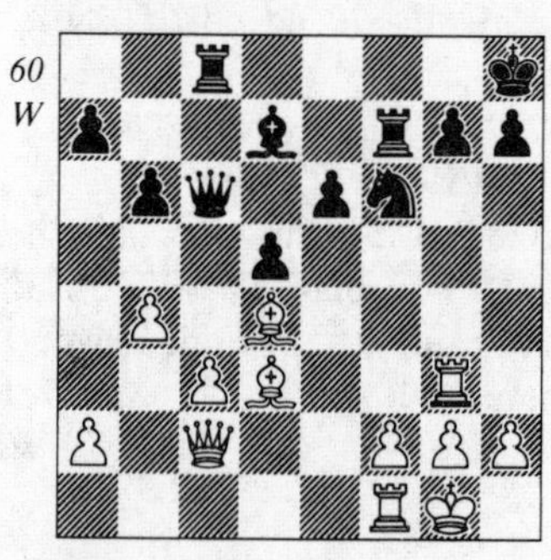

24	**♗xh7!**

A decisive strike which shatters the position of the enemy king. The bishop is immune to capture — 24 ... ♘xh7 25 ♕g6 ♔g8 26 ♗xg7 ♘f8 27 ♕h6 ♘h7 28 ♗f6+.

24	**...**	**e5**
25	**♗g6!**	**♖e7**
26	**♖e1**	**♕d6**
27	**♗e3**	**d4**
28	**♗g5**	

The extra pawn and the advantage of the two bishops practically guarantee a win for White.

28	**...**	**♖xc3**

29	**♖xc3**	**dc**
30	**♕xc3**	**♔g8**
31	**a3**	**♔f8**
32	**♗h4**	**♗e8**
33	**♗f5**	**♕d4**

White was threatening to play ♗g3.

34	**♕xd4**	**ed**
35	**♖xe7**	**♔xe7**
36	**♗d3**	**♔d6**
37	**♗xf6**	**gf**
38	**♔f1**	**♗c6**
39	**h4**	Black resigned.

Game No. 17

Afek–Psakhis

Israel 1990

1	**e4**	**e6**
2	**d4**	**d5**
3	**e5**	**c5**
4	**c3**	**♘c6**
5	**♘f3**	**♕b6**

A common continuation is 5 ... ♗d7 (see Game 1: Yanovsky–Kindermann).

6	**a3**	**♗d7?!**

A move which does not enjoy a good reputation. The usual continuation is: 6 ... a5!? 7 ♗d3 ♗d7 8 ♗c2 ♘ge7 9 0–0 cd 10 cd ♘f5, or 6 ... c4 7 g3 ♗d7 8 ♗h3 ♘a5 9 ♘bd2 ♘e7 10 0–0 h6 11 ♘h4 0–0–0 12 ♘g2 g6 13 ♘e3 h5 14 ♖b1 ♗h6 (Platonov–Ree, Kiev 1978).

7	**b4**	**cd**
8	**cd**	**♖c8**
9	**♗b2!**	

Also quite good is 9 ♗e3. After 9 ... ♘h6 10 ♗d3 ♘g4 11 0–0 ♗e7 12 ♘bd2 ♘xe3 13 fe 0–0 14 ♘b3 ♘b8 15 ♕e2 ♖c7 16 h4 h6 17 ♘c5 a6 18 ♘g5 White has gained a substantial advantage (Torre–Chernin, New Delhi 1990).

9	**...**	**♘a5!?**
10	**♘bd2**	**♘c4**
11	**♘xc4**	**dc**
12	**♖c1**	**♕a6**

After 12 … ♗b5 White can obtain an advantage with 13 ♘d2 c3 14 ♖xc3 ♖xc3 15 ♗xc3 ♗xf1 16 ♘xf1 ♘e7 17 ♘e3, or 13 d5 ed 14 ♕xd5. Black also fails to equalise after 12 … a5, in view of 13 ♘d2 ab 14 ♘xc4 ♕d8 15 ab b5 16 ♘d6+ (Sveshnikov–Lputian, Moscow 1991).

13 d5 ed
14 ♕xd5 ♗e6
15 ♕e4 ♘e7
16 ♗e2 ♗d5
17 ♕d4 b5
18 0–0 ♕b7
19 ♖fd1 ♗e6!

On 19 … ♗c6 an annoying reply is 20 e6! (20 … fe 21 ♘g5 ♗d5 22 ♗g4).

20 ♘g5 ♘f5
21 ♕f4 ♗e7
22 ♘xe6?!

Worth considering was 22 ♘e4 followed by 23 ♘d6.

22 … fe
23 ♗f3 ♕c7 *(61)*

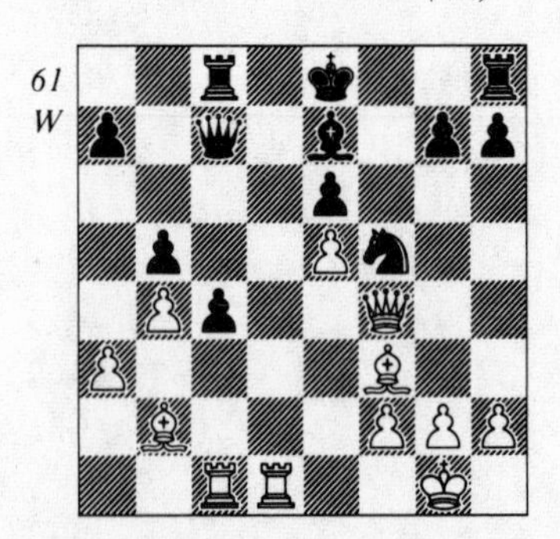
61
W

24 ♗d5! ♕b6!

After 24 … ed 25 ♕xf5 Black has no defence against 26 e6.

25 g4 ♖f8

Also possible was a different move order: 25 … ♘h4 26 ♗h1 ♖f8.

26 ♗h1 ♘h4
27 ♕g3

With the intention of playing 28 ♗d4 and 29 ♕e3.

27 … ♖d8

Worth considering was 27 ... a5!?.

28 ♖xd8+ ♕xd8

29 ♕e3

In the event of 29 ♗c6+ Black could have sacrificed a pawn: 29 ... ♔f7 30 ♗xb5 ♕a8, with a dangerous initiative.

29 ... a6

30 f4 ♔f7

31 ♗e4 ♔g8

Black has managed to castle artificially, but White has retained some advantage.

32 ♖f1

Threatening 33 f5 with a decisive attack.

32 ... ♕c8

33 ♗c3 a5

34 ♕b6

Not the best move; stronger was 34 ♕a7 or 34 ba.

34 ... ab

35 ab ♕d7

36 ♕c6?

But this is a serious mistake: in no circumstances should White have allowed the enemy queen to invade.

36 ... ♕a7+

37 ♔h1 ♕e3

38 ♗e1!

The only move. It was not good to play 38 ♕xe6+, because of 38 ... ♔h8!.

38 ... ♔h8

39 ♗g3 c3

40 ♖e1 ♕d2

41 ♕xe6 ♗xb4!

With passive play Black will be doomed to defeat, and so he makes the game sharper.

42 ♗xh4 c2

43 ♕c6?

White is playing with fire: it was essential to continue 43 ♗xc2, maintaining an advantage.

43 ... ♕xf4

With the extremely unpleasant threat of 44 ... ♕f1+ 45 ♖xf1 ♖xf1+ 46 ♔g2 c1(♕).

44 ♖g1 *(62)*

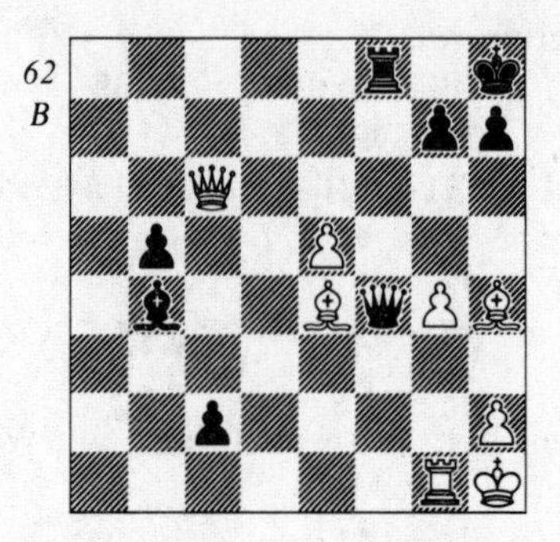

44	**...**	**♗c5!!**

A spectacular interference move on the c-file. On 45 ♕xc5 Black wins with 45 ... ♕xe4+ 46 ♖g2 ♖f1+; it doesn't help to play 45 ♗g3 ♕e3!.

45	**♗g5**	**♕xe5!**
46	**♖e1**	**♖f2**
47	**♕c8+**	**♗f8**
48	**♗f4**	**♕xf4**
49	**♗g2**	**♖d2**

White resigned.

Game No. 18

Boleslavsky–Ufimtsev

Moscow 1944

1	**e4**	**e6**
2	**d4**	**d5**
3	**♘c3**	**de**

Rubinstein's move. Black's concession of the centre guarantees White greater space and a more active position, on account of which this system is now adopted comparatively rarely.

4 ♘xe4 ♘f6

In the event of 4 ... ♘d7 White rapidly completes his development, obtaining an attacking position (see Game 10: Karpov–Speelman and Game 19: Spielmann–L'Hermet).

5 ♘xf6+ gf

It is risky to play 5 ... ♕xf6, because of 6 ♘f3 ♗d7 7 ♗g5 ♕g6 8 ♗d3 f5 9 h4 with advantage to White (Tarrasch–Lasker, sixth match game, World Ch., Munich 1908). Therefore instead of 6 ... ♗d7 Black has to lose time on the precautionary move 6 ... h6.

6 ♘f3 b6

The reply 6 ... c5 facilitates the transition to an ending which is good for White after 7 ♗e3 cd 8 ♕xd4.

7 ♗b5+ c6
8 ♗c4 ♗a6
9 ♗b3?!

White misguidedly declined to exchange bishops, which would have guaranteed him a small but lasting advantage.

9 ... ♕c7
10 c4 ♘d7
11 0–0 0–0–0
12 ♕e2 ♗d6
13 a4 ♖g8
14 a5 c5!

Preparing to include his bishop on a6 in the attack on the white king.

15 ab ♕xb6
16 ♗e3?

This is a serious error. After 16 ♗a4 cd 17 ♗xd7+ ♔xd7 18 b4 chances would have been roughly equal.

16 ... ♗b7
17 dc ♘xc5
18 ♗d1

Reinforcing the f3-square.

18 ... ♖g4
19 ♕d2 ♘e4
20 ♕a5 ♖dg8! *(63)*

63
W

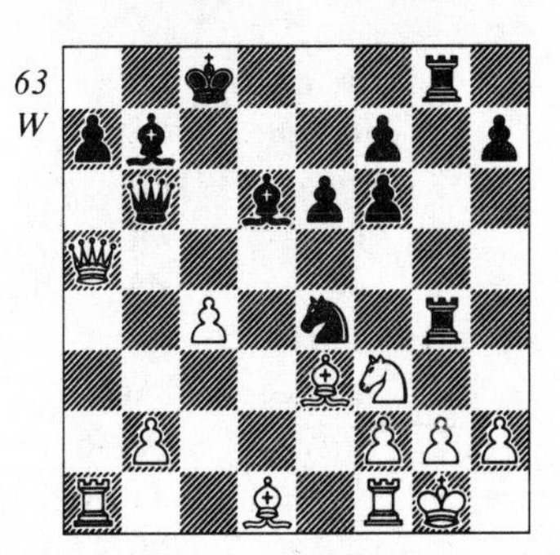

On 21 ♗xb6? Black would have ended the game in elegant fashion: 21 ... ♖xg2+ 22 ♔h1 ♖xh2+ 23 ♘xh2 ♘xf2 mate.

21 ♘e1 ♖xg2+
22 ♘xg2 *(64)*

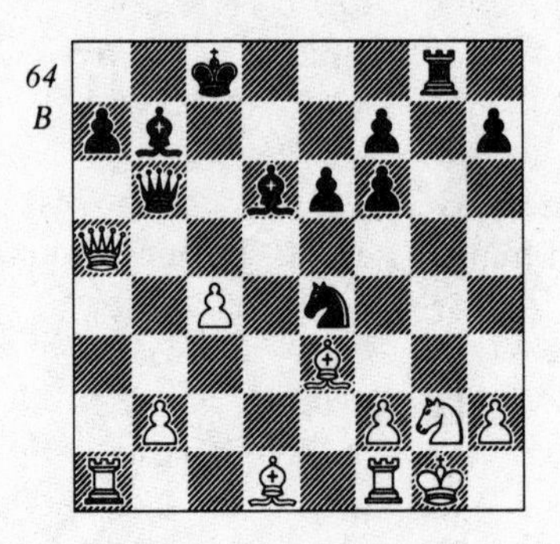
64
B

And now a brilliant finish.

22 ... ♘d2!!
23 ♕d5

In order to block off the troublesome bishop White has to give up his queen. After 23 ♗xb6 Black forces mate in three: 23 ... ♖xg2+ 24 ♔h1 ♖xh2+ 25 ♔g1 ♖h1 mate. White would also not save the game with the variation 23 f3 ♕xe3+ 24 ♖f2 ♘xf3+ 25 ♗xf3 ♗xf3.

23 ... ♗xd5
24 cd ♕xb2
25 ♗xd2 ♕xa1
26 ♗f3 ♗xh2+

White resigned.

Game No. 19
Spielmann–L'Hermet
Magdeburg 1927

1 e4 e6
2 d4 d5
3 ♘d2 de
4 ♘xd4 ♘d7
5 ♘f3 ♘gf6
6 ♘xf6+ ♘xf6
7 ♗d3 h6

Too passive. Usually Black plays 7 ... c5 at once (see Game 10: Karpov–Speelman), or 7 ... ♗e7 8 ♕e2 0–0 9 ♗g5 c5 10 0–0–0

♕a5 11 ♔b1 cd 12 h4 ♗d7! 13 ♘xd4 ♗c6 14 ♘xc6 bc 15 ♗d2 (Nunn–Skembris, Paris 1983).

8 ♕e2 ♗d6
9 ♗d2 0–0
10 0–0–0 ♗d7

Better prospects are offered by 10 ... b6, with the fianchetto of the light-squared bishop.

11 ♘e5 c5
12 dc ♗xe5
13 ♕xe5 ♗c6
14 ♗f4 ♕e7
15 ♕d4

A series of inaccurate moves by Black has given him a very difficult position. White has an extra pawn, the advantage of the two bishops, and pieces which are placed superbly.

15 ... ♖fd8
16 ♗d6 ♕e8
17 ♖hg1 b6
18 ♕h4 bc
19 ♗e5!

An interesting point in the game: White has chosen to reject the natural 19 ♗xc5 (although with this move he would have retained his extra pawn), preferring to launch a decisive attack on the king.

19 ... ♕e7
20 g4 c4
21 g5!

Now it is not good to play 21 ... hg because of 22 ♕xg5, and Black is also unable to play 21 ... ♘h7 — 22 ♗xh7+ ♔xh7 23 g6+.

21 ... ♘d7 *(65)*

It would appear that there is nothing particularly interesting in this position. White can win almost as he pleases: 22 ♗h7+ ♔f8 (22 ... ♔h8 23 ♗xg7+) 23 ♗d6, or at once 22 ♗xg7 cd 23 ♕xh6. Nonetheless, Spielmann finds the most elegant — and at the same time the most decisive — continuation of his attack, one incorporating a brilliant final thrust.

22 ♕xh6!!

What style!

22 ... gh

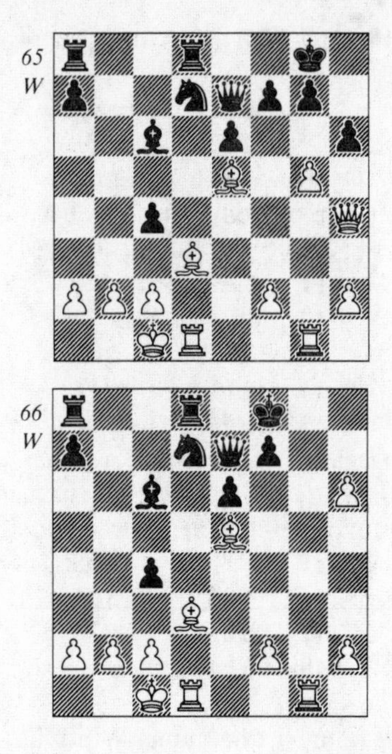

23	**gh+**	**♔f8** *(66)*
24	**♖g8+!**	Black resigned.

The black king is enticed onto the g8-square and the white h-pawn marches on triumphantly to be promoted and deliver checkmate: 24 … ♔xg8 25 h7+ ♔f8 26 h8(♕) mate (or even h8(♖) mate).

Game No. 20
Fischer–Kovacevic
Rovinj/Zagreb 1970

1	**e4**	**e6**
2	**d4**	**d5**
3	**♘c3**	**♗b4**
4	**a3**	

This move was adopted in matches for the World Championship by Alekhine against Euwe (Holland 1935) and by Smyslov against Botvinnik (Moscow 1954). Its merit is that White immediately clarifies the position in the centre and gets the advantage of the two bishops. The defect of this system is that White loses several tempi, allowing his opponent to get counterplay for his pieces.

4 … ♗xc3+
5 bc de
6 ♕g4 ♘f6
7 ♕xg7 ♖g8
8 ♕h6 ♘bd7

Frequently 8 … ♖g6 is played here, and now 9 ♕d2 b6 10 ♗b2 ♗b7 11 0–0–0 ♕e7 12 ♘e2 ♘bd7 13 c4 0–0–0 14 ♕e1 c5 15 ♘c3 cd 16 ♖xd4 ♘c5 leads to a roughly equal position (Sakharov–Dubinin, corr. 1977).

9 ♘e2

White's idea and the move played are both too passive. Worth considering is a continuation suggested by Hort: 9 f3!?.

9 … b6!

Also quite good is 9 … c5 10 ♘g3 ♕c7 11 ♕e3 ♕c6 12 a4 a6 13 dc ♕xc5 14 ♕xc5 ♘xc5 with drawish tendencies (Fischer–R. Byrne, USA Ch. 1966/67).

10 ♗g5?

A natural but, as it turned out, totally useless move. White loses two tempi and achieves nothing. He should have continued developing his kingside pieces: 10 ♘g3 and 11 ♗e2.

10 … ♕e7!

Threatening the annoying 11 … ♘g4, when there would follow 12 ♗xe7 ♘xh6 13 ♗h4 ♘f5.

11 ♕h4 ♗b7
12 ♘g3 *(67)*

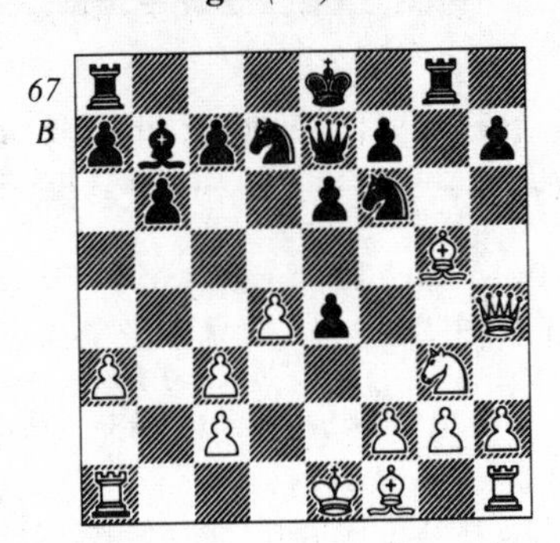

67
B

12 … h6!

A surprising move. The pawn cannot be captured, since 13 ♕xh6 loses a piece after 13 … ♘g4 14 ♗xe7 ♘xh6 15 ♗h4 ♖g4.

Also very unpleasant is 13 ♗xh6 ♖g4 14 ♕h3 0–0–0 15 ♗e2 ♖4g8 16 ♕h4 ♖h8.

13 ♗d2 0–0–0
14 ♗e2 ♘f8
15 0–0 ♘g6!

Black forces White to accept the sacrifice of the pawn on h6, which results in the h-file being opened up. Hardly any better was 16 ♕h3 ♘d5, with the threat of 17 ... ♘gf4.

16 ♕xh6 ♖h8
17 ♕g5 ♖dg8
18 f3!? *(68)*

The best practical chance. Removing the queen to b5 would lead after 18 ... ♘d5 to a very strong attack for Black on the kingside. The point of White's plan is that after the tempting 18 ... ♘h4? there would follow 19 fe!! ♖xg5 20 ♗xg5, when the nature of the conflict changes.

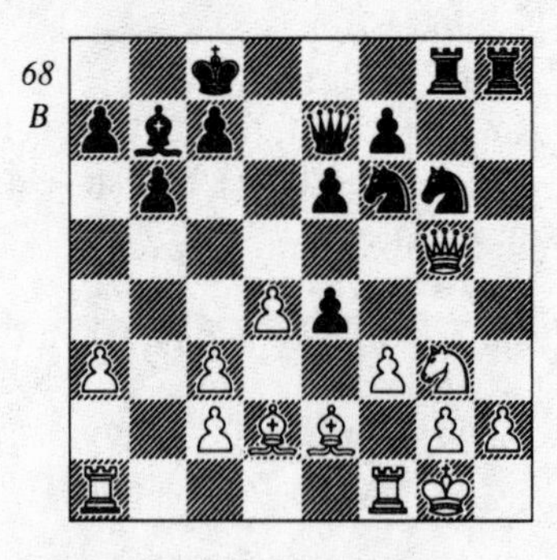

18 ... e3!!

Black prevents the f-file from being opened up and at the cost of a second pawn he gains time to develop his attack.

19 ♗xe3

Black's task would have been easier after 19 ♕xe3 ♘d5 20 ♕f2 (or 20 ♕g5 f6 21 ♕g4 ♖h4) 20 ... ♕h4 (analysis by Mednis).

19 ... ♘f8
20 ♕b5 ♘d5
21 ♔f2

There is nothing better. White loses after 21 ♗d2, because of 21 ... a6 (in order to prevent a queen check on e8) 22 ♕d3 ♕h4.

21 ... a6
22 ♕d3 ♖xh2

The start of the decisive phase of the attack.

23 ♖h1 ♛h4
24 ♖xh2 ♛xh2

But not 24 ... ♛xg3+? 25 ♔g1.

25 ♘f1 ♜xg2+
26 ♔e1 ♛h4+
27 ♔d2 ♞g6!

Yet another black piece is called up to take an active part in the attack.

28 ♖e1 ♞gf4
29 ♗xf4 ♞xf4
30 ♕e3 ♜f2! *(69)*

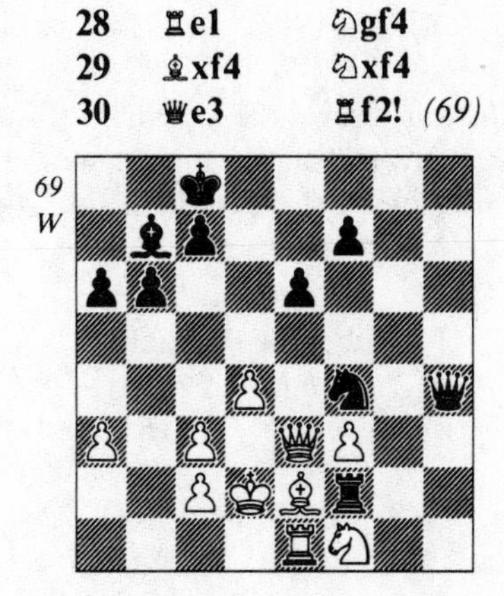

Black has too many threats: 31 ... ♞g2, 31 ... ♝xf3, 31 ... ♞xe2 32 ♖xe2 ♜xf1, so ...

White resigned.

5 The Positional Exchange Sacrifice

During the transition from the opening to the middlegame, exchange sacrifices are frequently played with a view to seizing the initiative or weakening the opponent's position.

Game No. 21
Ljubojevic–Vaganian
Belgrade 1974

1	**e4**	**e6**
2	**d3**	**d5**
3	**♘d2**	**♘f6**
4	**♘gf3**	**♘c6**
5	**c3**	**a5**
6	**e5**	

Vaganian has 'persuaded' his opponent to play a variation of the French Defence in a form which rather favours Black.

6	**...**	**♘fd7**
7	**d4**	**f6!**

The main counter-chance for Black in this system.

8 ♘h4?!

Theory does not approve of such activity on the kingside. Although White wins the exchange, he remains behind in development and his queen is shut out of the game for a long time. Worth considering was 8 ♗b5.

8	**...**	**♕e7**
9	**♗d3** *(70)*	
9	**...**	**fe!**

Forcing White to win the exchange.

10	**♕h5+**	**♕f7**
11	**♗g6**	**hg**

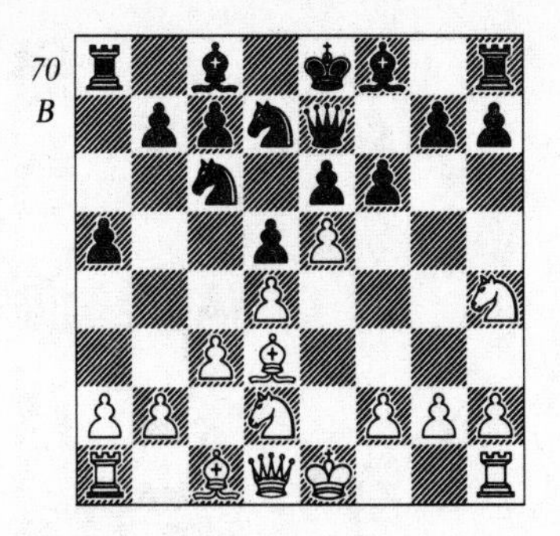

12 ♕xh8 e4!

Now, thanks to the threat of trapping the knight with 13 ... g5, Black succeeds in activating his forces even more and in gaining an overwhelming advantage.

13 ♘b1

If 13 ♘b3 then Black could have replied 13 ... a4, and on 13 ♕h7 g5 14 ♘g6 Black has the strong continuation 14 ... ♘f6!, winning material. If 13 f4 then 13 ... ♘f6 14 g3 ♗d7 15 ♘g2 0–0–0, with advantage to Black.

13 ... ♘f6
14 f3 ♗d7
15 fe de
16 0–0 0–0–0
17 g3 e5

The black pieces come into play with great effect. It was not so good to play 17 ... ♗e7, because of 18 ♕h7.

18 ♗e3 g5!

Trying to entice the white bishop onto g5, where it would have perished: 19 ♗xg5 ♗e7 20 ♕h7 ♘xh7 21 ♖xf7 ♘xg5.

19 ♘f5 ♘e7!
20 ♘h6 *(71)*

Ingenious, but insufficient; now the black queen is on the look-out for an opportunity on the kingside and it leads a decisive attack on the white king, abandoned by its pieces. A mating finish is inevitable.

20 ... ♕h5!
21 g4 ♘xg4!
22 ♖xf8 ♕xh2+
23 ♔f1 ♗b5+

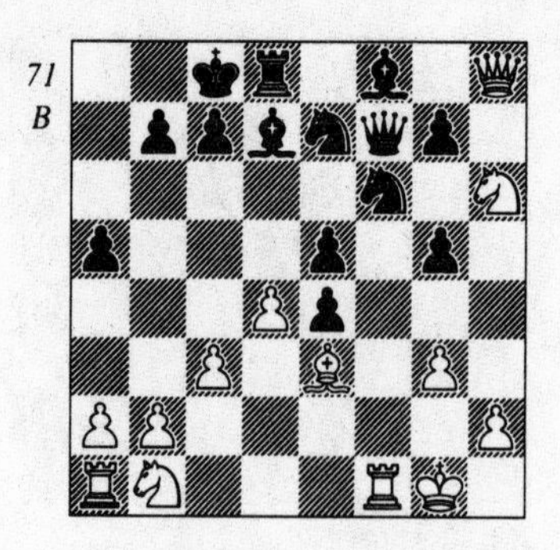

24	**♔e1**	**♕e2** mate.

Game No. 22
Frolov–Ulybin
Dimitrovgrad 1988

1	**e4**	**e6**
2	**d4**	**d5**
3	**♘d2**	**♘f6**
4	**e5**	**♘fd7**
5	**♗d3**	**c5**
6	**c3**	**♘c6**
7	**♘e2**	**cd**
8	**cd**	**f6**
9	**ef**	**♘xf6**
10	**♘f3**	**♗d6**
11	**0–0**	**0–0**
12	**♗f4**	

12 ♗g5 has been tried in recent games with this move order; for example: 12 ... ♗d7 13 ♖c1 ♗e8 14 ♗b1 ♕d7 15 ♘g3, and here the careless 15 ... ♘h5? was brilliantly refuted: 16 ♘xh5 ♗xh5 17 ♘e5!! ♘xe5 (it is bad to play 17 ... ♗xe5, in view of 18 ♗xh7+ ♔xh7 19 ♕h5+ ♔g8 20 de) 18 ♕xh5 (here 18 ♗xh7+ ♔xh7 19 ♕xh5+ ♔g8 20 de ♗xe5 only leads to equality) 18 ... g6 19 ♕h4 ♘f7 20 ♗d2! e5 21 de ♗xe5 22 b3 ♘d6 23 ♖cd1 d4 24 ♖fe1 and White's advantage is quite appreciable (Smrcka–Nesis, 10th corr. Ol. 1989/91).

12	**...**	**♗xf4**
13	**♘xf4**	**♘e4**

A new idea requiring further practical examination is 13 ... ♕b6

14 b3 g6 (Ivanchuk–Brenninkmeijer, Arnhem 1987/88).

14 Nh5

In the event of 14 Ne2 Black has the interesting sacrifice 14 ... Rxf3 (see Game 28: Kramnik–Ulybin).

We note that a line meriting consideration is 14 Qc1 Qd6 15 Ne2 e5 16 Qe3, when White's chances are to be preferred.

14 ... g6!

An excellent reply, casting doubt on the aggressive knight thrust.

15 Ng3 Nxg3
16 hg Qb6

The initiative is passing to Black.

17 Qb1

It seems that more accurate was 17 Qa4! a6 18 Rad1 Bd7 19 Qa3 Nxd4! 20 Nxd4 Qxd4 21 Bxg6 Qf6 22 Bb1 Bb5 23 Bd3 (Spasov–Ulybin, Tunja 1989).

17 ... Rf6
18 g4 Nxd4
19 Ne5

White is trying to alter the course of the game by tactical means.

19 ... Nc6
20 g5 *(72)*

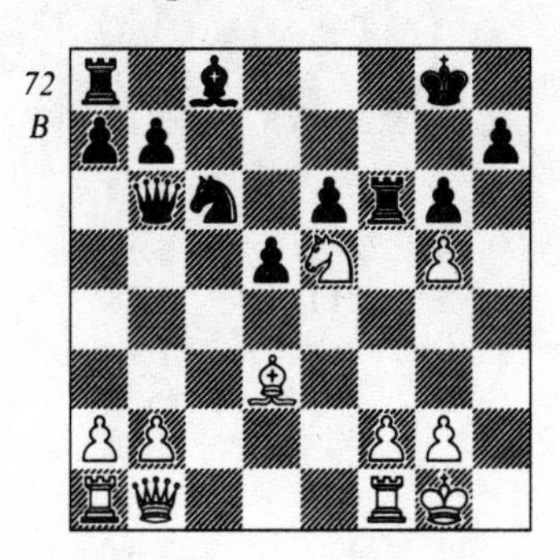

20 ... Rxf2!

Again we encounter an exchange sacrifice in this variation, although in a rather unusual form.

21 Rxf2 Nxe5
22 Be2 Bd7
23 Qc2 Rf8

After an exchange of rooks White has no chance of organising an attack, and the mighty pawn duo in the centre more than compensates Black for the loss of the exchange.

24	**♖f1**	**♜f5**
25	**g4**	**♜xf2**
26	**♖xf2**	**♞f7**
27	**♕d2**	**♛d6**
28	**♔f1**	**♝c6**

Black is ready to set his pawn centre in motion.

29	**♖f6**	**a5**
30	**♕e3**	**♝d7**
31	**♗d3**	**d4**
32	**♕f2**	**♞xg5**
33	**♗xg6** *(73)*	

A final attempt to 'muddy the waters'.

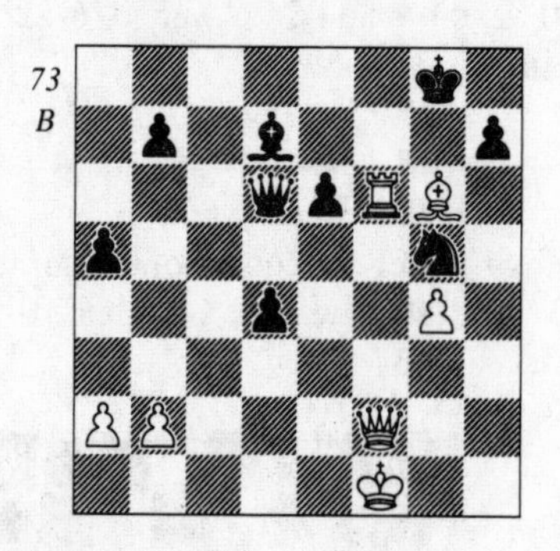

33	**...**	**♝b5+**
34	**♔g2**	**♝c6+**
35	**♔f1**	**d3!**

It is only possible to blockade the d-pawn at the cost of a piece.

36	**♗xh7+**	**♞xh7**
37	**♖g6+**	**♚h8**
38	**♕d2**	**♛e5**
39	**g5**	**♝e4**
40	**♖h6**	**♚g7**
41	**♖h4**	**♞xg5**

White resigned.

Game No. 23
Armas–Komarov
Bad Mergentheim 1989

1	**e4**	**e6**

2	**d4**	**d5**
3	**♘d2**	**♘f6**
4	**e5**	**♘fd7**
5	**c3**	**c5**
6	**♗d3**	**♘c6**
7	**♘e2**	**cd**
8	**cd**	**f6**
9	**ef**	**♘xf6**

9 … ♕xf6 leads after 10 ♘f3 ♗b4+ 11 ♗d2 ♗xd2+ 12 ♕xd2 0–0 13 0–0 e5 14 de ♘dxe5 15 ♘xe5 ♘xe5 16 ♘d4 to a position in which White has secured a small but lasting advantage.

10	**♘f3**	**♗d6**
11	**0–0**	**♕c7**
12	**g3**	

More often 12 ♘c3 a6 13 ♗g5 is played here (see Game 34: Rodriguez–Yusupov). Also worth considering is 12 h3!? 0–0 13 ♗e3 ♗d7 14 ♖c1 (Game 44: Barash–Monin).

12	**…**	**0–0**
13	**♗f4**	**♗d7**
14	**♖c1**	**♘g4**

An exchange sacrifice leads to interesting tactical play: 14 … ♘h5 15 ♗xd6 ♕xd6 16 ♘c3 g6 17 ♗b5 ♖xf3!? (Malevinsky–Komarov, Leningrad 1989). Also possible is 14 … ♖ac8 15 ♗b5 ♘e4 16 ♗xd6 ♕xd6 17 ♘e5 ♘xe5 18 de ♕e7 19 ♗xd7 ♕xd7 20 ♘d4 ♖c4! with equality (Gelfand–Dreev, USSR Jun. Ch., Riga 1987).

15 ♕d2!

A new continuation. Nijboer–Brenninkmeijer, Holland 1988/89, continued: 15 h3 e5!? (after the quiet 15 … ♘f6 16 ♗xd6 ♕xd6 17 ♘c3 White's position is to be preferred) 16 de ♘gxe5 17 ♗xh7+!? (more solid was 17 ♘xe5 ♗xe5 18 ♗xe5 ♕xe5 19 ♘f4, when the weakness of the isolated pawn on d5 becomes noticeable) 17 … ♔xh7? (after 17 … ♔h8! it is not easy for White to demonstrate that he has any advantage) 18 ♘g5+ ♔g6 (on 18 … ♔h8 decisive is 19 ♘d4 g6 20 ♘b5) 19 ♕xd5 ♖f6 20 ♘d4! with a very strong attack.

15 … ♖f6

A dubious continuation. Worth considering is 15 … a6, although also in this case White's chances are to be preferred.

16 b4! a6

17	**a4**	**♗xf4**
18	**♘xf4**	**♕d6**

An exchange sacrifice looks very tempting: 18 ... ♖af8 19 b5 ab 20 ab ♖xf4!? 21 gf ♖xf4, leading to a position in which it is not so easy to find one's way (see diagram 74).

74
W

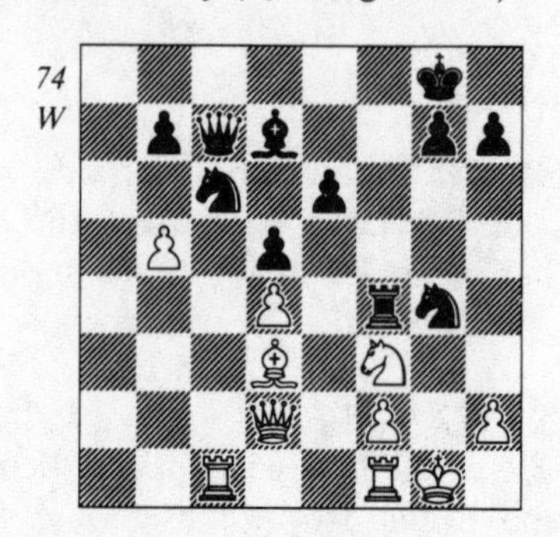

Let us examine the possible variations:

a) 22 ♔g2 ♖xf3! (another typical exchange sacrifice) 23 ♔xf3 ♘xd4+! 24 ♔xg4 ♔xh2, with the threats 25 ... e5+ and 25 ... h5+, not giving the white king any chance of a reprieve;

b) 22 ♘e5 ♘cxe5! 23 ♖xc7 (23 ♕xf4 ♘f3+!) 23 ... ♘f3+ 24 ♔g2 ♘xd2 25 ♖d1 ♖xf2+ 26 ♔g3 h5, winning;

c) 22 ♘e1 ♘xh2! 23 bc ♖g4+ 24 ♔h1 ♘xf1 25 ♗xf1 ♖h4+ 26 ♔g2 ♕h2+ 27 ♔f3 ♗xc6, when play is unclear;

d) 22 h3! ♖xf3 23 hg ♖h3 24 f4! ♕d8 25 bc ♖g3+ (25 ... ♕h4 26 ♕g2!) 26 ♔f2 ♕h4 27 cd! ♖xd3+ 28 ♔e2 and White wins.

19	**b5**	**ab**
20	**♗xb5?**	

An unfortunate continuation, letting White's advantage slip away. It was essential to play 20 ab ♘b4 (20 ... ♘xd4? is bad because of 21 ♘xd4 e5 22 ♘xd5!) 21 ♗e2! ♖a2 22 ♕d1 e5 23 de ♘xe5 24 ♘xe5 ♕xe5 25 ♘xd5! ♘xd5 26 ♗c4 with a material advantage for White.

In the event of 22 ... ♖xf4 (instead of 22 ... e5) 23 gf ♕xf4 sufficient is 24 ♖e3! (play is unclear after 24 h3?! ♘e3! 25 fe ♕xc3+ 26 ♖f2 ♖xe2 27 ♕xe2 ♕xc1+), after which Black does not have compensation for the sacrificed exchange.

20	**...**	**♖af8**
21	**h3** *(75)*	
21	**...**	**♖xf4!**

75
B

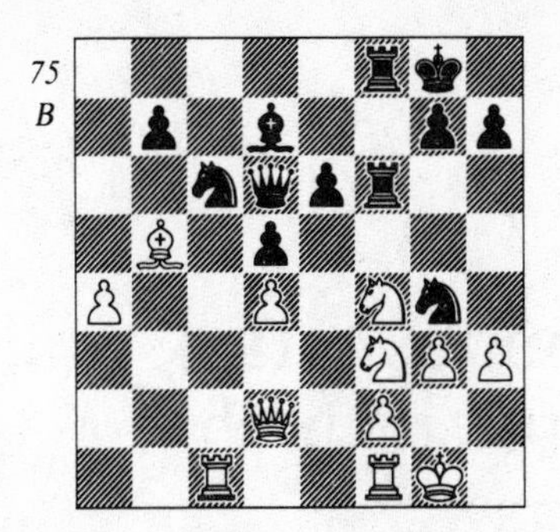

A sacrifice which occurs in many variations has finally appeared on the scene. After 21 ... ♘h6 22 ♗xc6 ♗xc6 23 ♘e5 there would be no doubt about White's advantage.

22 gf ♖xf4
23 hg ♖xf3

Now the threat is 24 ... ♖f4.

24 ♗xc6 ♗xc6
25 ♖fe1?!

An inaccuracy. More reliable was 25 ♖ce1 ♕f4 (worse is 25 ... ♗xa4 26 ♖e5) 26 ♕xf4 ♖xf4 27 f3.

25 ... ♖f4
26 ♕d1

In time-trouble White misses the draw that was possible after 26 ♕e2! ♖xd4 27 a5! (weaker would be 27 ♕xe6+ ♕xe6 28 ♖xe6 ♖xg4+, followed by 29 ... ♖xa4 and better prospects).

26 ... ♕b4!

The decisive thrust. White's position now falls apart.

27 ♕e2 ♖e4
28 ♕d1 ♖xd4
29 ♕f3 ♖xg4+
30 ♔f1 ♕xa4
31 ♖xe6 ♗b5+
32 ♔e1 ♖g1+
33 ♔d2 ♕d4+

White resigned.

6 Counter-Attack and Counterpunch

It is very important to make effective use of active defensive methods. By making sacrifices (or, conversely, by not accepting them — by returning sacrificed material) the aim is to change the nature of the game, to seize the initiative, to create counter-threats or to force the opponent to weaken his offensive.

Game No. 24

Kir. Georgiev–Dolmatov

Moscow 1990

1	**e4**	**e6**
2	**d4**	**d5**
3	**♘c3**	**♘f6**
4	**e5**	**♘fd7**
5	**f4**	**c5**
6	**♘f3**	**♘c6**
7	**♗e3**	**cd**

An interesting continuation is 7 ... ♕b6, followed by sacrificing the knight for three pawns (see Game 32: Timman–Yusupov).

8	**♘xd4**	**♕b6**

Or 8 ... ♗c5 9 ♕d2 0–0 10 0–0–0 a6 11 h4 ♕c7 12 h5 ♘xd4 13 ♗xd4 b5 14 h6 g6 15 ♘e2 with some advantage for White (de Firmian–Bareev, Novi Sad Ol. 1990).

9	**♕d2**	**♕xb2!?**

Black boldly captures the sacrificed pawn.

10	**♖b1**	**♕a3**
11	**♗b5**	**♘xd4**
12	**♗xd4**	**♗b4**
13	**0–0**	**a6**

Also possible is 13 ... 0–0 14 f5 ef, when it is not clear how

Black's fortress can be demolished.

14 ♖b3 ♕a5
15 ♖fb1

Now in the event of 15 ... ♗e7 16 ♗xd7+ ♗xd7 17 ♖xb7 White regains the pawn, retaining excellent attacking possibilities.

15 ... ♕xb5!
16 ♖xb4 ♕c6
17 f5 h6

Not allowing the white queen to come to g5; the variation 17 ... ef 18 ♕g5 ♕g6 19 ♕xg6 hg 20 ♘xd5 ♔d8 promises Black very little.

18 fe gf

In the event of 18 ... g5 a possible line is 19 ♖b6!? ♘xb6 20 ♖xb6 ♕c7 21 ♕e3, with a blockade on the dark squares.

19 ef ♕d6
20 a4 b5!? *(76)*

Expecting 21 ab a5 22 ♖a4 ♘b6 with sharp play.

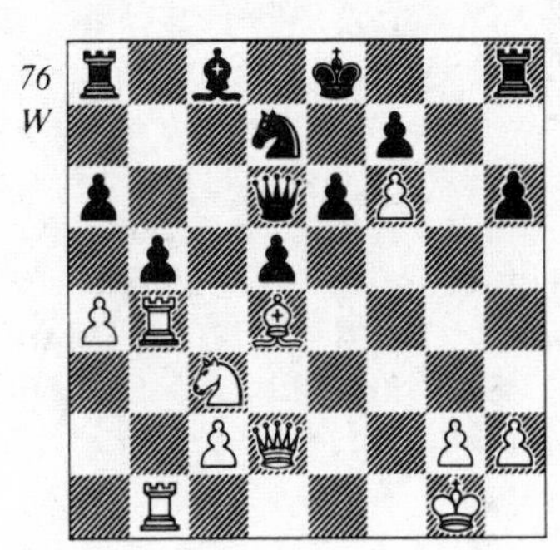
76
W

21 ♖xb5!?

A very interesting surprise! White does not begrudge giving up his rook in order to seize possession of the a3–f8 diagonal with tremendous effect. Now in the event of 21 ... ab 22 ♘xb5 ♕c6 23 ♕b4 ♘c5 a possible continuation is 24 ♕xc5 ♕xc5 25 ♗xc5 ♔d7 26 ♗e7 ♖xa4 27 ♘d6, when Black has a difficult position to defend.

21 ... ♖g8!

Taking advantage of the fact that White has no threats, Black has won time to bring his king's rook into play.

22 ♖e1

Forcing Black to accept the sacrifice of the rook on b5, but inserting the moves 21 ... ♖g8 and 22 ♖e1 clearly represents an achievement for Black, and thanks to this he manages to obtain counterplay.

22 ... ab
23 ♘xb5 ♕c6
24 ♕b4 ♘c5
25 ♗xc5 *(77)*

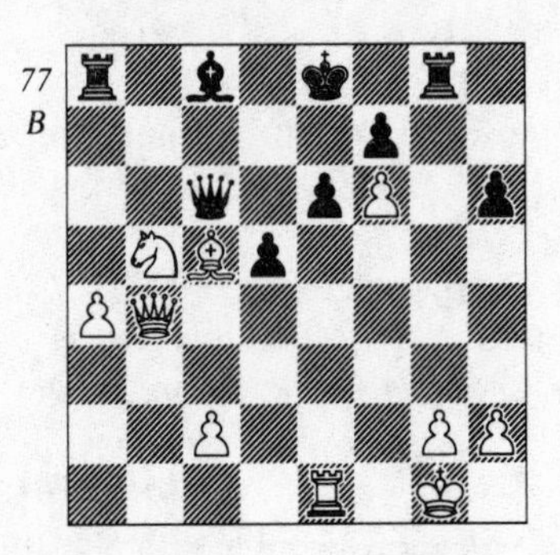

25 ... ♖xa4!

The only way to parry White's threats. In the event of 25 ... ♔d7 an unpleasant move would be 26 ♗f8.

26 ♕xa4 ♕xc5+
27 ♔h1 ♔d8

Not 27 ... ♔f8, because of 28 ♕a5 ♗d7 29 ♕d8+ ♗e8 30 ♘d6. Possible was 27 ... ♗d7 28 ♘d6+ ♕xd6 29 ♕a8+ ♗c8 30 ♕xc8+ ♕d8 31 ♕c6+ (but not 31 ... ♕d7 32 ♖xe6+! fe 33 f7+) and Black maintains the equilibrium.

28 ♕a5+ ♔d7 *(78)*

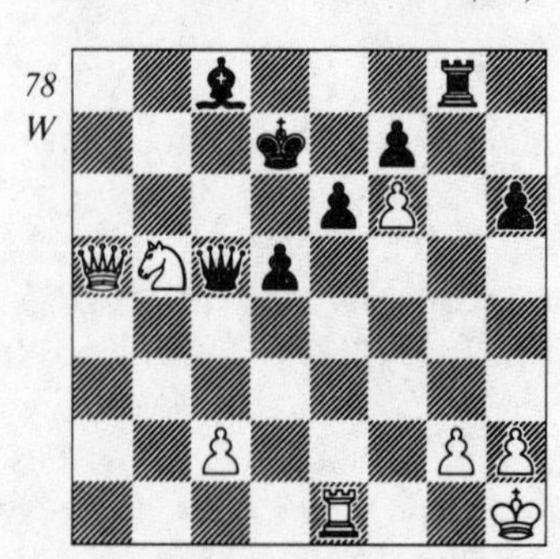

29 ♖e3!

White finds new attacking resources; the rook cannot be

captured, because of 30 ♕c7+ with mate next move.

29 ... ♖g4

Black reaps the rewards of his 21st move.

30 ♖c3 ♖b4!

Exploiting the weakness of the back rank.

31 g4 ♖b1+

In this extremely sharp position the players agreed a draw. Black has a guaranteed perpetual check: 32 ♔g2 ♕g1+ 33 ♔h3 ♕f1+ 34 ♔g3 ♕g1+ 35 ♔h3 ♕f1+, and he cannot count on anything more.

Drawn.

Game No. 25

Lukin–Cherepkov

Leningrad 1983

1	**e4**	**e6**
2	**d4**	**d5**
3	**♘c3**	**♗b4**
4	**e5**	**c5**
5	**a3**	**♗xc3+**
6	**bc**	**♘e7**
7	**♕g4**	**♕c7**

Black sacrifices two pawns on the kingside but begins a resolute counter-attack on the queenside.

An analogous plan may be carried out by playing 7 ... cd. For example: 8 cd ♕c7 9 ♖a2 ♘f5 10 ♘f3 ♘c6 11 ♗d3 h5 12 ♕g5 ♘cxd4 13 ♘xd4 ♕xc3+ 14 ♔f1 ♕xd4 15 ♗b2 ♕g4 16 ♕d2 with a roughly equal game (analysis by Suetin).

A line favouring White is 7 ... ♕a5?! 8 ♗d2 ♘g6 9 h4 h5 10 ♕g5 ♕d8 11 ♘f3 ♘c6 12 ♗d3 ♕xg5 13 hg ♗d7 14 a4 (Gurgenidze–Lutikov, USSR Ch., Leningrad 1960).

Interesting play also unfolds in the event of 7 ... 0–0 (see Game 13: Kruppa–Komarov and Game 39: Tischbierek–E. Vladimirov).

8 ♕xg7

White may also delay capturing the pawn — 8 ♗d3!?. In this case it is best for Black to reply 8 ... h5!? 9 ♕xg7 ♖g8 10 ♕h6 cd 11 ♘e2 dc! with roughly equal chances (Velimirovic–Uhlmann, Vrsac 1973). White achieved more in the game Velimirovic–Suetin, Belgrade 1977: 8 ♗d2!? cd 9 cd ♕xc2 10 ♖c1 ♕e4+ 11 ♕xe4 de 12 ♘e2 ♘bc6 13 g3 f5 14 ef gf 15 ♗g2, with somewhat better prospects for White.

8 ... ♖g8
9 ♕xh7 cd *(79)*

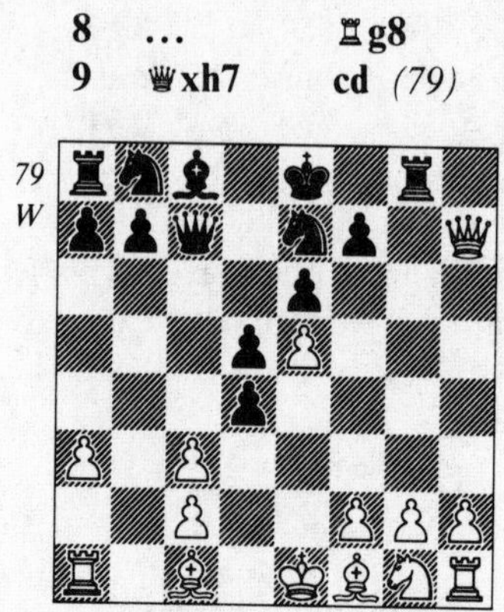

One of the key positions of this sharp opening system. Here White has two continuations of practically equal merit.

10 ♔d1!?

Euwe's recommendation. This variation was subject to intensive development at the end of the 1950s. The idea behind this move is the possibility of active play on the kingside for White, who has an attack against the f7-square in mind in some lines. But his loss of the right to castle gives Black additional opportunities to get counterplay.

A solid continuation is 10 ♘e2. White retains the possibility of castling and aims to reinforce the e5-square in order subsequently to organise a pawn offensive on the kingside: 10 ... ♘bc6 11 f4 ♗d7 12 ♕d3 dc 13 ♘xc3 a6 14 ♖b1 ♘a5 15 h4 ♘f5 16 ♖h3 0–0–0 17 h5 ♘c4 18 ♖b4 ♗c6 (Hort–Uhlmann, Hastings 1970/71).

10 ... ♘bc6
11 ♘f3 dc

Baffling complications with better chances for White ensue after 11 ... ♘xe5 12 ♗f4 ♕xc3 13 ♘xe5 ♕xa1+ 14 ♗c1 d3 15 ♕xf7+ ♔d8 16 ♕f6! dc+ 17 ♔d2 ♕d4+ 18 ♗d3 (Bronstein–Uhlmann, Zagreb 1965).

12 ♗g5!?

The strongest move is considered to be 12 ♗f4!. After 12 ... ♗d7 13 ♘g5 ♖xg5 14 ♗xg5 ♕xe5 15 h4 White has the advantage (Scriba–Dahl, corr. 1977).

12 ♘g5 is less successful, in view of 12 ... ♘xe5! 13 ♗f4 (it is not good to play 13 f4, because of 13 ... ♖xg5!) 13 ... ♕b6 14

♗xe5 ♖xg5 15 h4 ♖g8 16 ♔e1 ♗d7 with active play for Black.

12 ... ♗d7
13 ♗f6 0-0-0
14 h4 *(80)*

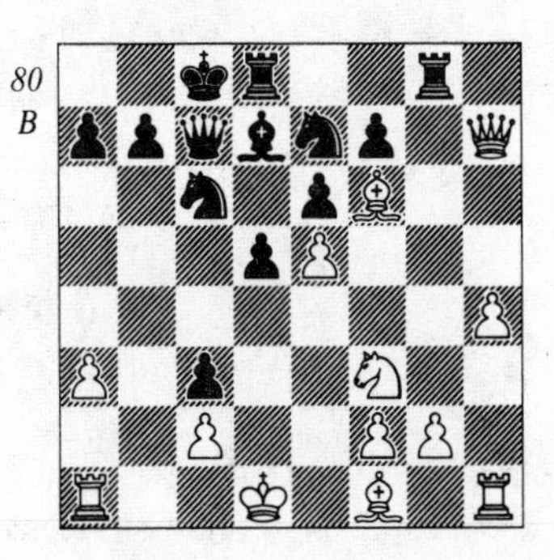

14 ... ♘g6!?

An interesting exchange sacrifice, giving Black good counter-chances. Also worth considering was 14 ... ♕b6 15 ♕d3 ♕xf2 16 ♕xc3 ♘f5! 17 ♗xd8 ♔xd8 18 ♕d2 ♕c5, when Black has excellent compensation for the sacrificed material.

15 ♗xd8 ♖xd8
16 ♕g7

More chances to cast doubt on Black's plan could have been obtained by playing 16 ♗b5, with a possible continuation being 16 ... ♘cxe5 17 ♗xd7+ ♖xd7 18 h5.

16 ... ♘gxe5
17 ♘xe5 ♘xe5
18 h5 d4

Black has obtained definite chances. Now, for example, in the event of 19 f4 there would follow 19 ... ♘c4 20 ♗xc4 ♕xc4 21 h6 ♗a4!, with the threat of 22 ... ♕d3+.

19 h6

More troublesome for Black was 19 ♖h3 ♗a4 20 ♗d3.

19 ... d3
20 ♗xd3 ♘xd3
21 cd ♗b5
22 h7

The continuation 22 ♖h4 ♖xd3+ 23 ♔e1 c2 24 ♖c1 would have posed Black definite problems.

22 ... c2+

23	**♔c1**	**♕f4+**
24	**♔b2** *(81)*	

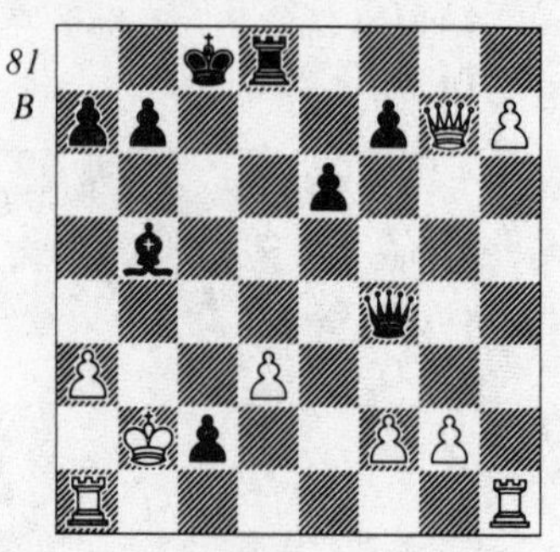

81
B

It seems that Black's attack has come to a dead end. On 24 ... ♕d2 decisive is 25 ♕c3+, exchanging queens, but nonetheless there is a saving continuation.

24	**...**	**e5!**

After this the white queen turns out to be isolated, cut off from the key square d4. The white king cannot avoid perpetual check.

25	**h8(♕)**

But not 25 ♔xc2?, because of 25 ... ♕xf2+ 26 ♔c1 ♗xd3 and White is mated.

25	**...**	**♕d4+**
26	**♔a2**	**♕d5+**
27	**♔b2**	**♕d4+**

Drawn.

Game No. 26

Fischer–Tal

Leipzig Ol. 1960

1	**e4**	**e6**
2	**d4**	**d5**
3	**♘c3**	**♗b4**
4	**e5**	**c5**
5	**a3**	**♗a5**
6	**b4**	**cd**
7	**♕g4**	**♘e7**
8	**ba**	**dc**
9	**♕xg7**	**♖g8**
10	**♕xh7**	**♘bc6**

Black does not achieve very much with the move 10 … ♘d7 (see Game 37: Smyslov–Botvinnik).

11 ♘f3

In Fischer's opinion the move 11 f4 would have strengthened the centre but would also have shut the bishop on c1 out of the game and resulted in the dark squares being weakened (see Game 14: Timman–Vaganian).

11 … ♕c7

Black gets a difficult position after 11 … ♕xa5, in view of 12 ♘g5 ♖f8 13 f4, followed by the march of the h-pawn.

12 ♗b5

Another possibility is 12 ♗f4, as in the game Unzicker–Dückstein, Zürich 1959, which continued: 12 … ♗d7 13 ♗e2 0–0–0 14 ♕d3 ♕xa5 15 0–0 ♖g4 16 ♗g3. In making the move in the text, Fischer considered that it would not be good for Black to continue 12 … ♖xg2 13 ♔f1! ♖g8 14 ♖g1! with a strong attack for White.

12 … ♗d7 *(82)*

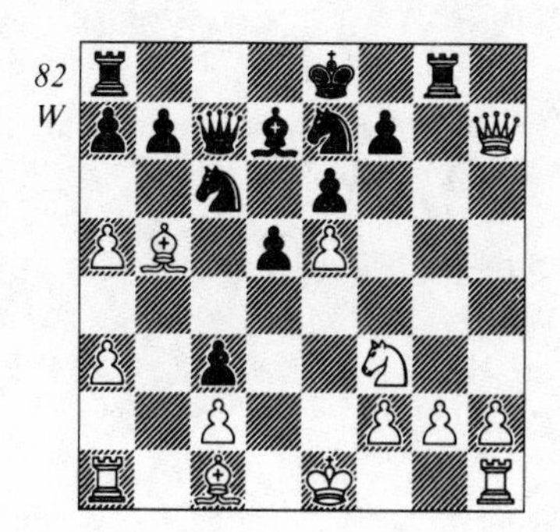

White is invited to continue 13 ♗xc6? ♗xc6 14 0–0 d4! 15 ♘g5 ♕xe5 16 ♕xf7+ ♔d7, when Black gets the better position.

13 0–0 0–0–0

Petrosian considered that 13 … ♘xe5 was a possibility, but after 14 ♘xe5 ♕xe5 15 ♗xd7+ ♔xd7 16 ♕d3! White has the advantage (if 16 … ♕e4? then 17 ♕xe4 de 18 f3!, winning a pawn).

14 ♗g5? *(83)*

Fischer himself gave this move a question-mark, considering that he should have played 14 ♗xc6! ♗xc6 (if 14 … ♕xc6 then 15 ♗g5 d4 16 h4!, or 14 … ♘xc6 15 ♖e1 followed by ♗c1–g5 and h2–h4, obtaining a decisive advantage) 15 ♕xf7, and now after 15 … d4 (it is not correct to play 15 … ♖xg2+!? 16 ♔xg2 d4 17 ♔g1 ♖g8+ 18 ♘g5) 16 ♕xe6+ ♗d7 (16 … ♔b8 17 ♘g5) 17 ♕xe7 ♖xg2+ 18 ♔xg2 ♗h3+ 19 ♔xh3 ♕xe7 20 ♗g5 White has a considerable advantage.

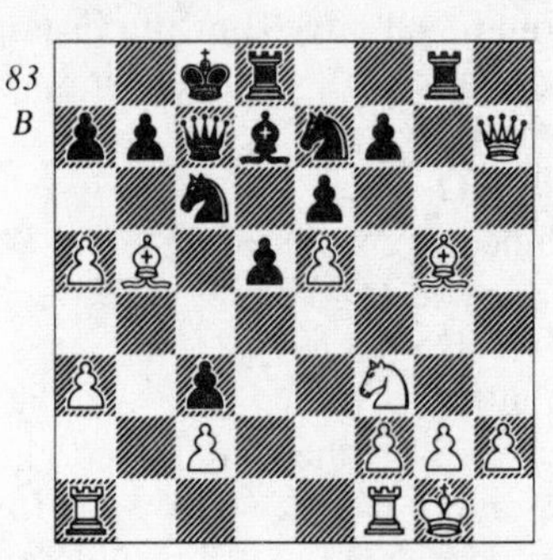

14 … ♘xe5!

The only chance for Black to free himself from White's pressure.

15 ♘xe5!

Now in the event of 15 ♗xd7+ Black would have had a pleasant choice between 15 … ♔xd7 and 15 … ♖xd7 16 ♘xe5 ♕xe5 17 ♗xe7? ♖h8, and White cannot play 15 ♗xe7 because of 15 … ♘xf3+ 16 ♔h1 ♖h8.

15 … ♗xb5!

Accurate play by Black; 15 … ♔xe5 would have led to an advantage for White after 16 ♗xe7 ♖h8 17 ♖fe1! (but not 16 ♖ae1 ♕b8!) 17 … ♕xe1+ 18 ♖xe1 ♖xh7 19 ♗xd8 ♔xd8 (or 19 … ♗xb5 20 ♗f6) 20 ♗xd7 ♔xd7 21 ♖e3! d4 22 ♖e4.

16 ♘xf7 ♗xf1

A very interesting variation, writes Tal, could have occurred in the event of 16 … ♖df8 17 ♗h6 (17 ♖fb1 ♗c6 18 ♘d6+! ♕xd6 19 ♔xe7 would lead to a roughly equal game) 17 … ♗xf1 18 ♗xf8 ♗xg2 19 ♘d6+! ♕xd6 20 ♗xe7, when it is not clear how Black can save the game.

17 ♘xd8 ♖xg5

18 ♘xe6 ♖xg2+ *(84)*

19 ♔h1!

Precisely so! 19 ♔xf1? ♖xh2 20 ♕f7 (20 ♘xc7 ♖xh7 and White remains a piece down) 20 … ♖h1+ would have given Black a decisive attack.

19 … ♕e5

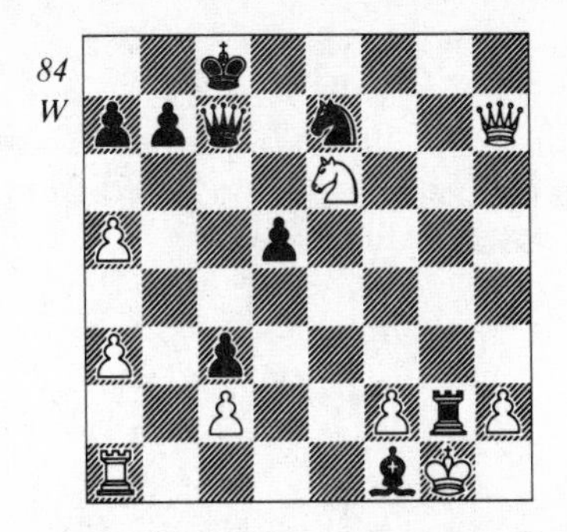
84
W

When beginning his combination with the move 14 ... ♘xe5, Black supposed that, besides the move in the text, which guarantees a draw, he also had the sharper line 19 ... ♛c4 20 ♛xe7 ♖g8, but he then discovered that after 21 ♘f4! d4 (if 21 ... ♛xf4? then 22 ♛e6+ ♔c7 23 ♛xg8) 22 ♛e4! the bishop stuck on f1 will be quite unable to get back into the game, whereas White has chances for an attack. Now, however, a draw is unavoidable.

20 ♖xf1 ♛xe6
21 ♔xg2 ♛g4+

Drawn by perpetual check.

Game No. 27
Karpov–Korchnoi
12th game, Candidates Final, Moscow 1974

1 e4 e6
2 d4 d5
3 ♘d2 c5
4 ed ed

In recent years capturing the pawn on d5 with the queen has been encountered more and more frequently, but not with any particular success for Black: 4 ... ♛xd5 5 ♘gf3 cd 6 ♗c4 ♛d6 7 0–0 ♘f6 8 ♘b3 ♘c6 9 ♘bxd4 ♘xd4 10 ♘xd4 a6 11 ♖e1 ♛c1 12 ♗b3 ♗d6 13 ♘f5 ♗xh2+ 14 ♔h1 ♔f8 15 g3 ef 16 ♗f4 (Psakhis–Pomes, Groningen 1990).

5 ♘gf3 ♘c6

Possible is 5 ... c4 with chances of equality: 6 b3 cb 7 ♗b5+ ♗d7 8 ♛e2+ ♛e7 9 ♗xd7+ ♘xd7 10 ab ♘gf6 11 ♘e5 ♛e6 12 0–0 ♗d6 (Beliavsky–Pr. Nikolic, Novi Sad Ol. 1990).

For 5 ... ♘f6 see Game 15: Godena–Bareev.

6	**♗b5**	**♗d6**
7	**0–0**	

The best continuation here is 7 dc (see Game 45: Psakhis–Vaganian), when energetic play is required from Black in order to overcome his opening difficulties.

7	**...**	**cd**
8	**♘b3**	**♘e7**
9	**♘bxd4**	**0–0**
10	**c3**	**♗g4**
11	**♕a4**	**♗h5**
12	**♗e3**	

White has hastened to develop his dark-squared bishop. As a result, Black saves a tempo by doing without ... h7–h6 and sets about directing his queen's knight towards the square c4 without further delay.

On 12 ♖e1 an unpleasant reply is 12 ... ♕c7, threatening to win the pawn on h2 after 13 ... ♘xd4. Black also has no great problems after 12 ♗d3 ♗c5 13 ♖e1 h6 14 ♗e3 ♕b6 (Karpov–Korchnoi, 14th match game, Moscow 1974).

12	**...**	**♕c7!**
13	**h3** *(85)*	

85
B

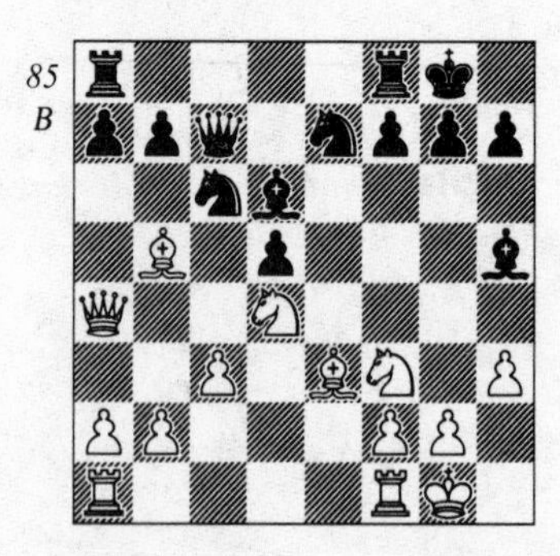

13	**...**	**♘a5!**
14	**♗d3**	

In the event of 14 ♖ad1 Black, in Botvinnik's opinion, was unable to reply 14 ... ♘c4 immediately, because of 15 ♗xc4 ♕xc4 16 ♕xc4 dc 17 ♘b5 ♗xf3 18 gf ♗b8 19 ♗c5, but with 14 ... a6 15 ♗d3 ♘c4 16 ♗c1 ♘e5 he would have obtained some initiative.

14	**...**	**♘c4!**

Black heads for a lively, forced game.

15 ♘b5 ♕d7

Worth considering was 15 ... ♕c6 16 ♘fd4 ♕d7, and if 17 ♗xc4 dc 18 ♕xc4 ♗b8 then Black has some positional compensation for the sacrificed pawn.

16 ♗xc4 dc

17 ♖fd1 ♘f5

After 17 ... a6 18 ♖xd6 ♕xb5 19 ♕xb5 ab 20 ♘d4 White has a lasting advantage.

18 ♕xc4 ♗xf3

19 gf ♘xe3

20 fe *(86)*

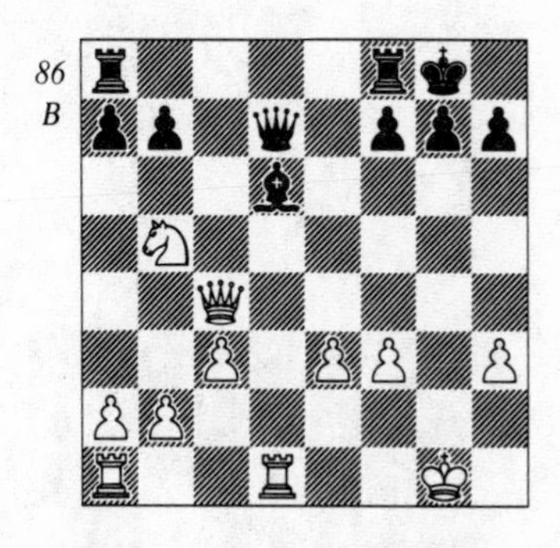

86
B

20 ... ♕xh3!

When Black decided to go for this position he had of course taken into account the sacrifice of the bishop on d6. Now White is unable to avoid perpetual check.

21 ♘xd6

Nothing is changed by 21 ♖xd6 ♕g3+ 22 ♔f1 ♕xf3+ 23 ♔g1 a6, when the white knight cannot retreat, in view of the possibility of ... ♕f3–♕g3+, winning the rook on d6.

21 ... ♕g3+

22 ♔f1 ♕xf3+

23 ♔e1

Tempting Black with the possibility of playing for a win with 23 ... ♕xe3+, but after 24 ♕e2 ♕g3+ 25 ♕f2 he would not have obtained anything substantial.

23 ... ♕g3+!

Forcing a draw, since the white king cannot cross onto the d-file because of 24 ... ♕xd6+.

Drawn.

Game No. 28

Kramnik–Ulybin

USSR Ch., Moscow 1991

1	**e4**	**e6**
2	**d4**	**d5**
3	**♘d2**	**♘f6**
4	**e5**	**♘fd7**
5	**♗d3**	**c5**
6	**c3**	**♘c6**
7	**♘e2**	**cd**
8	**cd**	**f6**
9	**ef**	**♘xf6**
10	**0–0**	**♗d6**
11	**♘f3**	**0–0**
12	**♗f4**	**♗xf4**
13	**♘xf4**	**♘e4**
14	**♘e2** *(87)*	

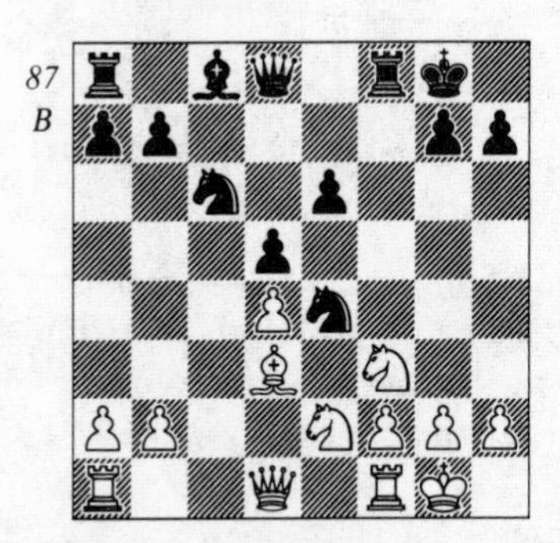

White invites his opponent to sacrifice the exchange, and the game enters a period of great complications. (See Game 22: Frolov–Ulybin for 14 ♘h5.)

14 … ♖xf3!?

15 gf

It can hardly be good to play 15 ♗xe4, because of 15 … de 16 gf ef 17 ♘g3 ♘xd4 18 ♖e1 ♕d5 19 ♔h1 ♗d7 20 ♖e4 (better was 20 ♕d3!?) 20 … e5 21 ♕e1 ♘e2! 22 ♕b4 ♗h3 with a clear advantage to Black (Malishauskas–Ulybin, Uzhgorod 1988).

15 … ♘g5

16 ♔h1

In the event of 16 ♔g2 e5!, or 16 ♘g3 ♘xd4, Black gets a

dangerous initiative, and on 16 f4 it is best for Black to choose 16 … ♘f3+! (16 … ♘h3+ is inferior, because of 17 ♔h1 ♕h4 18 ♕e1 ♘xf4 19 ♘xf4 ♕xf4 20 ♕e3 with advantage to White) 17 ♔g2 ♕h4 18 ♔xf3 ♕h3+ 19 ♘g3 e5, when Black's attack is very strong.

16 … e5

It is not good to play 16 … ♘xf3 at once, in view of 17 ♗xh7+ ♔xh7 (or 17 … ♔h8 18 ♘f4) 18 ♕d3+ and 19 ♕xf3.

17 de ♘xf3

Inferior is 17 … ♘xe5 18 ♘g1 ♕f6 19 ♗e2 ♗e6 20 ♕d4 with advantage to White.

18 ♗xh7+ ♔h8!

19 ♘g1

Worth considering was 19 ♘f4!?, and now on 19 … ♘cxe5 a possible continuation is 20 ♘g6+ ♘xg6 21 ♕xf3 ♔xh7 22 ♕h5+. However, 19 … ♗g4 would appear to be an improvement — translator's note.

19 … ♘cd4! *(88)*

88
W

20 ♘xf3!

White has no choice.

20 … ♗g4

21 ♘xd4!

White loses after 21 ♕xd4, because of 21 … ♗xf3+ and 22 … ♕g5+, with mate.

21 … ♗xd1

22 ♖axd1 ♔xh7

23 f4

In the game Timoshenko–Gleizerov, Chelyabinsk 1989/90, White played 23 ♖d3, and Black, though not without some difficulty, nevertheless salvaged half a point. Here too, extremely accurate play is required from Black.

23	**...**	**♕b6**
24	**f5**	**♕xb2**
25	**♖d3**	**♖c8!**
26	**f6**	**♖c1**

Black has managed to generate counterplay just in time.

27 ♖h3+ ♔g6

27 ... ♔g8? loses to 28 f7+ and 29 ♖h8+.

28 ♖g3+ *(89)*

Drawn.

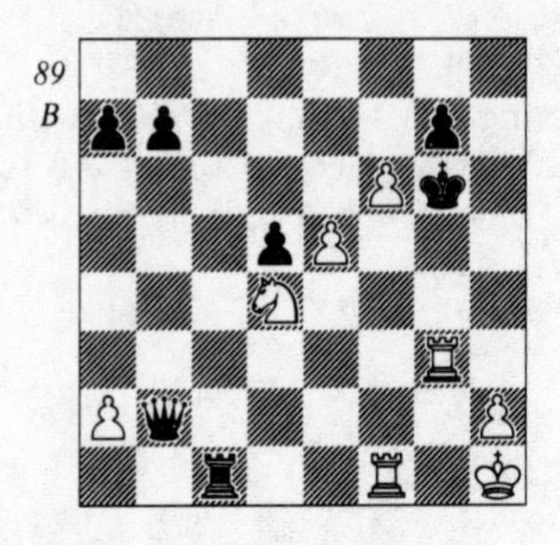

Black saves the game with 28 ... ♔h5!, when 29 ♖xc1 ♕xc1+ 30 ♖g1 ♕e3 guarantees Black perpetual check.

7 Interference and Isolation

In combinations on the theme of interference, either the connection between opposing pieces on the same line is broken or their access to a key square is barred by means of a sacrifice.

The tactical device of isolation does not occur in combinations quite so often. Outwardly it resembles the idea of interference, but isolation refers to a situation in which the connection between one of the defending side's pieces and a particular square or object is severed by a piece or pawn of the active side — there is no interference caused by a piece or pawn of the defending side.

This is the essential difference between isolation and interference.

Worth some attention is the following very short but extremely eventful game:

Kunin–Oksengoit

Moscow 1958

1 e4 e6 2 d4 d5 3 ♘c3 ♗b4 4 ♗d2 de 5 ♕g4 ♕xd4 6 0–0–0 f5

Black's strongest reply here, casting doubt on this gambit variation, is 6 … h5!.

7 ♗g5 ♕e5

It was simpler and also more sound to exchange queens: 7 … fg 8 ♖xd4 ♗e7.

8 ♖d8+ ♔f7 9 ♘f3!

The exchange of queens leads to mate (9 … fg 10 ♘xe5 mate). Black decided not to take the knight — 9 … ef 10 ♕xb4 — fearing an attack. For example: 10 … ♘c6 11 ♖f8+ ♔g6 12 ♕h4 ♘d4 13 g4!, or 10 … ♕e1+ 11 ♖d1 ♕xf2 12 gf. But a possibility was 10 … c5! and if 11 ♕h4 then 11 … ♘c6, after which 12 ♗f4 ♕f6 13 ♗g5 ♕e5 14 ♗f4 only gives White a draw.

9 … ♕a5 *(90)*

Black obviously supposed that the queen had to retreat.

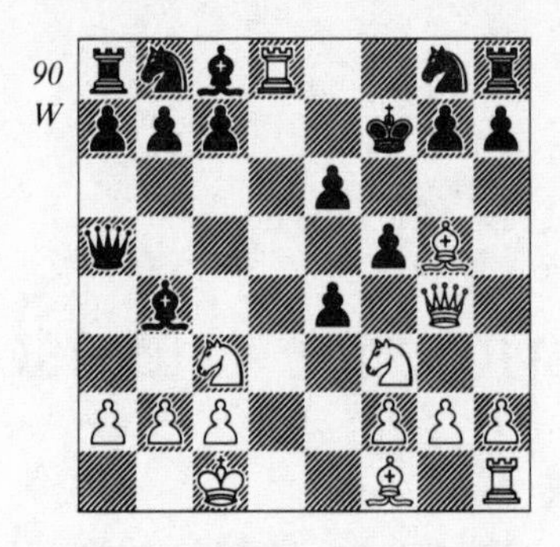

90
W

10 ♗b5!!

An astonishing move. The black queen is cut off from the e5-square and the immediate threat is mate in two: 11 ♘e5 mate or 11 ♗e8+ ♔f8 12 ♗g6 mate. If 10 ... ♘f6 White wins with 11 ♕h5+! g6 (11 ... ♘xh5 12 ♘e5 mate) 12 ♘e5+ ♔e7 13 ♖xh8! gh 14 ♖e8+ ♔d6 15 ♘f7+ ♔c5 16 ♗e3 mate.

The most stubborn continuation was 10 ... g6. Then there could have followed: 11 ♘e5+ ♔g7 12 ♕h4 c6 (12 ... ♗xc3 13 ♗h6+! ♘xh6 14 ♕e7+ ♘f7 15 ♕xf7+ ♔h6 16 ♖xh8) 13 ♖xc8 cb 14 ♖xg8+ ♔xg8 (14 ... ♖xg8 15 ♕h6+ and 16 ♘f7 mate) 15 ♗d8! ♗xc3 (otherwise 16 ♕f6) 16 ♗xa5 ♗xe5 17 ♕e7, winning.

10 ... ♘c6 11 ♘e5!+

Forcing Black to remove his knight from the a4–e8 diagonal.

11 ... ♘xe5 12 ♗e8+ ♔f8 13 ♗g6 mate.

Game No. 29

Euwe–Maróczy

6th match game, Bad Aussee 1921

1	**e4**	**e6**
2	**d4**	**d5**
3	**♘c3**	**♘f6**
4	**♗g5**	**♗b4**

This move characterises the MacCutcheon Variation, which leads to a very sharp and complicated game.

5 e5

Weaker is 5 ed ♕xd5 6 ♗xf6 gf 7 ♕d2 ♕a5 8 ♘ge2 ♘d7 9 a3 ♘b6! 10 ♖d1 ♗e7 with a good position for Black. On 5 ♘e2 Black gets equal chances with 5 ... de 6 a3 ♗e7 7 ♗xf6 ♗xf6

8 ♘xe4 e5!, or he can make the game sharper with 7 ... gf 8 ♘xe4 b6 9 g3 ♗b7 10 ♗g2 c6.

5 ... h6

6 ♗d2

Janowski's move 6 ♗e3 is associated with the sacrifice of a pawn, but accurate defence is required from Black; for example: 6 ... ♘e4 7 ♕g4 g6 8 a3 ♗xc3+ 9 bc ♘xc3 10 ♗d3 ♘c6 11 h4 ♕e7 12 h5 g5 13 f4 with an initiative for White (Klovan–Makarychev, USSR 1978). Chigorin recommended 6 ef hg 7 hg ♖g8 8 h4 gh 9 ♕h5.

6 ... ♗xc3

If 6 ... ♘fd7 then 7 ♕g4 ♗f8 8 ♘f3 c5 9 ♘b5 favours White (see Game 11: Nezhmetdinov–A. Chistyakov).

7 bc

After 7 ♗xc3 ♘e4 White will be unable to safeguard his dark-squared bishop against exchange: 8 ♗b4 c5 9 dc? ♘xf2!.

7 ... ♘e4

8 ♕g4

The critical position of the MacCutcheon System.

8 ... g6

The alternative is 8 ... ♔f8, with a possible continuation being 9 h4 f5 10 ♕f4.

9 h4 c5

10 ♗d3 ♘xd2

11 ♔xd2 ♕a5 *(91)*

In the game Euwe–Bogoljubow, Budapest 1921, Black first played 11 ... ♘c6, and after 12 ♖h3 ♕a5 there followed 13 ♗xg6! ♖f8 14 ♖f3 cd 15 ♗xf7+ ♔d8 16 ♕g7 with an easy win.

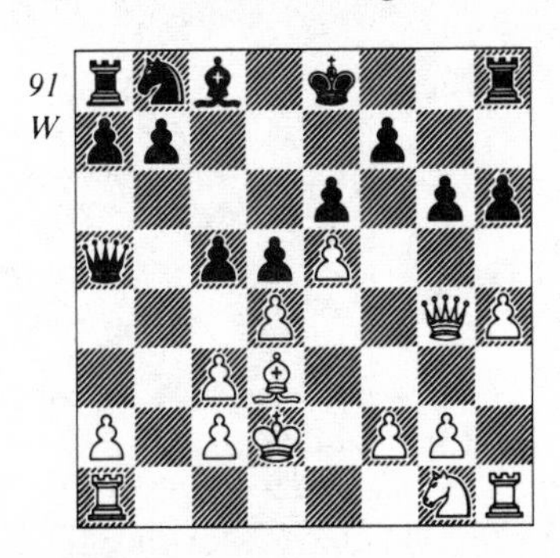
91
W

12 ♖h3!?

Also worth considering is 12 ♘f3 ♘c6 13 ♕f4 b6 14 ♖hb1 ♗a6 15 a4 ♗xd3 16 cd a6 17 dc ♕xc5 18 d4 ♕a5 19 ♔d3! with advantage to White (Aseev–Piskov, Berlin 1990).

12 ... cd

13 ♗xg6!

The first stage in the destruction of the black king's position.

13 ... ♕c7

14 ♖f3 ♖g8! *(92)*

Black's defence rests on this move. White cannot play 15 ♗xf7+ because of 15 ... ♕xf7.

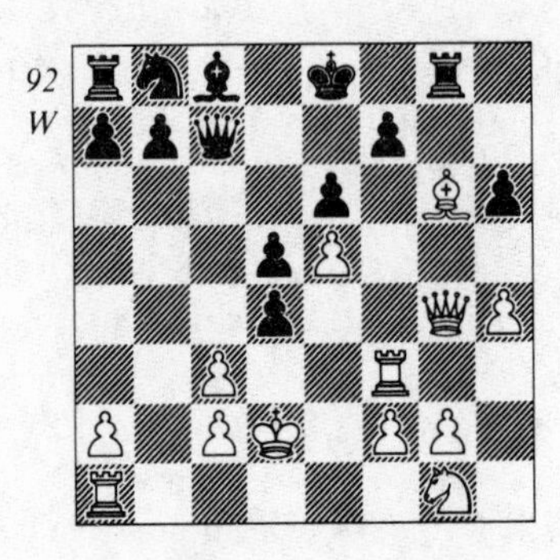

92
W

15 ♖xf7! ♕xc3+

16 ♔e2 d3+

17 cd ♕xe5+

18 ♔f3! ♖f8

In the event of 18 .. ♕xa1 there follows 19 ♖g7+ ♔f8 20 ♕f4+! and the black king is enticed onto g7, after which it is mated.

19 ♖f5+ ♔d7

20 ♖xf8 ♕xa1

21 ♖f7+ ♔d8

22 ♕b4 ♘d7

23 ♕d6

With the threat of 24 ♖f8 mate.

23 ... ♕h8

24 ♘e2 e5 *(93)*

25 ♘f4!!

The white knight sacrifices itself merely for the sake of deflecting a black pawn onto the f4-square, blocking the f-file.

25 ... ef

93
W

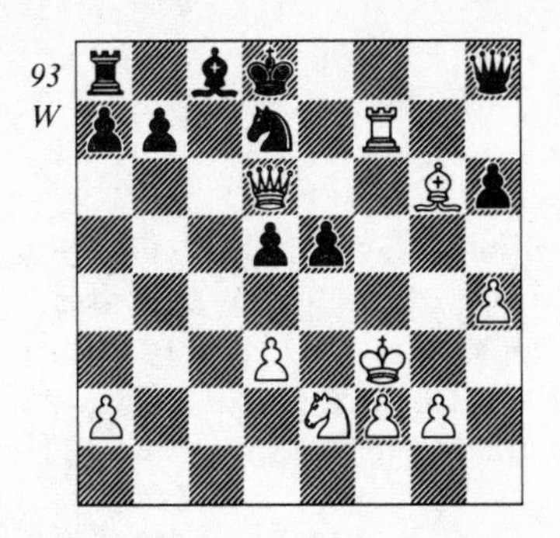

26	**♗f5**	**♕e8**
27	**♗xd7**	

This is the point: if the knight had not been sacrificed on move 25, the black queen would have captured the rook on f7 with check!

27	**...**	**♗xd7**
28	**♖f8**	Black resigned.

Game No. 30
Duras–Spielmann
Piestany 1912

1	**e4**	**e6**
2	**d4**	**d5**
3	**♘c3**	**♘f6**
4	**e5**	**♘fd7**
5	**♘ce2**	

In recent years the system with 5 f4 has been a more usual continuation (see Game 24: Kir. Georgiev–Dolmatov, and Game 32: Timman–Yusupov).

Also encountered is 5 ♘f3, when Black obtains an equal position with accurate play: 5 ... c5 6 dc ♘c6 7 ♗f4 ♗xc5 8 ♗d3 f6! (weaker is 8 ... h6 9 ♗g3! a6 10 0–0 b5 11 ♖e1 0–0 12 ♘e2 with advantage to White in Gufeld–Spassky, USSR Ch., Leningrad 1960) 9 ef ♘xf6 10 0–0 0–0 11 ♘e5 ♗d7 12 ♘xc6 (after 12 ♕e2 ♕e7 13 ♖ae1 ♖ae8 14 a3 a6 15 ♔h1 ♗d4 Black seizes the initiative: Ljubojevic–Petrosian, Las Palmas 1972) 12 ... ♗xc6 13 ♕e2 ♘e4 (Vogt–Farago, Kecskemét 1979).

5	**...**	**c5**
6	**f4**	**♘c6**

7 c3 ♕b6

Emanuel Lasker usually continued 7 ... b5 here, and only then brought his queen out to b6.

8 ♘f3 ♗e7

Stronger is the immediate 8 ... f6, and if 9 g3 then 9 ... cd 10 cd ♗b4+ 11 ♘c3 0–0 12 ef ♘xf6 with a satisfactory game. In the event of 9 a3 possible is 9 ... ♗e7 10 b4 (10 ♘g3 0–0 11 ♗d3 fe 12 fe cd 13 cd a5!) 10 ... cd 11 cd 0–0 12 ♕d3 a6 13 ♗e3 ♕d8 14 g3 ♘b6 with equality (Enevoldsen–Koch, Helsinki Ol. 1952).

9 g3 f6

10 ♗h3 f5?

Black displays a degree of inconsistency. The pawn advance ... f7–f5 could have been played one move ago, without wasting a tempo. Here it looks more logical to play 10 ... cd, when White cannot play 11 ♗xe6 because of 11 ... ♘dxe5 12 ♗xd5 ♘xf3+ 13 ♗xf3 dc, when Black has an excellent game. Also possible is 11 cd fe 12 fe 0–0 13 ♗xe6+ ♔h8 14 ♗xd5 ♘dxe5! 15 de ♗g4 with a strong attack.

11 0–0 0–0

Worth considering was 11 ... h5 or 11 ... ♘f8, but also in this case White's position is to be preferred, since Black experiences difficulties associated with the fact that his queenside is undeveloped.

12 g4 g6

13 gf gf

It would be bad to play 13 ... ef, leaving the pawn on d5 undefended, and White would also get a defended passed pawn on e5.

14 ♔h1 ♔h8

15 ♖g1 ♖f7

It was not good to play 15 ... ♖g8, since there would have followed 16 ♖xg8+ ♔xg8 17 ♕g1+ ♔h8 18 ♘g5 ♗xg5 19 ♕xg5, with a big advantage.

16 ♘g5 ♗xg5

17 ♖xg5 cd

18 ♕g1

The idea of this move is to force Black to play either 18 ... ♖f8, after which White will get the opportunity to attack the rook on f8 with his dark-squared bishop along the a3–f8 diagonal and will also have the move ♖g5–g7, or 18 ... ♘e7, forfeiting control over the d4-square.

18 ... ♘e7

19 ♘xd4 ♘f8

A passive move. Black fails to take advantage of the opportunity to improve his position by playing 19 ... ♘c5 and 20 ... ♘e4.

20 ♗f1

Tarrasch considered that 20 ♕g2 was stronger, simultaneously defending the pawn on b2 and facilitating the development of his queenside pieces: ♗c1–e3 and ♖a1–g1.

20 ... ♗d7

21 ♗e2 ♘fg6

22 ♕g3 ♖g8

23 b3 ♘c6

24 ♗e3

Also quite good was 24 ♘b5, when Black cannot reply 24 ... ♘xe5 because of 25 ♗e3.

24 ... ♘xd4

25 ♗xd4 ♕a5

26 a4!

This move makes 26 ... ♗b5 impossible, permits the rook to be transferred from a1 to g1, and threatens 27 b4 and 28 ♗xa7.

26 ... a6

27 ♖g1 ♕d8

28 h4 ♕f8

29 h5 ♕h6

30 ♗f3

With the threat of 31 ♗xd5, when the bishop cannot be captured because of 32 e6+. But stronger still was 30 ♕h2 ♘e7 31 ♗c5 ♖xg5 32 fg ♕f8 33 g6 ♖g7 34 h6 ♖xg6 35 ♖xg6 hg 36 ♕h4. On the other hand, 30 ♖g2? would have led to trouble for White after 30 ... ♖fg7 31 ♔g1 ♘xf4!.

30 ... ♖fg7 *(94)*

31 ♕h2!

Now 31 ... ♘xf4 is not playable, in view of 32 ♖xg7 ♖xg7 33 ♖xg7 ♔xg7 34 ♗e3. The tempting 31 ♗c5? ♘xf4 32 ♗e7 would have lost, in view of 32 ... ♖xg5 33 ♗xg5 ♘xh5! 34 ♕h4 ♖xg5 35 ♕xg5 (or 35 ♖xg5) 35 ... ♘g3+.

31 ... ♘e7

32 ♗c5 ♘c6

33 ♕h4

94
W

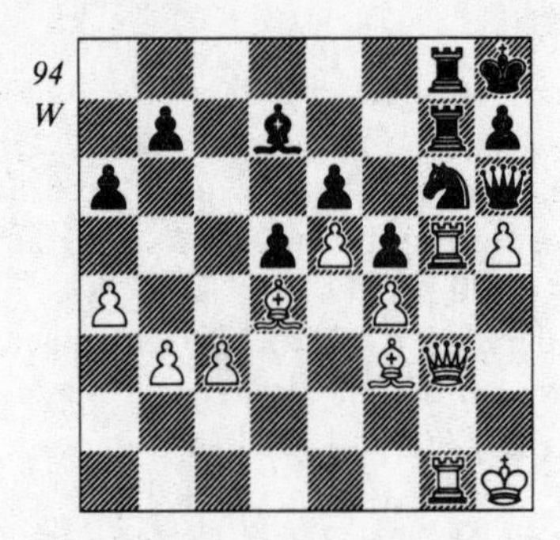

Threatening 34 ♗f8, which could not be played at once because of 33 ... ♖xg5 34 ♗xh6 ♖xg1+.

33 ... ♖g6
34 ♖1g2

Many years later, a chessplayer from Voronezh, Bubnov, discovered a quick win for White: 34 ♗f8!, and if 34 ... ♖xf8 then 35 ♖xg6 hg 36 ♖xg6 ♕h7 37 ♕g5 ♖g8 38 ♕f6+ ♖g7 39 ♖h6.

34 ... ♗e8
35 b4 b5

Preventing 36 b5, after which White's dark-squared bishop would have reached f6 via e7.

36 ab ab
37 ♔h2!

Setting off to defend the queen, and so Black is forced to exchange rooks.

37 ... ♖xg5
38 fg ♕g7
39 ♕f4 ♘xe5?

Black's position is extremely difficult (in particular, White threatens the breakthrough g5–g6), and so he risked a move which was virtually suicidal: he opened up the a1–h8 diagonal for White's dark-squared bishop.

40 ♗d4 ♘xf3+
41 ♕xf3 e5
42 h6!

This is the whole point! Now on 42 ... ♕c7 a double pin is decisive: 43 ♕f4!!.

42 ... ♕e7
43 ♖e2 ♖xg5

No better was 43 ... ♖f8 44 ♖xe5 ♕c7 45 ♕f4 ♔g8 46 ♗c5.

44 ♖xe5

Also quite good was 44 ♗xe5+ ♔g8 45 ♗f4.

44 ... ♕d6! *(95)*

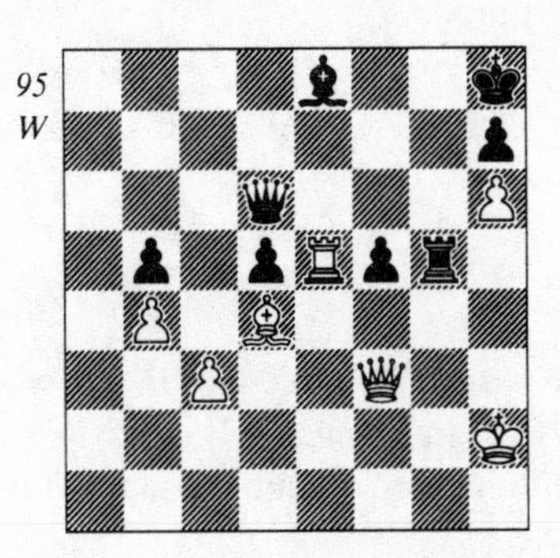

The impression is that White has miscalculated, since the white king has no retreat-squares — after the pawn on h6 is captured it will be mate.

45 ♕g3!!

The tactical device of interference comes into operation: not 45 ... ♖xg3, because of 46 ♖xe8 mate.

45 ... ♕xh6+
46 ♕h3 ♕d6

46 ... ♕xh3+ results in the loss of a piece: 47 ♔xh3 ♔g8 48 ♖xe8+ ♔f7 49 ♖b8.

47 ♔h1 ♔g8
48 ♖xe8+ ♔f7
49 ♖h8 Black resigned.

Game No. 31
Rachels–Penkalski
USA 1991

1 e4 e6
2 d4 d5
3 ♘d2 ♘c6

Worth considering is the flexible 3 ... ♗e7!?, not hurrying to commit the king's knight; for example: 4 ♗d3 c5 5 dc ♘d7 6 ed ed 7 ♘b3 ♘xc5 8 ♘f3 ♘f6 9 ♘xc5 ♗xc5 10 0–0 (10 ♗g5 would have given White a small advantage) 10 ... 0–0 11 c3 ♗g4 12 ♗g5 ♖e8 13 ♗c2 h6 14 ♗xf6 ♕xf6 15 ♕xd5 ♗xf3 16 ♕xf3

♕xf3 17 gf ♖e2 with a drawn ending (Jansa–Gausel, Gausdal 1991); or 4 ♘gf3 ♘f6 5 ♗d3 c5 6 e5 ♘fd7 7 c3 ♘c6 8 0–0 cd 9 cd a5 10 ♘b1 a4 11 ♘c3 ♘b6 12 ♗f4 ♘b4 13 ♗e2 ♗d7 14 a3 ♘c6 15 ♗d3 ♘a5 with an excellent position for Black (Efimov–Gausel, Gausdal 1991).

4 ♘gf3

Less testing is 4 c3 e5 5 ed ♕xd5 6 ♘gf3 ed as in Game 38: Fischer–R. Byrne.

4 ... de
5 ♘xe4 ♘f6
6 ♘xf6+ gf

Inserting the moves ♘f3 and ... ♘c6 in this well-known position rather favours White. In Game 18: Boleslavsky–Ufimtsev, Black's queen's knight remained on its initial square and Black had played ... b6 instead.

7 ♗b5 a6
8 ♗xc6+ bc
9 ♕e2 ♖b8

9 ... c5 10 ♗e3 cd 11 ♘xd4 ♗b7 12 0–0–0 gives White good attacking chances.

10 0–0 c5
11 ♖d1 ♕d5
12 dc

In the event of 12 c4? ♕h5 13 d5 e5 Black has seized the initiative.

12 ... ♕xc5
13 ♗e3 ♕b5

It would be worse to play 13 ... ♕h5? 14 ♕c4 ♗d6 15 ♗a7 ♕b5 16 ♕h4.

14 c4 ♕h5

Black would lose after 14 ... ♕xb2? 15 ♕d3 ♗d6 16 ♖db1.

15 ♗a7!

15 ♗d4 would have given Black the advantage: 15 ... ♗b7! 16 ♗xf6 ♖g8 17 ♕d3 ♗d6; White would not achieve anything with 15 ♖d5?! ♕g4 16 h3 ♕e4 17 ♘g5 (in the hope of 17 ... fg 18 ♗xg5!) 17 ... ♕g6.

15 ... ♖a8? *(96)*

After 15 ... ♖b7 16 ♗d4 ♗e7 17 ♕e4 0–0 18 ♕c6 e5 19 ♗c3 White would have had some advantage but Black would have had an entirely defensible position.

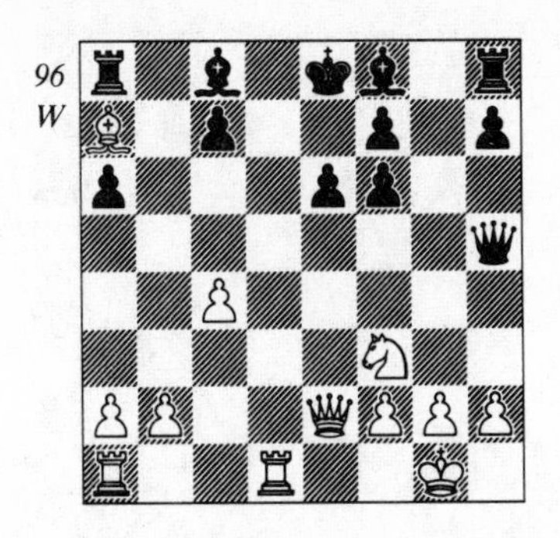
96
W

16 ♕e4!

White sacrifices a piece but gains a tempo in order to break through Black's defences. In addition, Black's rook is enticed onto the square a7, where it is placed very badly and is vulnerable.

16 ... ♖xa7

Black has no choice.

17 ♕c6+ ♔e7
18 ♖d5!!

The idea behind this move is that it either destroys Black's fortifications in the centre or it cuts the black queen off from the key square c5.

18 ... ed

In the event of 18 ... f5 there could have followed: 19 ♕c5+ ♔f6 (19 ... ♔e8 20 ♕xa7 ed 21 ♕xc7) 20 ♕xa7 ed 21 ♕d4+; if 18 ... ♕g4 then 19 h3! (but not 19 ♕c5+ ♔e8 20 ♕xa7 ed 21 ♕xc7 ♕d7! 22 ♖e1+ ♗e7) 19 ... ♕g6 (19 ... ♕f4 20 ♖e1 ♖b7 21 ♘d4 f5 22 g3 ♕g5 23 ♘xf5+ ♔f6 24 ♘e7 wins) 20 ♕c5+ ♔e8 21 ♕xa7 ed 22 ♕xc7 ♗e6 23 ♖e1.

19 ♖e1+ ♗e6
20 cd ♔d8

No better was 20 ... ♗h6 21 de ♖d8 22 ef+ ♔xf7 23 ♕e6+ ♔g6 24 ♘e5+ ♕xe5 25 ♖xe5 ♖d1+ 26 ♖e1, or 20 ... ♕g4 21 h3! ♕f5 22 ♘d4 ♕d3 23 ♖xe6+ fe 24 ♕xe6+ with mate (analysis by Rachels).

21 de ♕b5 *(97)*

On 21 ... fe White would play 22 ♕xe6, with the threats 23 ♕xf6+ and 23 ♘d4.

22 ♘d4!

The knight comes into play at just the right time and with

97
W

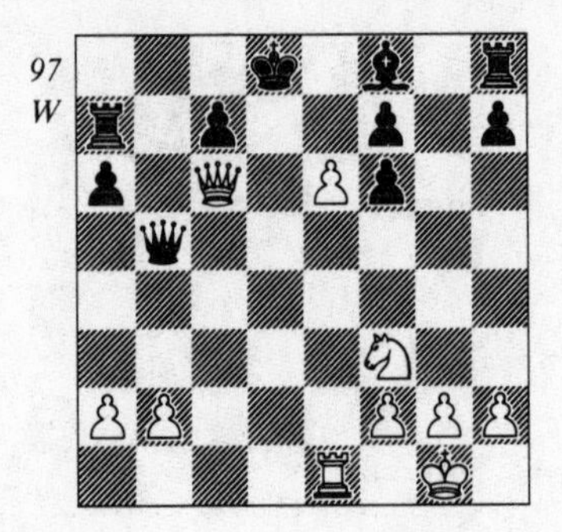

decisive effect.

22	**...**	**♕xc6**
23	**♘xc6+**	**♔c8**

23 ... ♔e8 24 ♘xa7 ♗c5 25 ♘c6 fe 26 ♖xe6+ ♔f7 27 ♖e2 and the extra pawn guarantees a win for White.

24	**♘xa7+**	**♔b7**
25	**e7!**	

Precisely so! The move 25 ef would have led to a win for Black after 25 ... ♗c5! (but not 25 ... ♔xa7 26 ♖e8) 26 ♖e8 ♖f8 27 ♘c8 ♖xf7 28 ♔f1 ♖f8!.

25	**...**	**♗xe7**
26	**♖xe7**	**♖d8**
27	**♔f1**	**♖d2**
28	**♖xf7**	**♖xb2**
29	**a4**	**♖a2**

After 29 ... ♖b4 30 a5 ♖a4 31 ♖xf6 ♔xa7 32 ♖f5 White wins easily.

30	**♘b5**	**ab**
31	**ab**	**♖b2**
32	**♖xf6**	**♖xb5**
33	**♔e2**	**♖h5**
34	**h3**	**c6**
35	**♔e3**	**♔b6**
36	**♔d4**	**♔b5**
37	**♖f7**	

White finds a very precise way to win.

37	**...**	**♖d5+**
38	**♔c3**	**h5**
39	**h4**	**c5**

40	**♖f4**	**♖e5**
41	**g3**	**♖d5**
42	**♖f8**	**♖d1**
43	**♖f5**	**♖f1**
44	**♔b3**	**♔c6**
45	**♔c4**	**♖c1+**
46	**♔d3**	**♖f1**
47	**♔e2**	**♖h1**
48	**♖xh5**	

And on move 60 Black ended his resistance. (Notes based on those by Stuart Rachels in *Informator* 52.)

8 Combinations on the Theme of the Pin

The idea of the pin is that a piece is totally or partially unable to move. The pinning motif is widely exploited in practice in conjunction with other tactical devices. For example, by sacrificing pieces the active side may create a pin or utilise an existing pin in order to derive other advantages.

Of particular interest are combinations on the theme of the double pin, when a piece of the defending side is tied down to a particular square by means of pins along two lines at once (see the note to the 42nd move of Game 30: Duras–Spielmann).

Let us examine an example where a pin was created as the result of a fascinating combination.

Spielmann–Wahle
Vienna 1926

1 e4 e6 2 d4 d5 3 ♘c3 ♘f6 4 ed ed 5 ♗g5 ♗e7 6 ♗d3 ♘c6 7 ♘ge2 ♘b4 8 ♘g3 ♘xd3+ 9 ♕xd3 g6 10 0–0 c6 11 ♖ae1 0–0? *(98)*

Black underestimates the perilous nature of his position.

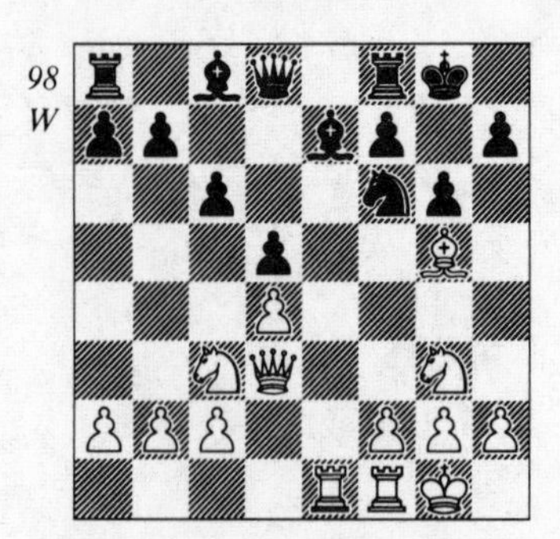

12 ♖xe7! ♕xe7 13 ♕f3 ♔g7

Black was unable to save himself with 13 ... ♗f5 14 ♘xf5 gf 15 ♕g3!, since on 15 ... ♔g7 there follows 16 ♗xf6++ ♔xf6 17 ♕h4+ ♔e6 18 ♖e1+.

The pinned knight on f6 is attacked twice and defended twice. By sacrificing a knight, White creates a new threat to the f6-square, and this time it is decisive.

14 ♘ge4! de 15 ♘xe4 ♕e6

There appears to be nothing better.

16 ♗xf6+ ♔g8 17 ♕f4 Black resigned.

There is no defence against 18 ♕h6.

Game No. 32

Timman–Yusupov

4th match game, Tilburg 1986

1 d4 e6
2 e4 d5
3 ♘c3 ♘f6
4 e5

This continuation, favoured by Steinitz, leads to a sharp fight with good counter-chances for Black.

4 ... ♘fd7
5 f4

The Gledhill Attack, 5 ♕g4, is not good, because of 5 ... c5 6 ♘b5 cd 7 ♘f3 ♘c6 8 ♘d6+ ♗xd6 9 ♕xg7 ♗xe5 10 ♘xe5 ♕f6, or 6 ♘f3 cd 7 ♘xd4 ♘xe5 8 ♕g3 ♘bc6 9 ♗b5 a6! (but not 9 ... ♗d7, because of 10 ♗xc6 ♘xc6 11 ♘db5 ♖c8 12 ♗f4 ♕b6 13 ♗c7 ♕c5 14 ♗d6! ♕b6 15 ♗xf8 ♔xf8 16 ♕d6+ ♔e8 17 0–0–0 with an irresistible attack).

A more highly regarded alternative to the standard 5 f4 is 5 ♘ce2 (see Game 30: Duras–Spielmann).

5 ... c5
6 ♘f3 ♘c6
7 ♗e3 ♕b6

Black in effect consents to exchange a piece for three pawns. In recent games a more common continuation has been 7 ... cd (see Game 24: Kir. Georgiev–Dolmatov), or 7 ... a6 8 ♕d2 b5 9 dc ♗xc5 10 ♗xc5 ♘xc5 11 b4 ♘xb4 12 ♘xb5 0–0! 13 ♕xb4 ♕b6 14 a4 ab 15 a5! ♕a7 16 ♘d4 ♗d7 17 ♗d3, when play is unclear (Boll–Jezek, corr. 1988/90).

The fourth game of the Candidates match Anand–Dreev,

Madras 1991, continued: 7 ... a6 8 ♕d2 b5 9 h4 ♗b7 10 h5?! b4! 11 ♘a4?, and now 11 ... ♘xd4 12 ♘xd4 cd 13 ♗xd4 ♗c6 would have given Black the advantage.

8 ♘a4 ♕a5+

9 c3 cd

Also possible is 9 ... c4 10 b4 ♕c7 11 ♗e2 b5 12 ♘c5 ♘xc5 13 dc a5 14 a3 ♗e7 15 0–0 0–0, with an equal game (Kruppa–Dokhoian, USSR Ch., Moscow 1991).

10 b4 *(99)*

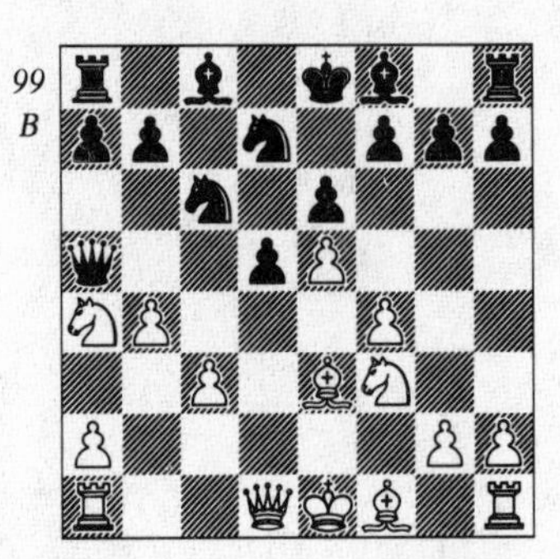

10 ... ♘xb4

After 10 ... ♕c7 (or 10 ... ♕d8) 11 ♘xd4 White stands better.

11 cb ♗xb4+

12 ♗d2 ♗xd2+

Also possible is 12 ... b6, waiting for White to play 13 ♖b1 or 13 ♔f2, insofar as 13 ♗xb4 ♕xb4+ 14 ♔f2 can be followed by 14 ... b5.

13 ♘xd2 b6

Stronger is 13 ... g5! 14 ♘b2 gf 15 ♘d3 b6 16 ♔f2 ♗a6 17 ♘f3 ♖c8! with an excellent position for Black (Anand–Dreev, sixth match game, Madras 1991).

14 ♕c2

White solves the problems associated with the knight on a4 by tactical means. As Makarychev notes, it is not good for Black to straighten out his pawn structure by playing 14 ... ♘c5 15 ♘xc5 bc, since 16 ♔f2 (with the threat of 17 ♘b3) 16 ... c4 17 ♗xc4! dc 18 ♘xc4 and 19 ♘d6+ ensures a dangerous initiative for White.

14 ... ♗b7

14 ... 0–0 15 ♕c6 ♖b8 16 ♕b5 leads to an exchange of queens in a situation favouring White, and 14 ... ♗a6 15 ♗xa6 ♕xa6

16 ♕c6 amounts to transposition.

15	**♕c7**	**♗a6**
16	**♗xa6**	**♕xa6**
17	**♕c6**	**♖c8** *(100)*

100
W

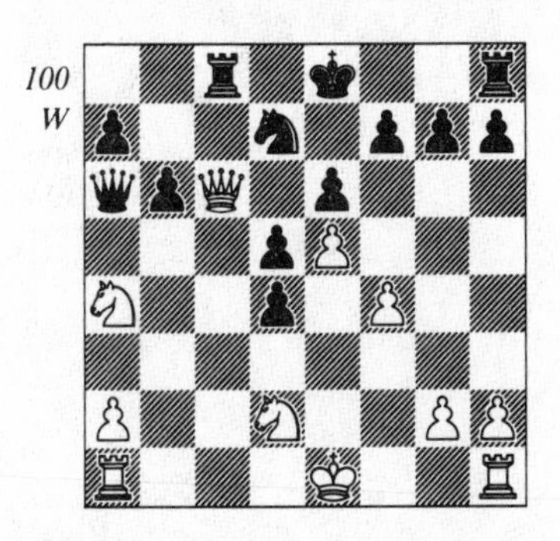

18 ♘c5!!

Not too difficult to find but very elegant. White exploits a double pin: of the knight on d7 along the diagonal, and of the pawn on b6 along the sixth rank.

18	**...**	**♖xc6**
19	**♘xa6**	**g5**

A typical method. Black's lead in development permits him to demolish a blockade type of position which, had it been preserved, would have meant that White's extra piece would have told in the end. Black needs to exchange a large number of pawns, not just to enable his pawn mass in the centre to become mobile but also to ensure his own safety. With a limited amount of material remaining on the board, converting an extra piece into a win can prove to be extremely difficult.

20 0–0

In the event of 20 g3 gf 21 gf f6!? 22 ef (or 22 ♘f3 fe 23 fe ♖c4 24 ♔d2 ♖f8 25 ♖f1 ♔e7) 22 ... ♖c3! 23 ♘h3 ♘c5 Black has risked nothing.

20	**...**	**gf**
21	**♖xf4**	**♘xe5**
22	**♖xd4**	**♖g8**
23	**♘b4**	**♖c3** *(101)*

Black's three pawns for a knight and the active positions of his pieces mean that any attempt by White to play for a win would be both futile and dangerous. The tempting 24 ♖e1 achieves

101
W

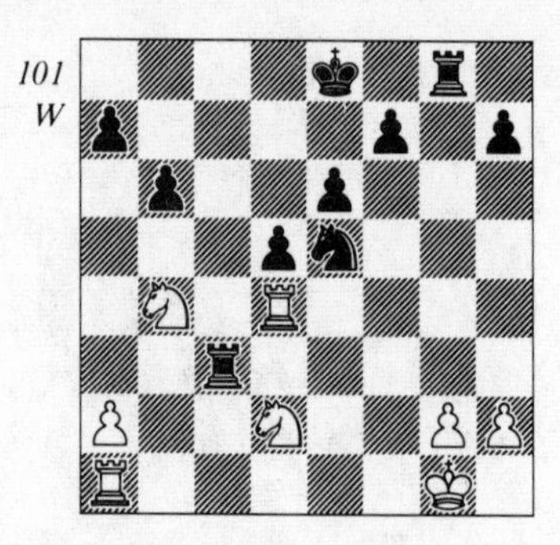

nothing, because of 24 … f6. Therefore Timman decides to give back the piece and force a draw.

24	**♘xd5**	**ed**
25	**♖xd5**	**♖c5!**

Weaker was 25 … f6 26 ♘e4 ♖c6 27 ♘xf6+, or 25 … ♘g6 26 ♘e4 ♖c6 27 ♘d6+ ♔f8 28 ♘f5 ♖c8 29 ♖ad1 with a definite initiative for White.

26	**♖xc5**	**bc**
27	**♘e4**	**♔e7**
28	**♘xc5**	**♖c8**
29	**♘b3**	

The active position of the black rook can have no influence on the final outcome. The limited material remaining makes a draw inevitable.

29	**…**	**♖c2**
30	**♘d4**	**♖c4**
31	**♖e1**	**f6**
32	**♘f3**	**♔e6**
33	**♘xe5**	**fe**
34	**♖e3**	**♖a4**
35	**♖h3**	**♖xa2**
36	**♖xh7**	**e4**

The game gets a little sharper, but no more than that.

37	**h4**	**e3**
38	**♔f1**	**a5**
39	**h5**	**♖f2+**
40	**♔e1**	**♖xg2**

Drawn.

Game No. 33

G. Timoshenko–Styrenkov

Budapest 1991

1	**e4**	**e6**
2	**d4**	**d5**
3	**♘c3**	**♗b4**
4	**e5**	**b6**

The point of this move is to exchange off the important light-squared bishop, but it also blocks the a5–d8 diagonal which in many variations Black makes use of in order to bring his queen into play.

5 a3

A natural and strong move is 5 ♕g4. In the game Mokry–Ravikumar, Dieren 1990, there followed: 5 ... ♗f8 6 ♘f3 ♕d7 7 ♗b5 c6 8 ♗e2 ♗a6 9 0–0 ♘e7 10 ♖d1 ♘f5 11 a3 ♕b7 12 b3 ♘d7 13 ♘b5! and White obtained a good attacking position.

5	**...**	**♗f8**
6	**♗b5+**	**♗d7**
7	**♗d3**	**c5**
8	**♘f3**	**♘c6**
9	**0–0**	**♘ge7**
10	**♗g5!?**	

An interesting idea. Previously the continuation 10 ♘b5 had been encountered (Cabrilo–G. Dizdar, Yugoslav Ch. 1990).

10 ... a6? *(102)*

Black has failed to anticipate White's plan. Otherwise he would have played 10 ... ♕b8 11 ♖e1 ♘g6 with a solid position.

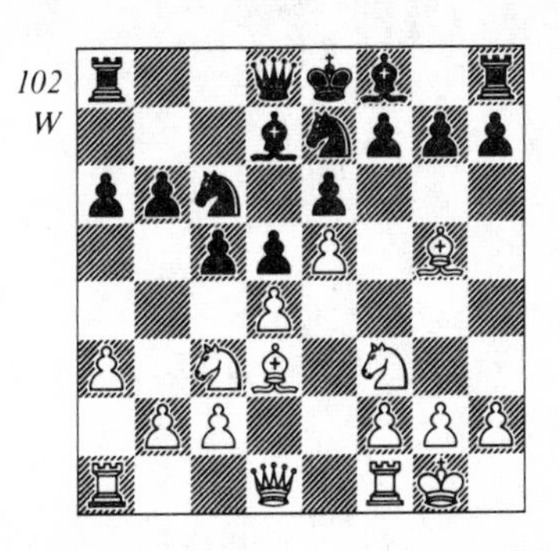

11 ♗xa6!!

The pin of the knight on e7 becomes noticeable. On 11 ... ♖xa6 there follows 12 ♘b5 ♗c8 13 ♘d6+ ♔d7 14 ♘xf7 ♕e8 15 ♘xh8 ♖a8 16 c3, with advantage to White. Still worse is 11 … ♘xe5, because of 12 ♘xe5 ♖xa6 13 ♕f3! f6 14 ♗xf6.

11 … ♕b8
12 ♗d3 ♘xd4
13 ♘xd4 cd
14 ♘b5 ♘g6

White would have obtained a very strong attack after 14 … ♕xe5 15 f4! ♕b8 16 f5 e5 (in the event of 16 … ♘xf5 there follows: 17 ♖xf5 ef 18 ♘c7+ ♕xc7 19 ♕e2+ ♗e6 20 ♗b5+ ♕d7 21 ♗xd7+ ♔xd7 22 ♕b5+ ♔c7 23 ♗f4+ ♔b7 24 b4, with a decisive advantage) 17 f6 ♘g6 (or 17 … ♘c6 18 fg ♗xg7 19 ♖xf7! ♔xf7 20 ♕f3+ with a mating attack) 18 ♘xd4! ♗c5 19 fg ♗xd4+ 20 ♔h1 ♖g8 21 ♕f3 ♘f4 (21 … f5 22 ♗xf5 ♗xf5 23 ♕xd5 ♖xg7 24 ♖xf5) 22 ♗xf4 ef 23 ♖ae1+ ♗e6 24 ♕xd5 ♗e3 25 ♖xe3 fe 26 ♗b5+ ♔e7 27 ♕g5+ ♔d6 28 ♖d1+ with mate (analysis by G. Timoshenko).

15 ♖e1 ♘xe5?!

Stronger was 15 … h6 16 ♗d2 ♗e7, although here too there is no doubting White's advantage after 17 f4.

16 ♗f4 f6 *(103)*

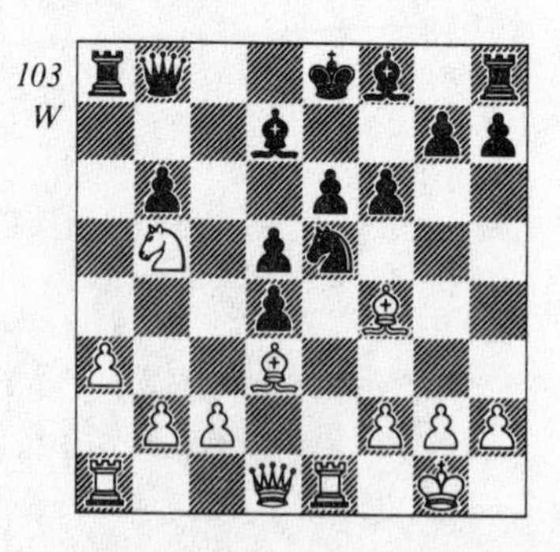
103
W

17 ♖xe5!

The second phase of the attack. The variation 17 ♗xe5 fe 18 ♕h5+ g6 19 ♗xg6+ hg 20 ♕xh8 ♗xb5 21 ♖xe5 ♔f7 leads to an unclear position.

17 … fe
18 ♕h5+ g6

Or 18 … ♔d8 19 ♗xe5 ♕b7 20 ♗xg7 ♗xg5 21 ♗xh8.

19 ♕xe5! ♕xe5

20 ♗xe5 ♖a5
21 ♘c7+ ♔f7

If 21 … ♔d8 White plays 22 ♘xe6+.

22 ♗xh8 ♗d6
23 ♘xe6 Black resigned.

The two extra pawns are quite sufficient to win.

Game No. 34
R. Rodriguez–Yusupov
Thessaloniki Ol. 1988

1 e4 e6
2 d4 d5
3 ♘d2 ♘f6
4 e5 ♘fd7
5 ♗d3 c5
6 c3 ♘c6
7 ♘e2 cd
8 cd f6
9 ef ♘xf6
10 0–0 ♗d6
11 ♘f3 ♕c7
12 ♘c3

The immediate 12 ♗g5 guarantees Black a good game after 12 … 0–0 13 ♖c1 ♘g4 14 ♘g3 g6 15 ♗b5 ♗d7 16 ♘h4 ♘f6 17 ♕d3 ♖f7 18 ♖fe1 ♘g4 19 ♘f3 ♖e8 (A. Sokolov–Yusupov, ninth match game, Riga 1986).

Other typical alternatives are 12 g3 (see Game 23: Armas–Komarov) and 12 h3 (see Game 44: Barash–Monin).

12 … a6
13 ♗g5 0–0

Black gets a difficult position after 13 … ♘g4 14 ♘h4 ♗xh2+ 15 ♔h1 ♗g1 16 g3 ♘xf2+ 17 ♖xf2 ♗xf2 18 ♕h5+ g6 19 ♗xg6+ ♔d7 20 ♘xd5 (A. Sokolov–Bystrov, USSR 1981).

14 ♗h4

Weaker is 14 ♖c1; for example: 14 … ♗d7 15 ♖e1 (here too, 15 ♗h4 is possible) 15 … ♘g4 16 g3 (the only move: on 16 h3? a decisive continuation is 16 … ♗h2+ 17 ♔f1 ♘xf2! 18 ♔xf2 ♕g3+ 19 ♔e3 ♖xf3+) 16 … h6 17 ♗e3 ♖f6 18 ♗f1 ♖af8 19 ♗g2 ♗e8 and Black stands better; the game Semeniuk–Komarov, Novosibirsk 1989, developed in very interesting fashion, though it was not free from errors: 20 ♘h4! (weaker was 20 h3 ♗h5! 21 hg ♗xg4) 20 ... ♗h5 (considerably stronger was 20 ... ♘xe3 21 ♖xe3 ♕b6, when Black has the better chances) 21 ♗h3 ♘xf2 22 ♗xe6+! ♖xe6 23 ♕xh5 ♘d3 24 ♕xd5 ♖e8 25 ♗f4 ♘xe1 26 ♖xe1 ♘b4 (a dangerous manoeuvre; worth considering was 26 ... ♕f7!? 27 ♖xe6 ♖xe6 28 ♗xd6 ♖e1+ 29 ♔g2 ♖e2+! 30 ♔h3 ♕xd5 31 ♘xd5 ♘xd4 and, despite his material deficit, Black ought not to lose) 27 ♖xe6? (an exchange of courtesies; White could have won with 27 ♕b3! ♕f7 28 ♖xe6 ♖xe6 29 ♗xd6 ♘d3 30 ♘e4) 27 ... ♘xd5 28 ♖xe8+ ♔f7 29 ♘xd5 ♕a5!, and after 30 ♗xd6? ♔xe8 31 ♘c3 ♕b6 Black won.

14 ... ♘h5

A fashionable continuation. Lines previously played in this position are: 14 ... ♗d7 15 ♖e1 ♔h8 16 ♗g3 ♗xg3 17 hg ♕b6 18 ♘a4 ♕a7 19 ♗b1! with a small advantage to White (Balashov–Vaganian, USSR Ch., Moscow 1976); or 14 ... ♗f4 15 ♖e1 ♔h8 16 ♗g3 ♘h5 17 ♘e2 ♘xg3 18 ♘xf4 ♘e4 19 a3 ♖xf4 20 gf ♕xf4 21 ♗xe4 de 22 ♘e5 with a clear advantage to White (Karpov–Chen De, Hannover 1983).

15 ♖e1

Also possible is 15 ♖c1, maintaining the other rook on the f-file. For example: 15 ... g6 16 ♗b1 ♕g7 17 ♘a4 ♗d7 18 ♘c5 ♗xc5 19 ♖xc5 ♖xf3 20 gf ♖f8 with complicated play.

15 ... g6
16 ♗f1

Worth considering is 16 ♗g5 ♕g7 17 ♗e3 ♗d7 18 ♗f1 ♖f7 19 g3 (more accurate is 19 ♘g5!, with the advantage) 19 ... h6 20 ♗g2 ♖af8 21 ♕e2 ♘f6 22 ♖ad1 g5 23 ♖f1 Drawn (Ivanchuk–Komarov, Kramatorsk 1989).

16 ... h6
17 ♗g3 ♘xg3
18 hg ♖f6

Black plans to increase his pressure along the f-file.

19 ♕d2 g5
20 ♘h2 ♕g7
21 ♗e2 ♗c7

Black manoeuvres very purposefully. The bishop is being transferred to the square b6, creating a threat against the isolated pawn and, after this has been won, also the very important square f2.

22 ♗h5 ♗b6

23 ♘f3 ♗d7
24 ♖f1

In connection with the threat of g5–g4, White is forced to switch to the defence of the pawn on f2.

24 ... ♖af8
25 ♘a4 ♗a7
26 ♖ac1 *(104)*

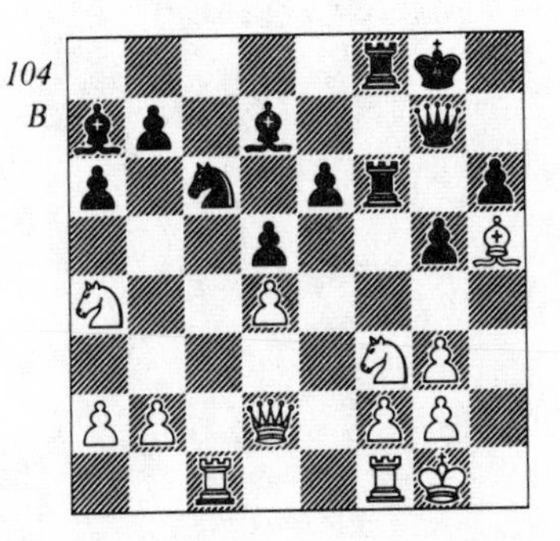
104
B

Black has mobilised his forces superbly and willingly brings about tactical complications which are very typical of this variation.

26 ... ♘xd4!

Now on 27 ♘xd4 there follows 27 ... ♖xf2 28 ♖xf2 ♕xd4, with a decisive advantage.

27 ♖c7 ♘b5
28 ♖xb7 g4
29 ♗xg4 ♕xg4
30 ♖xd7 ♕xa4
31 b3 ♕g4
32 a4 *(105)*

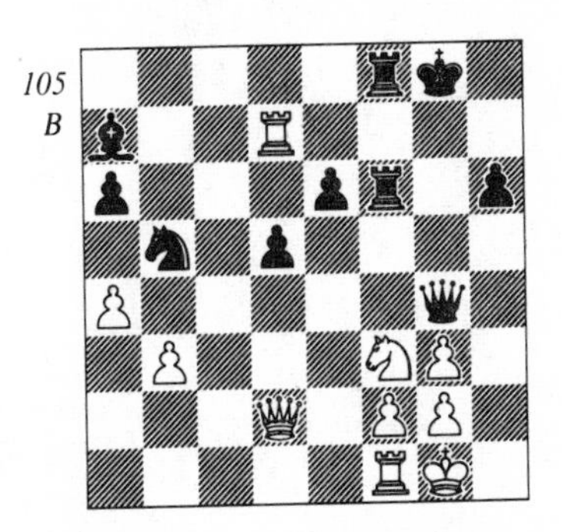
105
B

The impression is that White is winning back his piece. But Black had foreseen everything.

32 ... ♖xf3!

Now on 33 gf there follows 33 ... ♕xg3+.

33 ♕xh6 ♖3f7
34 ♖xf7 ♖xf7
35 ab ab

White resigned.

9 The Back Rank

The weakness of the back rank is a common tactical motif, serving as the basis for many combinations. As a rule, such operations either involve a sacrifice to deflect the enemy pieces defending the back rank or they exploit the fact that these pieces may be overloaded by having various functions to perform.

A classic example is provided by the finish of the following game *(106)*:

Bernstein–Capablanca
Moscow 1914

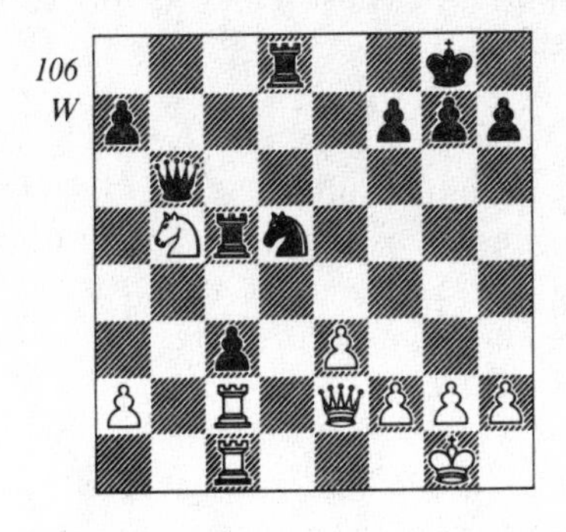

106
W

White decided to gobble up a pawn, little suspecting the possible consequences.

1 ♘xc3 ♘xc3 2 ♖xc3 ♖xc3 3 ♖xc3 *(107)*

Now Black achieves nothing with 3 ... ♕b1+, in view of 4 ♕f1 (4 ... ♖d1?? 5 ♖c8+), but the weakness of the back rank tells in the end nonetheless.

3 ... ♕b2! 4 ♖c2 (or 4 ♕e1 ♕xc3!) **4 ... ♕b1+** and White loses a rook.

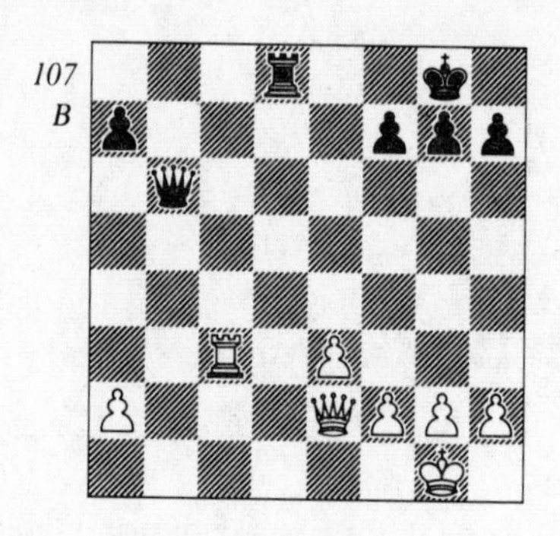

Game No. 35

Capablanca–Alekhine

1st game, World Ch., Buenos Aires 1927

1	**e4**	**e6**
2	**d4**	**d5**
3	**♘c3**	**♗b4**
4	**ed**	

This insipid exchange rapidly leads to equality and is no longer seen much in practice. "If White has any fighting ambitions", comments Alekhine, "he must avoid in this variation the pawn exchange on the fourth move."

4	**...**	**ed**
5	**♗d3**	

Black gets the advantage after 5 ♕f3?! ♕e7+! 6 ♕e3 (or 6 ♗e3 ♘f6 7 ♗d3 c5!: Mestrovic–Maric, Yugoslav Ch., Kraljevo 1967) 6 ... ♘c6 7 ♗b5 ♗f5 8 ♕xe7+ ♘xe7 9 ♗f4 ♗xc2 10 ♗xc7 ♖c8 (Zakharov–Antoshin, Sochi 1966).

5	**...**	**♘c6**
6	**♘ge2**	

White gets nowhere with 6 a3, because of 6 ... ♗e7!? 7 ♘ce2 ♗f6. Play is sharp and unclear after 6 ... ♗xc3+ 7 bc ♘f6 8 ♗g5 ♕e7 9 ♘e2 ♗d7 10 0–0 h6 11 ♗f4 0–0–0 12 c4 ♗e6 13 c5 g5 (Miles–Short, British Ch., Chester 1979).

6	**...**	**♘ge7**
7	**0–0**	**♗f5**
8	**♗xf5**	

The nature of the game is not really any different after 8 ♘g3 ♗xd3 9 ♕xd3 ♕d7 10 ♗f4 0–0 11 ♖ad1 ♖fe8 12 a3 ♗d6, with equality (A. Rabinovich–Yudovich, Moscow 1934).

8	**...**	**♘xf5**
9	**♕d3**	**♕d7**
10	**♘d1**	

White aims to exchange off the knight on f5, but such passive tactics with the idea of simplification ultimately allow Black to take the initiative. Play would have become sharper after 10 ♗f4 0–0–0 11 ♘a4.

10	**...**	**0–0**
11	**♘e3**	**♘xe3**
12	**♗xe3**	**♖fe8**
13	**♘f4** *(108)*	

An unsuccessful thrust. By playing 13 ♗f4 and 14 c3 Capablanca would have obtained a position leading most probably to a draw.

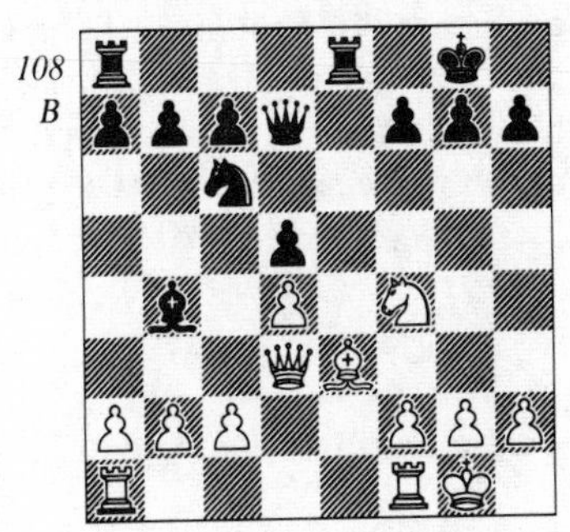

13	**...**	**♗d6!**

Inviting the variation 14 ♘xd5 ♗xh2+ 15 ♔xh2 ♕xd5 16 c4 ♕h5+ 17 ♔g1 ♖ad8 18 d5 ♖d6, when unpleasant threats hang over the white king (analysis by Kotov).

14	**♖fe1**	

Another inaccuracy, allowing Black to develop dangerous pressure. White should have consolidated his position with 14 c3.

14	**...**	**♘b4**
15	**♕b3**	

Better here was 15 ♕d2, defending the knight on f4 once more.

15	**...**	**♕f5**
16	**♖ac1?** *(109)*	

White's position is already difficult. Alekhine gives the following possible continuations: 16 ♖ec1 a5! 17 a3 a4 18 ♕c3 ♘c6 19 ♘d3 ♖e6; or 16 ♘d3 ♘xd3 17 ♕xd3 ♕xd3 18 cd ♗b4 19 ♖ec1 c6 and then ... a7–a5! with advantage to Black.

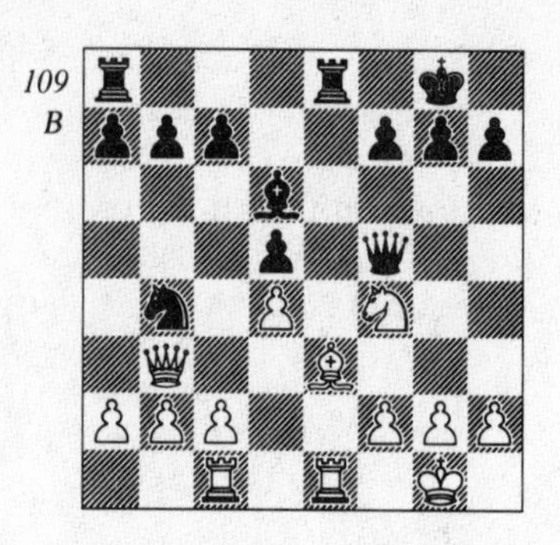

16 ... ♘xc2!
17 ♖xc2 ♕xf4!

A subtlety not foreseen by Capablanca. He had apparently only expected 17 ... ♗xf4, after which the pawn may be regained with 18 ♖c5 c6 19 ♕xb7. But with the move played Black has won a pawn by exploiting the weakness of the back rank.

18 g3 ♕f5
19 ♖ce2 b6
20 ♕b5 h5
21 h4 ♖e4

Threatening to create mating threats after 22 ... ♖xh4!.

22 ♗d2!

Sacrificing another pawn in order to complicate the game.

22 ... ♖xd4
23 ♗c3 ♖d3
24 ♗e5 ♖d8
25 ♗xd6 ♖xd6
26 ♖e5 ♕f3
27 ♖xh5!

White has achieved some measure of success, and Black now needs to play accurately in order not to fall into a trap. For example: 27 ... ♖e6? 28 ♕e8+ and 29 ♖xe8 mate.

27 ... ♕xh5
28 ♖e8+ ♔h7
29 ♕xd3+ ♕g6
30 ♕d1 ♖e6!

Dislodging the white rook from the only open file, since an exchange of rooks would not be to White's advantage.

31 ♖a8 ♖e5

32 ♖xa7

White has even succeeded in re-establishing material equilibrium, but Black's strong passed pawn decides the outcome.

32 ... c5
33 ♖d7

This alleviates Black's task. But also after 33 ♔g2 d4 White's position would still have been dismal.

33 ... ♕e6
34 ♕d3+ g6
35 ♖d8 d4
36 a4 ♖e1+

Black could have won even more quickly with 36 ... ♕e7 37 ♖b8 ♕c7, when the white rook is trapped: on 38 ♖a8 Black plays 38 ... ♕c6, threatening not only to capture the rook but also to give checkmate on the back rank.

37 ♔g2 ♕c6+
38 f3 ♖e3
39 ♕d1 ♕e6
40 g4 ♖e2+
41 ♔h3 ♕e3
42 ♕h1 ♕f4
43 h5 ♖f2
White resigned

Game No. 36
A. Sokolov–Yusupov
3rd game, Candidates Final, Riga 1986

1 e4 e6
2 d4 d5
3 ♘c3 ♗b4
4 e5 ♘e7
5 a3 ♗xc3+
6 bc c5
7 ♘f3 b6

Also perfectly playable is 7 ... ♗d7 (see Game 9: Hazai–Uhlmann).

8 a4

More to the point strategically is 8 ♗b5+ ♗d7 9 ♗d3, avoiding the exchange of bishops. After 8 ♘g5?! h6 9 ♕h5 g6 10 ♕h3 ♕c7! 11 ♗d2 cd 12 cd ♕xc2 13 ♖c1 ♕b2 14 ♗d3 ♕xd4

White has no compensation for the sacrificed material (Nunn–Hertneck, Munich 1991).

8 ... ♗a6
9 ♗xa6

Black also has no difficulties after 9 ♗b5+ ♗xb5 10 ab ♘d7 11 0–0 ♕c7 12 ♕d3 h6 13 ♗a3 0–0 14 c4 dc 15 ♕xc4 ♖fc8 (Kavalek–Portisch, Montreal 1979).

9 ... ♘xa6
10 0–0 ♘b8

In a Candidates quarter-final match between Geller and Spassky (Sukhumi 1968) this position was encountered several times. In the third game Geller played 11 ♗a3, but achieved nothing substantial after 11 ... ♘d7 12 ♕d3 ♖c8 13 ♖fd1 0–0 14 a5 h6.

11 dc bc
12 c4 0–0
13 cd ♘xd5

A comparative novelty. In the fifth game of the match mentioned above Black continued 13 ... ♕xd5, when there followed: 14 ♕e2 ♘d7 15 ♖fd1 ♕b7. By playing 16 ♖a3 here Geller could have obtained the better chances, creating threats such as 17 ♘g5 and, in some lines, 17 ♖ad3.

14 ♕d3 h6
15 c4 ♘e7
16 ♕e4 ♘d7
17 ♖b1?!

Worth considering was 17 a5, in order after 17 ... ♕c7 to continue 18 ♗b2, followed by occupying the d-file.

17 ... ♕a5!
18 ♖d1 ♖ad8!

Avoiding a trap: 18 ... ♖fd8 19 ♖xd7, and after 18 ... ♕xa4?! 19 ♗xh6! gh 20 ♖a1 ♕c6 21 ♕xc6 ♘xc6 22 ♖xd7 the game is level.

19 ♕c2? *(110)*

White has failed to take his opponent's brilliant riposte into account. But, as Yusupov has pointed out, White was already unable to defend his weaknesses: 19 ♖d6 ♘xe5!! 20 ♕xe5 ♘c6! 21 ♕g3 (on 21 ♖xc6 there follows 21 ... ♖d1+, with mate) 21 ... ♖xd6 22 ♕xd6 ♖d8 23 ♗d2 ♖xd6. Better for White was 19 h3 ♕xa4 20 ♗e3.

19 ... ♘xe5!!

110
B

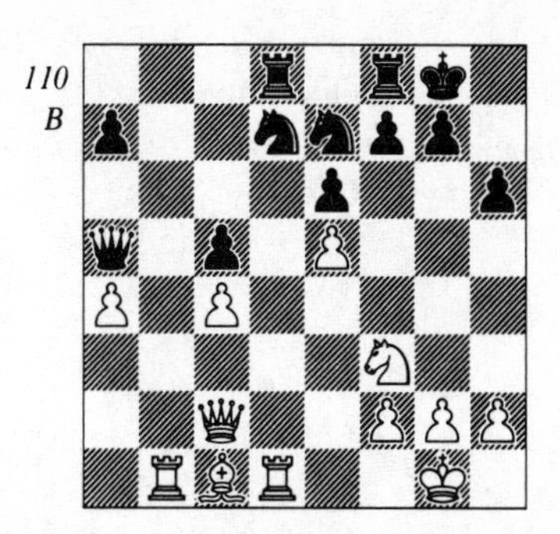

A superb combination, based on the weakness of the back rank.

20	**♘xe5**	**♛c3!**
21	**♕e2**	

21 ♖xd8 was not sufficient, because of 21 ... ♛xc2 22 ♖xf8+ ♚xf8 23 ♖b8+ ♞c8 24 ♖xc8+ ♚e7 with a decisive lead in material for Black.

21	**...**	**♛xe5**
22	**♗e3**	**♞f5**
23	**♕f3**	**♜xd1+**
24	**♖xd1**	**♞d4**
25	**♗xd4?**	

The last chance was 25 ♕b7, although also in this case after 25 ... ♞c2 26 ♕f3 ♞xe3 Black would have retained the advantage. Now, however, Black gets a technically won ending.

25	**...**	**cd**
26	**♕d3**	**♜d8**
27	**g3**	**♛c5**
28	**f4**	**♛b4**
29	**♖a1**	**a5**
30	**h4**	**h5**

A Zugzwang position has arisen. Now any move results either in the advance of Black's passed d-pawn or in further loss of material.

31	**♖b1**	**♛xa4**
32	**♖b5**	**g6**
33	**♔f2**	**♛a2+**
34	**♔f3**	**a4**

And White resigned on move 41.

Game No. 37
Smyslov–Botvinnik
9th game, World Ch., Moscow 1954

1	**e4**	**e6**
2	**d4**	**d5**
3	**♘c3**	**♗b4**
4	**e5**	**c5**
5	**a3**	**♗a5**
6	**b4**	**cd**
7	**♕g4**	**♘e7**

On 7 ... ♔f8 a very strong continuation is that pointed out by Lilienthal and Zagorovsky: 8 ba dc 9 a4!, followed by 10 ♗a3+.

8	**ba**	**dc**
9	**♕xg7**	**♖g8**
10	**♕xh7**	**♘d7**

This move, associated with the transfer of the knight to f8, results in the loss of a tempo; stronger was 10 ... ♘bc6 (see Game 14: Timman–Vaganian and Game 26: Fischer–Tal).

11	**♘f3**	**♘f8**

In a book devoted to the games of this match Botvinnik recommended 11 ... ♕c7. But White had the strong reply 12 ♗b5!. Now it is dangerous to play 12 ... ♖xg2, because of 13 ♔f1 ♖g8 14 ♖g1, and after the exchange of rooks the situation of Black's king proves to be desperate. On 12 ... a6 there would have followed 13 ♗xd7+ ♗xd7 14 0–0, when White retains a positional advantage.

12	**♕d3**	**♕xa5**
13	**h4**	**♗d7**
14	**♗g5!**	

The bishop is very well-placed. It not only prevents Black from castling but also totally dominates the weakened dark squares. Now both kings remain in the centre of the board, but White's advantage is indisputable. As Smyslov observes, the most significant factor is the possibility of an attack with the h-pawn.

14	**...**	**♖c8**
15	**♘d4**	

The knight has taken up an excellent position, at the same time eliminating the threat of ... ♖c8–c4–e4+. Now, as Smyslov points out, after 15 ... ♖c4 there would follow 16 ♕e3 ♖a4 17 ♖b1 ♖xa3 18 ♘b5, with an attack.

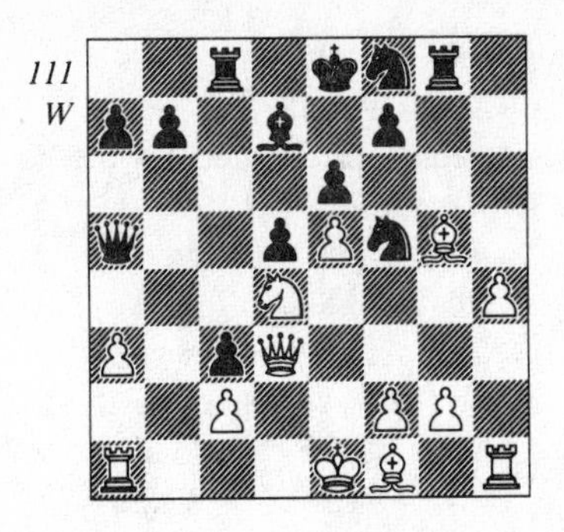

15 ... ♘f5 *(111)*
16 ♖b1!

Black had renewed the threat of ... ♖c4 and would also not have minded exchanging light-squared bishops with 16 ... ♘xd4 17 ♕xd4 ♗b5. It is not good for White to exchange on f5, since Black would then get the convenient square e6 for his knight on f8. The move 16 ♖b1! not only parries Black's threats, it also creates the right conditions for an attack.

16 ... ♖c4

It would have been better to settle for the variation 16 ... b6 17 g4 ♘xd4 18 ♕xd4 ♕xa3, although after 19 ♗d3 there is no doubt about White's advantage.

17 ♘xf5 ef
18 ♖xb7 ♖e4+ *(112)*

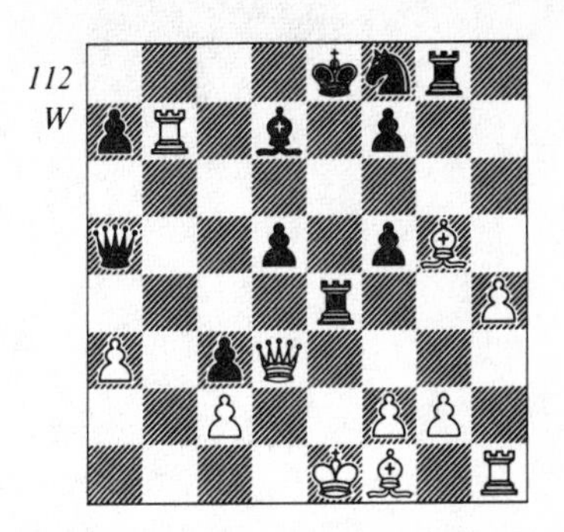

Black has finally accomplished his idea, but this has resulted in disaster. The game could have been prolonged, but not saved, by playing 18 ... ♖xg5. After 19 hg ♖e4+ 20 ♗e2 ♘g6 (or 20 ... ♘e6 21 g6! fg 22 ♖h8+ ♔e7 23 ♖h7+) 21 ♔f1! ♘f4 22 ♕a6

White remains the exchange ahead.

19 ♕xe4!!

This spectacular queen sacrifice decides the game. It turns out that Black's king is in a mating net.

19	**...**	**de**
20	**♖b8+**	**♗c8**
21	**♗b5+**	**♕xb5**

Of course, not 21 ... ♘d7 because of 22 ♖xc8+.

22	**♖xb5**	**♘e6**
23	**♗f6**	**♖xg2**
24	**h5**	**♗a6**
25	**h6**	Black resigned.

10 The Intermediate Move

When using the term 'intermediate move' one has in mind an unexpected move, one which does not follow from the logic of the position but which is capable of upsetting the planned course of events abruptly and of cutting short a forced variation.

In an instructive example, suggested by Neishtadt in 1979, the opening moves **1 e4 e6 2 d4 d5 3 ♘c3 de 4 ♘xe4 ♘f6 5 ♘xf6+ ♕xf6 6 ♘f3 b6 7 ♗d3 ♗b7?** (it is essential to play 7 ... h6) lead to the following position *(113)*:

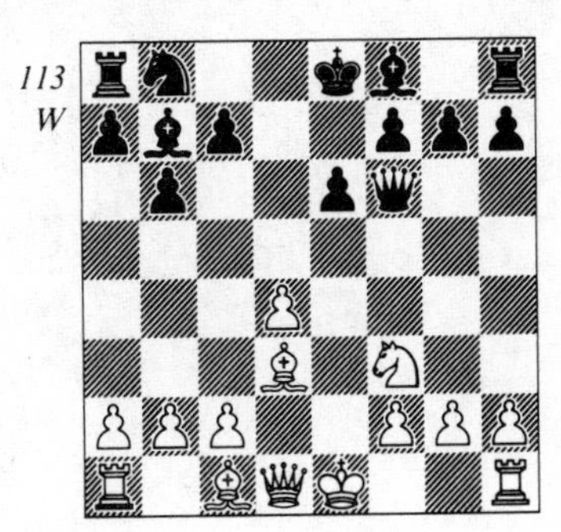

8 ♗g5 ♗xf3

Has White actually miscalculated here? After the natural 9 ♕xf3 the queens will be exchanged with 9 ... ♕xf3, when Black has the better endgame. But now comes a surprise:

9 ♕d2!

And Black loses his queen, since the pawn on d4 cannot be captured because of 10 ♗b5+.

Game No. 38
Fischer–R. Byrne
USA Ch., New York 1965
1 e4 e6!

Fischer lost very rarely, especially with White, but the French Defence was always a stumbling-block for him.

2 d4 d5

3 ♘d2 ♘c6

A move which was introduced into practice by the Argentine Grandmaster, Guimard, the idea being to get immediate piece play in the centre.

4 c3

This move falls in with Black's plans. Greater chances of gaining an advantage are offered by 4 ♘gf3 ♘f6 5 e5 ♘d7 6 ♗b5 (see Game 42: Ermenkov–Kovacevic).

4 ... e5!

The natural reaction to White's piece formation.

5 ed ♕xd5

6 ♘f3 ed

It is a mistake to play either 6 ... ♗g4? 7 ♗c4 ♗xf3 8 ♕b3! with a considerable advantage to White (Keres–Botvinnik, USSR Ch., Moscow 1955), or 6 ... e4? 7 ♗c4 ♕f5 8 ♕e2 ♘f6 9 ♗d3.

7 ♗c4 ♕h5

Also playable is 7 ... ♕f5 8 ♘xd4 ♘xd4 9 cd ♗e6 10 ♕a4 ♗d7 11 ♕b6 0–0–0 as in Jansa–J. Sørensen, Herning 1991.

8 0–0 ♘f6!

Black does not wish to lose time in gaining a pawn. After 8 ... dc 9 ♖e1+ ♗e7 10 bc, followed by 11 ♗a3, White has a sufficient initiative.

9 ♕e1+?

An unnatural move; for the sake of pinning the black bishop (a pin which was in any case quite illusory!) White adopts an unsuccessful formation for his pieces. White had nothing better here than 9 cd ♗e7 10 a3 0–0 11 b4 ♗d6 with approximate equality (Bouwmeester–Hort, Varna Ol. 1962).

9 ... ♗e7

10 ♘xd4 0–0!! *(114)*

A brilliant move. The whole point is that after 11 ♘xc6 Black has the excellent intermediate move 11 ... ♗d6!, and after 12 ♘e7+ ♔h8 13 ♘f3 ♗g4 Black's attack is very strong.

11 ♗e2 ♗g4

12 ♘xc6?

In this position Black's idea can be implemented with even greater force. It was essential to play 12 ♗xg4 ♘xg4 13 ♘2f3

114
W

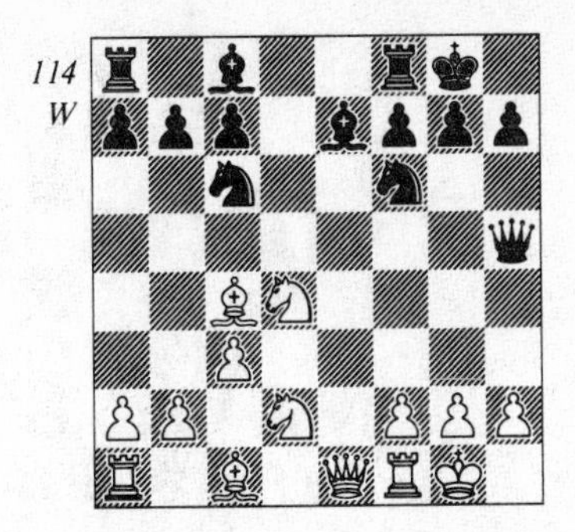

♘xd4 14 cd, when Black stands better, but not so much better as to be in a position to win.

12	**...**	**♗d6!**
13	**h3**	

Altogether bad for White was 13 f4 ♗xe2 14 ♖f2 ♘g4!.

13	**...**	**♗xe2**
14	**♘d4**	**♗xf1**
15	**♕xf1**	

As a result of all this, the game has reached the stage where a material advantage can be converted into a win by tactical means.

15	**...**	**♖fe8**
16	**♘2f3**	**a6**
17	**♗g5**	**♕g6**
18	**♖d1**	**♖e4**
19	**♗e3**	**♘d5**
20	**♗c1**	**♖ae8**

In addition to everything he has already gained, Black now also dominates the only open file.

21	**♘d2**	**♖4e7**
22	**♘c4**	**♗f4**

The start of a mass exchange of pieces.

23	**♘f3**	**c6**
24	**♘b6**	

Spectacular, but not sufficient to obtain any counterplay.

24	**...**	**♗xc1**
25	**♘xd5**	**cd**
26	**♖xc1**	**♖e2**
27	**♖b1**	**♕c2!** *(115)*

This is not an oversight: on 28 ♘d4 Black plays 28 ... ♕xb1!

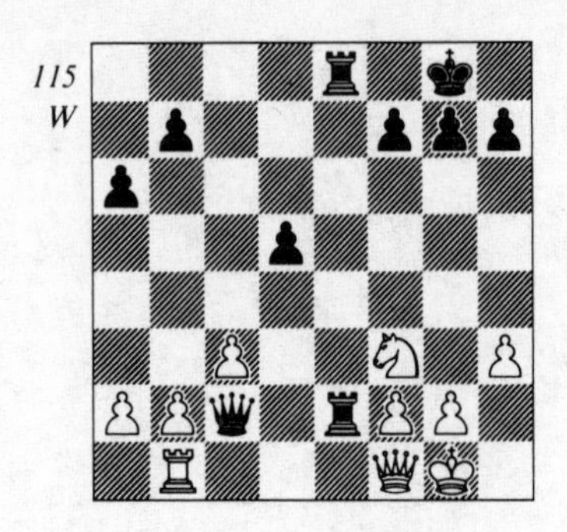

29 ♕xb1 ♖e1+. On the other hand, Black now threatens 28 ... ♖xf2! 29 ♕xf2 ♕xb1+.

28	**♖c1**	**♕xb2**
29	**♖b1**	**♕xc3**
30	**♖xb7**	**♖xa2**

At this point one may bring the curtain down — Black won.

11 Combining Tactical Methods

In practical play tactical operations are very often based not on a single idea but on two or more. For example, the demolition of the kingside is frequently associated with methods for enticing the enemy king into the line of fire of the pieces that are attacking or with the deflection of the pieces defending. In many cases exploitation of the weakness of the back rank also involves the deflection of the pieces defending it.

Quite a number of such combinations are encountered in games opening with the French Defence. For instance, a cascade of tactical tricks was seen in the following game:

Nimzowitsch–Alapin

St. Petersburg 1914

1 e4 e6 2 d4 d5 3 ♘c3 ♘f6 4 ed ♘xd5 5 ♘f3 c5 6 ♘xd5 ♕xd5 7 ♗e3 cd 8 ♘xd4 a6 9 ♗e2 ♕xg2 10 ♗f3 ♕g6 11 ♕d2 e5 12 0–0–0! ed 13 ♗xd4 ♘c6 *(116)*

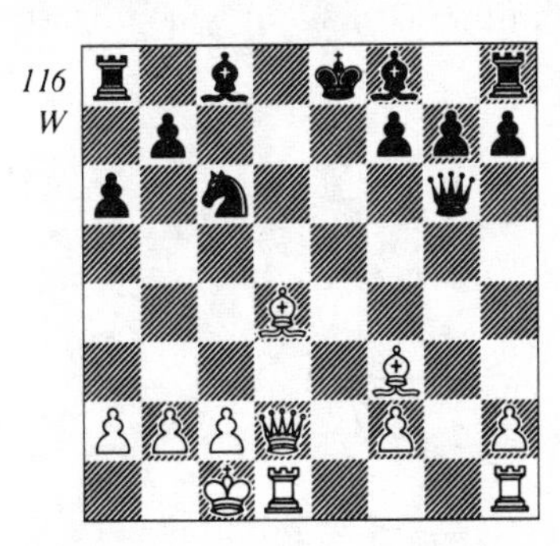

Having sacrificed first a pawn and then a piece, White has obtained an enormous lead in development. Moreover, both of the central files are open. All of this enables White to conclude the game with an elegant combination based on tactics involving the vacating and opening of lines, as well as a pin.

14 ♗f6!

The bishop sacrifices itself for the sake of vacating the d-file.

14 ... ♕xf6 15 ♖he1+ ♗e7

Because of the pin it is no use playing 15 ... ♗e6, because of 16 ♕d7 mate.

16 ♗xc6+ ♕f8

If 16 ... bc then 17 ♕d8 mate (again a pin!), and on 16 ... ♗d7 there follows a beautiful variation: 17 ♕xd7+ ♔f8 18 ♕d8+! ♖xd8 19 ♖xd8+ ♗xd8 20 ♖e8 mate.

17 ♕d8+ ♗xd8 19 ♖e8 mate.

Another game worth some attention was played in the 13th Olympiad, which Alekhine called "a pearl of a tournament".

Pleci–Endzelins

Buenos Aires Ol. 1939

1 e4 e6 2 d4 d5 3 ♘d2 c5 4 ♘gf3 de 5 ♘xe4 ♘d7 6 dc ♘xc5 7 ♕xd8+ ♔xd8 8 ♗g5+ f6? 9 0–0–0+ ♔e8 10 ♗b5+ ♔f7 11 ♖d8!

Black cannot take any of the sacrificed pieces, in view of the check on e5 (11 ... fg 12 ♘e5+ ♔e7 13 ♖e8 mate, or 11 ... ♘xe4 12 ♘e5+ ♔e7 (12 ... fe 13 ♗e8 mate) 13 ♖e8+ ♔d6 14 ♘f7+ ♔c5 15 ♗e3+ ♔xb5 16 ♖xf8 and White wins material.

11 ... ♗e7 *(117)*

An attempt by Black to free himself, but White now plays a beautiful combination, the idea of which consists in vacating the h4–d8 diagonal.

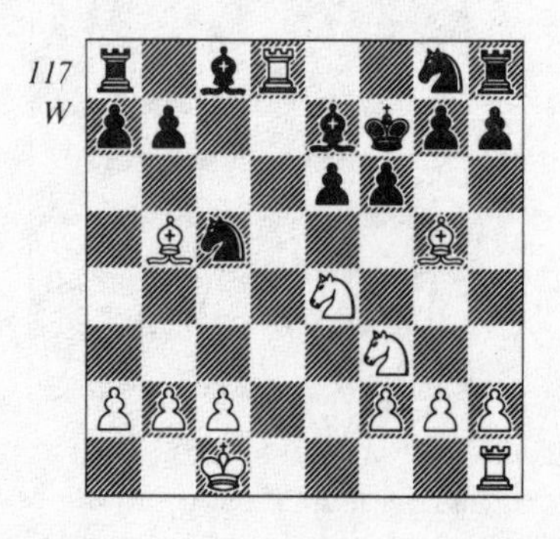

12 ♘e5+! fe 13 ♘d6+!

If the knight is captured, the finish is 14 ♗e8+ ♔f8 15 ♗g6 mate.

13 … ♔g6 14 ♗xe7

And White won.

Demolition and Enticement

Game No. 39
Tischbierek–E. Vladimirov
Berlin 1989

1	**e4**	**e6**
2	**d4**	**d5**
3	**♘c3**	**♗b4**
4	**e5**	**c5**
5	**a3**	**♗xc3+**
6	**bc**	**♘e7**
7	**♕g4**	**0–0**
8	**♗d3**	**f5!?**

The variation 8 … ♘bc6 9 ♕h5 was encountered in Game 13: Kruppa–Komarov.

9	**ef**	**♖xf6**
10	**♕h5**	

10 ♗g5 leads after 10 … e5!? 11 ♕h4 e4 12 ♗xf6 gf 13 ♗e2 ♘f5 14 ♕f4 cd 15 cd ♘xd4 16 ♕d2 ♘bc6 17 ♖d1 ♗e6 18 ♘h3 ♘xe2 19 ♕xe2 ♗xh3 20 gh ♘e5 to a position where Black has sufficient compensation for the loss of the exchange (Emunds–Piskov, Münster 1991).

10	**…**	**h6**

The move 10 … g6 results in a substantial weakening of the dark squares around Black's king.

11	**g4**	

A quieter continuation is 11 ♘f3; after 11 … ♘bc6 12 0–0 ♗d7 13 ♖e1 c4! 14 ♗e2 ♗e8 15 ♕h3 ♕a5 16 ♗d2 ♗g6 Black has been permitted to take the initiative (Lau–E. Vladimirov, Moscow 1989).

11	**…**	**♘bc6**
12	**g5** *(118)*	
12	**…**	**g6!**

Inviting the variation 13 ♕xh6 ♖f7 14 ♗xg6 ♖g7 15 ♗d3 c4

118
B

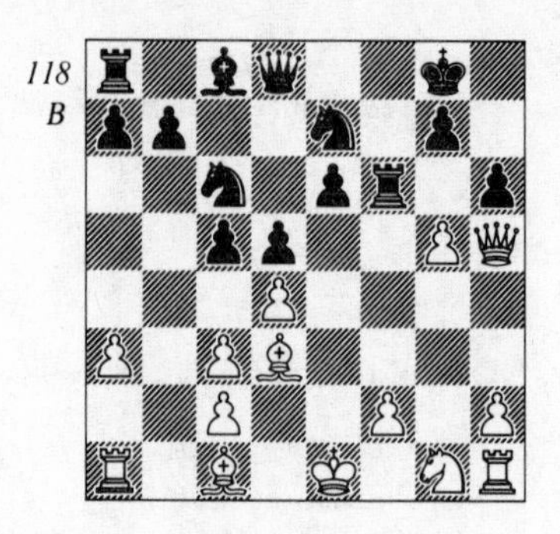

16 ♗e2 ♖h7 17 ♕f6 ♖f7, with a draw by repetition.

13 ♕h4?

White has underestimated the manoeuvre which Black now carries out. Worth considering was 13 ♕d1 ♖f7 14 gh, with complications.

13	**...**	**♘f5**
14	**♗xf5**	**♖xf5**
15	**♕xh6**	**♘e7**
16	**♘e2**	**♖f7!**

The unfortunate position of the queen is the main reason for White's subsequent difficulties.

17 ♕h3

No better was 17 ♕h4 ♘f5 18 ♕g4 e5!.

17	**...**	**e5**
18	**♕g2**	**♗f5**
19	**f3**	

The threat was 19 ... ♗e4, and in the event of 19 0–0 Black could have played 19 ... ♕d7, with the threat of 20 ... ♗h3.

19	**...**	**♘c6**
20	**de**	**♘xe5**
21	**0–0**	**♗xc2**
22	**♘f4**	**♗d3**
23	**♖e1**	**♕d6!**
24	**♗d2**	

24 ♖xe5 ♕xe5 25 ♘xd3 ♕xc3 26 ♘b2 ♖e8 would have led to an easy win for Black.

24	**...**	**c4**
25	**♗e3**	**♖af8**
26	**♕g3**	

White would have achieved nothing with 26 ♗d4, because of 26 ... ♘c6 27 ♘xd3 ♘xd4 28 cd cd 29 ♖e3 ♕b6 30 ♖xd3 ♖xf3!.

26 ... ♖f5!

27 ♔g2 *(119)*

White wards off the threat of 27 ... ♖xg5 28 ♕xg5 ♘xf3+. It was not good to play 27 h4, because of 27 ... ♘c6 28 ♘e2 ♕xg3+ 29 ♘xg3 ♖xf3.

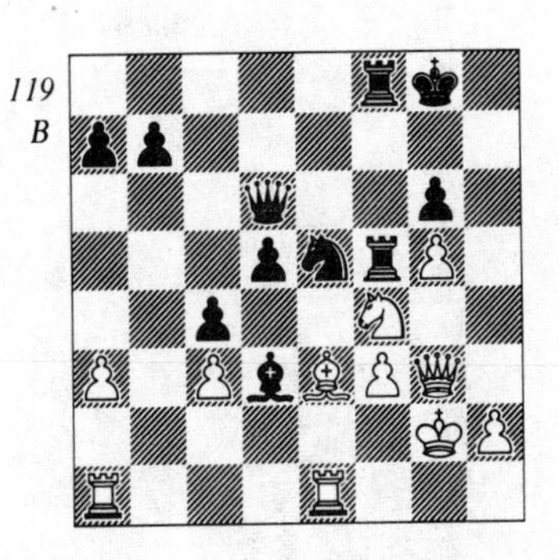

119
B

27 ... ♘xf3!!

Demolishing the white king's protective screen and enticing it onto the f-file.

28 ♔xf3

Not 28 ♕xf3 because of 28 ... ♗e4.

28 ... ♕e5!

29 ♔f2

There could have been a spectacular finish in the event of 29 h4: 29 ... ♗e4+ 30 ♔g4 ♖xf4+ 31 ♗xf4 ♕f5 mate.

29 ... ♗e4

30 ♖e2 ♖xg5

31 ♕h4 ♖g2+

32 ♔f1 g5!

This puts an end to White's resistance.

33 ♕h5 ♖xf4+

Now 34 ♔e1 ♕xc3+ or 34 ♗xf4 ♕xf4+ with mate.

White resigned.

Game No. 40

Kotronias–Short

Novi Sad Ol. 1990

1 e4 e6

2	**d4**	**d5**
3	**♘d2**	**♘f6**
4	**e5**	**♘fd7**
5	**c3**	**c5**
6	**♗d3**	**b6?!**

A dubious plan; usually Black plays 6 ... ♘c6 (see, for example, Game 28: Kramnik–Ulybin).

7	**♘e2**	**♗a6**
8	**♗xa6**	**♘xa6**
9	**0–0**	**b5**

Possibly 9 ... ♘ab8 is better.

10	**♘f4**	**♗e7**
11	**♕g4**	**g6** *(120)*

120
W

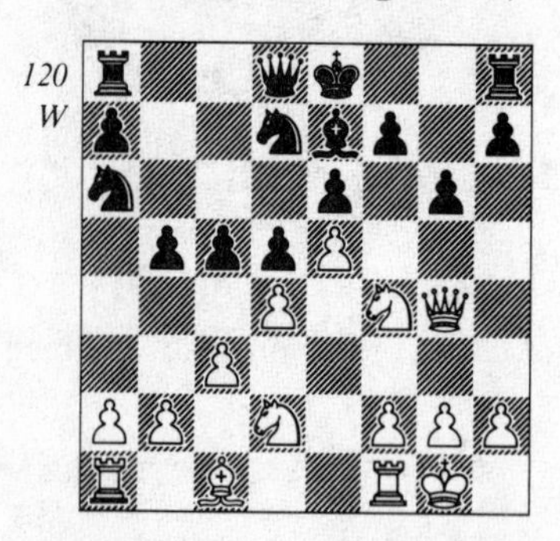

12	**h4!**	**h5**

But not 12 ... ♗xh4? because of 13 ♘xe6! fe 14 ♕xe6+ and 15 ♕xa6.

13	**♕e2**	

Also quite good was 13 ♕h3!? cd 14 cd ♖c8 15 ♘f3 (15 ♘xe6? fe 16 ♕xe6 is not playable, because of 16 ... ♕b6! 17 ♕xd5 ♘b4).

13	**...**	**cd**
14	**cd**	**♗xh4**

Better was 14 ... ♘c7.

15	**a4!**	**♕b6**
16	**ab**	**♘c7**
17	**♘f3**	**♗d8**
18	**♘h3**	

Vacating the g5-square for the dark-squared bishop.

18	**...**	**♘xb5**

Nothing is changed by 18 ... ♕xb5 19 ♕c2 ♕c4 20 ♕b1,

followed by 21 ♗g5.

19	**♖d1**	**♘b8**
20	**♗g5**	**♘c6**
21	**♕d2**	**♗xg5**
22	**♕xg5**	**♕d8**

In the event of 22 ... ♘bxd4 a pin is decisive: 23 ♘xd4 ♘xd4 24 ♕e3!.

23	**♕f4**	**♘e7**

It would be bad to play 23 ... 0–0, because of 24 ♕h6 and 25 ♘hg5, but worth considering was 23 ... ♔f8 followed by ... ♔g7.

24	**♘hg5**	**♘f5**
25	**♘h4**	**♕e7**

Stronger was 25 ... ♘c7!, preparing to castle kingside. It was not good to play 25 ... 0–0 at once, in view of 26 ♘xf5 ef 27 e6!.

26	**♘xf5**	**gf**
27	**♖dc1**	**♔d7**
28	**♖c5**	**a6**
29	**♖ac1**	**h4?** *(121)*

Black prepares to play ... ♖h5, but in so doing he underestimates his opponent's combinational idea. Interesting play could have unfolded after 29 ... ♖ac8: 30 ♖xd5+! ed 31 ♕xf5+ ♕e6 32 ♘xe6 ♖xc1+ 33 ♔h2 fe 34 ♕f7+ ♔c6 35 ♕xe6+ ♔b7 (35 ... ♔c7 36 ♕xa6) 36 ♕xd5+ ♔a7 e6 with advantage to White (analysis by Andrianov).

121
W

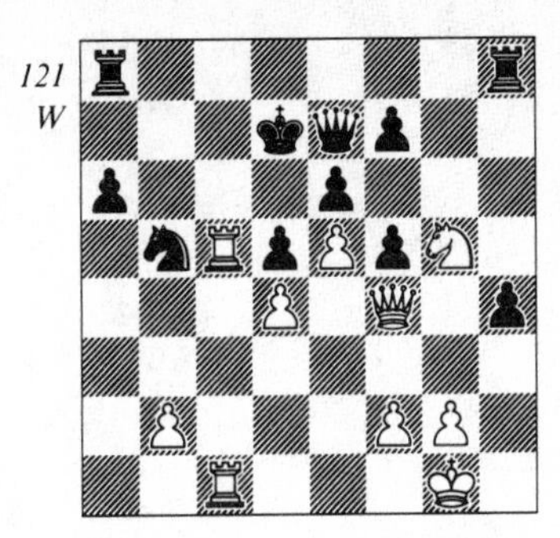

30	**♖xd5+!**	

A temporary rook sacrifice, motivated by the absence of good retreat-squares for the black king.

30	**...**	**ed**
31	**♕xf5+**	**♔e8**

No better was 31 ... ♔d8 32 ♘xf7+.

32	**♖c8+!**	**♖xc8**
33	**♔xc8+**	**♕d8**
34	**♕xd8+**	**♔xd8**
35	**♘xf7+**	**♔d7**
36	**♘xh8**	**♘xd4**

In the course of just seven moves a full board of pieces has become deserted, and as a result White has an extra pawn and improved winning chances.

37	**♘g6**	**♘f5**
38	**♔f1**	**a5**
39	**♔e2**	**a4**
40	**♔d3**	**♔c6**
41	**e6?**	

White would have had a simple win after 41 ♘f4! ♔c5 42 ♘e6+ ♔b4 43 ♘d4 ♘e7 44 f4, or 41 ♔c3! ♔c5 42 e6 ♔d6 43 e7 ♘xe7 44 ♘xe7 ♔xe7 45 ♔b4! ♔d6 46 ♔xa4 ♔c5 47 ♔b3! ♔d4 48 ♔c2.

41	**...**	**♔d6**
42	**e7**	**♘xe7**
43	**♘xh4**	

Now 43 ♘xe7 ♔xe7 44 ♗c3 ♔d6 45 ♔b4 ♔e5 46 ♔xa4 ♔d4! 47 ♔b4 ♔d3 48 ♔a5 d4 49 ♔d5 ♔e2! 50 ♔xd4 ♔xf2 51 b4 ♔xg2 leads to a draw.

43	**...**	**♔c5**
44	**f4**	**♔b4**
45	**f5?**	

White would still have had winning chances after 45 ♔d2 ♔b3 46 ♔c1 d4 47 ♘f3 d3 48 g4.

45	**...**	**♔b3**
46	**f6**	**♘c6!**
47	**♘g6**	

Not 47 f7, because of 47 ... ♘e5+.

47	**...**	**♘d8**
48	**♘e7**	**♔xb2**
49	**♘xd5**	**a3**
50	**♘c3**	

And, not waiting for the obvious 50 ... ♘f7, the players agreed a draw.

Enticement and Double Attack

Game No. 41
Zapata–E. Vladimirov
Salamanca 1991

1	**e4**	**e6**
2	**d4**	**d5**
3	**♘d2**	**a6**
4	**ed**	

It is hard for White to reckon on any opening advantage with this move. Usually 4 ♘gf3 and sometimes 4 e5 is played, with the following possible continuation: 4 e5 c5 5 c3 ♘c6 6 ♘df3 cd 7 cd ♘ge7 8 ♗d3 ♘f5 9 ♘e2 ♗e7 10 a3 ♕b6 11 h4 ♗d7 12 ♖b1 ♘a5 13 ♗g5 (Kupreichik–Dolmatov, Erevan 1982).

4	**...**	**ed**
5	**♗d3**	**♗d6**
6	**♘e2**	**♘c6**
7	**c3**	**♕f6!?**

Black does not content himself with the immediate 7 ... ♘ge7, with guaranteed equality.

8	**0–0**	**♘ge7**
9	**♖e1**	

On 9 ♘f3 an unpleasant reply is 9 ... h6, followed by ... ♗g4.

9	**...**	**♗f5**

Also quite good is 9 ... ♗g4 10 ♘f1 0–0.

10	**♗xf5**	**♕xf5**
11	**♘g3**	**♗xg3**

It looks more attractive to play 11 ... ♕g6.

12	**hg**	**0–0**
13	**♘f1**	**♕d7**
14	**♗f4**	**♘g6**
15	**♕h5**	**♖fe8**
16	**♘e3**	**♖ad8**

The position is absolutely equal, and after 17 ♖ad1 it would have looked rather drawish. It would be a mistake to play 17 ♘xd5?, in view of 17 ... ♖xe1+ 18 ♖xe1 ♕xd5 19 ♖e8+ ♘f8. The continuation 17 ♕f5 (or 17 ♕g4) can be spectacularly refuted by 17 ... ♖xe3!, when on 18 ♕xd7 Black plays 18 ... ♖ce1+.

17	**♖e2?!**	**♖e4**

The threat is 19 ... ♖xf4.

18 ♕f3? *(122)*

White should have played 18 ♗g5, though here too after 18 ... ♖de8 Black would have obtained some advantage.

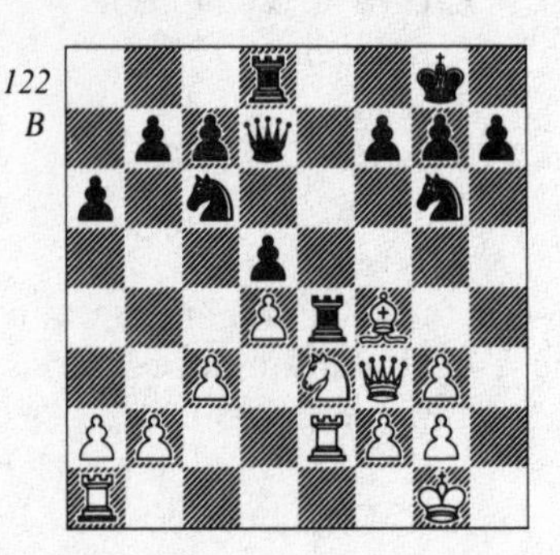

122
B

18 ... ♖xd4!
19 cd

Black would have had an advantage after 19 ♗g5 f6 20 ♗xf6 gf 21 cd ♘xd4 22 ♕h5 ♘xe2+ 23 ♕xe2, or 19 ♘c2 ♘xf4 20 gf ♖e4 21 ♖xe4 de 22 ♕xe4 ♖e8.

19 ... ♘xd4
20 ♕h5 ♘xf4
21 gf g6
22 ♕h4?

The best move in this position is 22 ♕g5, attempting to provoke Black into the continuation 22 ... f6 23 ♕h4! ♘xe2+ 24 ♔f1 ♕b5 25 a4 ♘g3++ 26 ♔g1 ♘e2+ 27 ♔f1, with a draw, but 25 ... ♕xb2 gives Black excellent chances (translator's note) and 22 ... ♘xe2+ 23 ♔f1 ♘d4 24 ♘g4 ♕d6 leads to a considerable advantage for Black (analysis by E. Vladimirov).

22 ... ♘xe2+
23 ♔f1 ♘d4
24 ♖d1

White gets nowhere with 24 ♘g4 ♘f5! 25 ♘f6+ ♔g7.

24 ... c5
25 f5 ♕d6
26 f6 ♖e8

Of course, the two extra pawns guarantee a win for Black, but all the same White tries to find some counter-chances.

27 ♖xd4 cd
28 ♘f5 ♕e5

But not 28 ... gf?? because of 29 ♕g5+ with mate.

29	**♘e7+**	**♔h8**
30	**f4**	**♕h5**
31	**♕xh5**	**gh**
32	**♔e2**	**♖d8**
33	**♔d3**	

No better was 33 ♘f5 h6 34 ♘xh6 ♖d7 (followed by 35 ... ♔h7).

33	**...**	**♖d6**
34	**♔xd4**	**♖xf6**
35	**f5**	**♔g7**
36	**♔e5**	**d4**
37	**♘d5**	**d3!**
38	**♘xf6**	**d2**

White resigned.

The Passed Pawn and Enticement

Game No. 42
Ermenkov–Kovacevic
Kavala 1990

1	**e4**	**e6**
2	**d4**	**d5**
3	**♘d2**	**♘c6**
4	**♘gf3**	**♘f6**

Much stronger than the 4 ... de of Game 31: Rachels–Penkalski.

5	**e5**	**♘d7**
6	**♗b5**	**a5**
7	**c3**	

Also possible is 7 a4 ♘cb8!? 8 0–0 ♗e7 9 ♖e1 b6 10 c3 ♗a6, when White has a minimal advantage.

7	**...**	**♘a7**
8	**♗d3**	**c5**
9	**0–0**	**♘c6**
10	**♖e1**	

On 10 a4 Black continues 10 ... cd 11 ♘b4, followed by 12 ... b6 and 13 ... ♗a6.

10	**...**	**cd**
11	**cd**	**a4!?**

In the event of 11 ... ♕b6?! 12 a3! ♘xd4 13 ♘xd4 ♕xd4 14

♘f3 ♕b6 15 ♕a4 White has considerable compensation for the sacrificed pawn.

12 ♘f1

The knight sets off in the wrong direction. The variation 12 ♘b1?! ♗e7 13 ♘c3 ♘b6 14 ♗c2! ♗d7 15 a3 0–0 16 ♖b1 guarantees White an advantage.

12 ... ♗e7
13 ♘g3 h5
14 ♘e2 ♘b6
15 g3

White achieves nothing by 15 ♘c3 ♗d7 16 ♗c2 ♘b4 17 ♗b1 ♗c6 18 a3 ♘a6 19 ♗c2 ♘c7.

15 ... ♘b4!

With a different move order White succeeds in beginning active operations: 15 ... ♗d7?! 16 h4 ♘b4 17 ♗g5!.

16 ♗b1 ♗d7

If 16 ... h4?! then 17 g4!, followed by ♘e2–f4–h3 and ♗g5.

17 h4 ♘c4
18 ♘f4 ♕b6
19 ♔g2 ♔d8!

The king runs away to the queenside.

20 ♘g5 ♗xg5
21 hg g6
22 ♘e2 ♘c6
23 ♖h1 ♔c7!

It would have been rather hasty to play 23 ... ♘xb2?! at once, in view of 24 ♕d2 a3 25 ♕f4 ♔c7 26 ♕xf7 ♘c4 27 ♕xg6.

24 ♖h4 ♘xb2
25 ♕d2 a3
26 ♕f4 ♖hc8!

Black does not waste time on 26 ... ♖hf8; this would have been met by 27 ♕f3 and then 28 ♖f4.

27 ♕xf7 ♖f8
28 ♕xg6 ♘d1!

The tempting 28 ... ♘xe5? would have led to loss of material by Black after 29 ♗f4! ♖xf4 30 ♕c2+.

29 ♖f4?! *(123)*

This natural move comes up against an elegant refutation. But other continuations also favoured Black: 29 ♕c2 ♖xf2+ 30 ♔g1 ♖af8 31 ♖f4 (31 ♕d1 ♖f1+ 32 ♕xf1 ♖xf1+ 33 ♔xf1 ♕b2!) 31

... ♜8xf4 32 gf ♜xe2; or 29 ♗c2 ♜xf2+ 30 ♔h3 ♛b4! 31 ♛d3 ♘b2 32 ♗xb2 ab 33 ♖b1 ♜xa2 34 ♘c3 ♜a1 (analysis by Kovacevic).

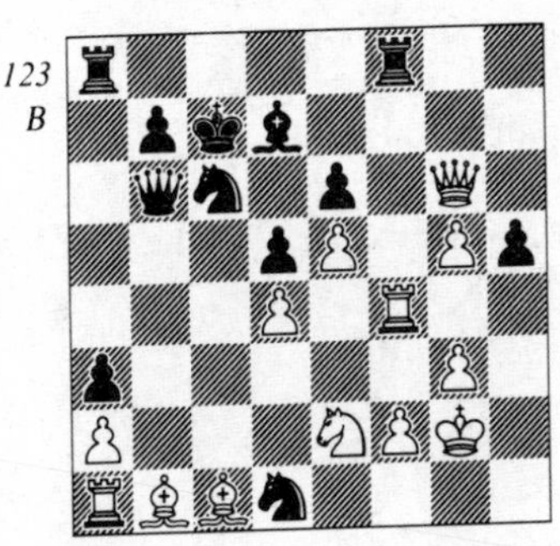

123
B

29 ... ♛b2!!

A move which could almost be the solution to a study! In the event of the queen being captured the white bishop is enticed onto a square where it can be taken by the rook's pawn.

30	**♗c2**	**♛xa1**
31	**♗xd1**	**♜xf4**
32	**gf**	**♛xa2**

The black a-pawn is destined to decide the game.

33	**f5**	**♛b1**
34	**♘c3**	**♛xc1**
35	**fe**	**♛xc3**
36	**ed**	**♛xd4**
37	**♕d6+**	**♚b6**
38	**e6**	**a2**
39	**♗f3**	**♛c5**

White resigned.

Vacating a File and Exploiting the Weakness of the Back Rank

Game No. 43
Short–Bareev
Tilburg 1991

1	**e4**	**e6**
2	**d4**	**d5**
3	**e5**	**c5**
4	**♘f3**	

A system associated with the sacrifice of a pawn, for which White by no means always obtains sufficient compensation.

4 … cd
5 ♗d3

The continuation 5 ♘xd4 ♘c6 6 ♘xc6 bc 7 ♗d3 ♗a6! guarantees Black an equal game.

5 … ♘e7

Black also has good prospects in the event of 5 … ♘c6 6 0–0 ♗c5 7 ♘bd2 ♘ge7 8 ♘b3 ♗b6 9 ♗f4 ♘g6 10 ♗g3 f5 11 h4 0–0 12 h5 ♘h8 13 ♗h4 ♕e8.

6 0–0 ♘g6
7 ♖e1 ♘c6
8 a3 ♗d7

Also worth considering is 8 … a5.

9 b4 ♕c7
10 ♕e2 ♗e7
11 b5 ♘a5
12 ♗g5 ♘c4

It looked clearly preferable to exchange bishops first.

13 ♗xe7 ♔xe7
14 g3 ♗xb5
15 h4

White, having totally lost the strategic battle, pins all his hopes on an attack on the black king stranded in the centre.

15 … ♖hc8
16 ♘bd2

Threatening the manoeuvre ♘d2–b3xd4. Black must play with extreme caution.

16 … ♘xd2
17 ♕xd2 ♗xd3
18 cd ♕c3
19 ♕g5+ ♔f8
20 h5 h6!

It would have been bad for Black to continue 20 … ♘e7 21 h6 g6 22 ♕f6 ♕xd3 23 ♘g5 ♕f5 24 ♕g7+ ♔e8 25 ♘xh7.

21 ♕g4 ♘e7
22 ♘xd4 ♘c6?

Black has conducted his defence well, but here he totally overlooked the simple 22 … ♕xd3, after which White would have had no compensation for the loss of two pawns; for example: 23

♖e3 ♕h7 24 ♖f3 ♘c6 25 ♘xe6+ ♔g8.

23 ♘b5 ♕xd3

Stronger was 23 ... ♘xe5 24 ♕e2 ♕c5 25 d4 ♘f3+.

24 ♘d6 ♖c7
25 ♖ad1 ♕a6 *(124)*

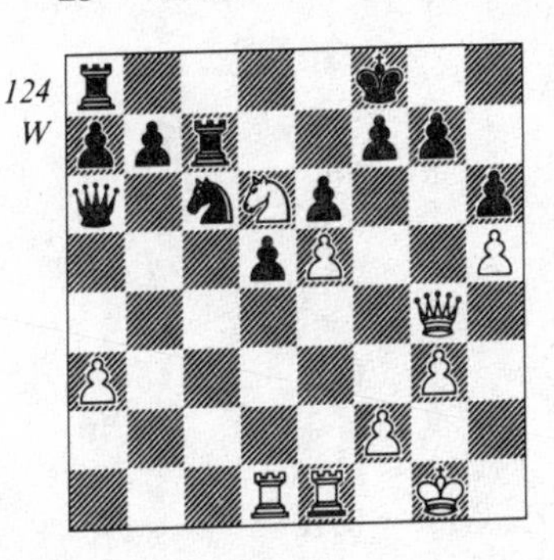

124
W

26 ♖xd5!?

Now on 26 ... ed an unpleasant reply would be 27 ♘f5, with a strong attack, but the preliminary 26 ... ♘xe5 27 ♖exe5 (28 ♖dxe5 ♕xd6) 28 ... ed would have resulted in a win for Black.

26 ... ♖d8
27 ♖dd1 ♘xe5? *(125)*

The simple 27 ... ♔g8 would have maintained Black's advantage. But now comes a stunning blow.

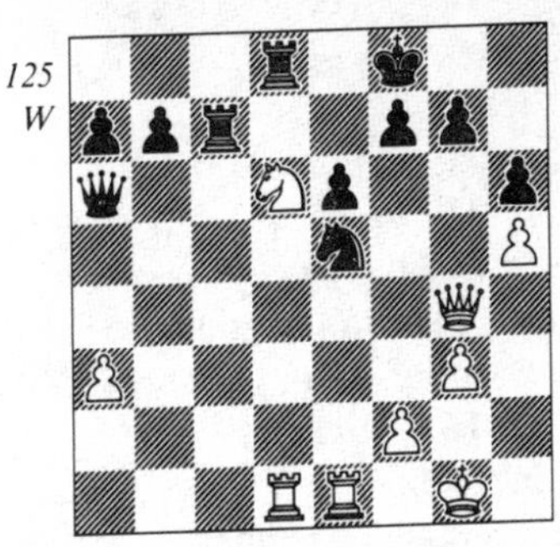

125
W

28 ♘f5!! Black resigned.

The d-file is opened up and the weakness of the back rank is decisive: 28 ... ♘xg4 29 ♖xd8 mate; 28 ... ♖xd1 29 ♕xg7+ ♔e8 30 ♕g8+ ♔d7 31 ♖xd1+ ♘d3 32 ♕xf7+; 28 ... ef 29 ♖xd8+ ♔e7 30 ♕d4 f6 31 f4.

Exploiting the Weakness of the Back Rank and Interference

Game No. 44
Barash–Monin
17th USSR corr. Ch. 1986/88

1	**e4**	**e6**
2	**d4**	**d5**
3	**♘d2**	**♘f6**
4	**e5**	**♘fd7**
5	**♗d3**	**c5**
6	**c3**	**♘c6**
7	**♘e2**	**cd**
8	**cd**	**f6**
9	**ef**	**♘xf6**
10	**♘f3**	**♗d6**
11	**0–0**	**♕c7**

Another common continuation is 11 … 0–0 (see Game 22: Frolov–Ulybin and Game 28: Kramnik–Ulybin).

12	**h3**	**0–0**
13	**♗e3**	

White implements the strategic plan which is most successful in such positions, maintaining his control over the central squares whilst also preparing to attack first on one flank and then on the other.

13	**…**	**♗d7**
14	**♖c1**	**♖ae8**

A line worth considering is 14 … ♗e8 15 ♘g5 ♕d7 16 f4 h6 17 ♘f3 ♘e4 18 ♘e5 ♗xe5 19 de ♗g6 20 ♘d4 ♘xd4 21 ♗xd4 ♗h7 (Spasov–Gdanski, Tunja 1989).

15	**a3**	**♖e7?** *(126)*

A serious mistake, and the prime reason for Black's defeat. With this move he allows the white knight to establish itself on the square e5. It was essential to play 15 … ♕b8!.

16	**♘e5!**	

Now Black cannot play 16 … ♗xe5 17 de ♕xe5, because of 18 ♗c5, when he loses the exchange.

16	**…**	**♗e8**
17	**f4**	

White has obtained a perceptible positional advantage. His immediate task is to organise an offensive on the queenside by making use of the c-file.

126
W

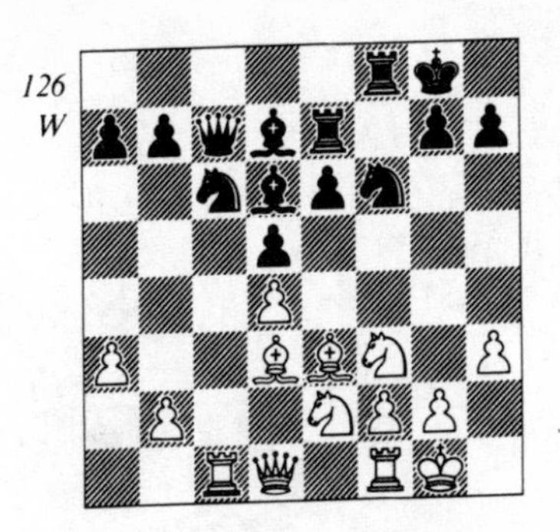

17	**...**	**♕b6**
18	**♕d2**	**♘a5**
19	**♕e1**	**♗b5**

Black seeks salvation in simplification, attempting by such means at least to free himself from the positional bind.

20	**♗xb5**	**♕xb5**
21	**♘c3**	

An illusory pawn sacrifice: in the event of 21 ... ♕xb2? 22 ♖b1 ♕c2 (22 ... ♕xa3 is bad, because of 23 ♘b5) 23 ♖f2 ♕f5 24 g4 Black is forced to give up his knight to avoid losing his queen.

21	**...**	**♕b3**
22	**♘b1**	**♖c7**
23	**♖xc7**	**♗xc7**
24	**♗d2**	

White does not permit his opponent to eliminate the centralised knight.

24	**...**	**♕b6**
25	**♗b4**	**♖e8**
26	**♗xa5!**	

A timely exchange, forestalling Black's plans of attacking the central squares by means of 26 ... ♘c6.

26	**...**	**♕xa5**
27	**♘c3**	**♕b6**
28	**♕d2**	**♕b3**
29	**♕e2**	**♗b6**
30	**♘f3**	

White has regrouped his forces and built up pressure against the weak pawn at e6. The queen is now centralised in place of the knight.

30	**...**	**♘h5**
31	**♕e5**	**♘g3**
32	**♖e1**	**♘f5**

Black has improved the position of his pieces, but even so the initiative is still in White's hands.

33	**♘xd5!**	**♕xb2** *(127)*

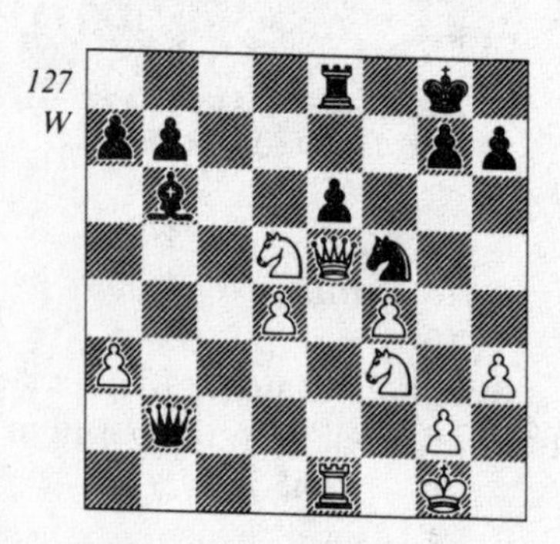

The impression is that Black's game is quite in order, but White had prepared a stunning blow, exploiting the weakness of the back rank.

34	**♘e7+!!**	**♘xe7**

34 ... ♖xe7 35 ♕b8+ ♔f7 36 ♘e5+ leads to mate.

35	**♕xe6+**	**♔h8**
36	**♕f7**	Black resigned.

On 36 ... ♖g8 there follows 37 ♖xe7 ♕b5 38 ♔h2, when Black has a hopeless task.

Vacating a File and Defending the Back Rank

Game No. 45
Psakhis–Vaganian
Moscow 1981

1	**e4**	**e6**
2	**d4**	**d5**
3	**♘d2**	**c5**
4	**ed**	**ed**
5	**♘f3**	**♘c6**
6	**♗b5**	**♗d6**
7	**dc**	

This is stronger than 7 0–0 (see Game 27: Karpov–Korchnoi).

7 ... ♗xc5

Unsuccessful is 7 ... ♕e7+?!, because of 8 ♕e2! (Black easily equalises after 8 ♗e2 ♗xc5 9 0–0 ♘f6 10 ♘b3 ♗b6 11 ♗g5 0–0 12 ♕d2 ♕e6: Ostojic–Vaganian, Vrnjacka Banja 1971) 8 ... ♕xe2+ 9 ♔xe2 ♗xc5 10 ♘b3 ♗d6 11 ♗g5 f6 12 ♗h4 (Vaganian–Bronstein, USSR Ch., Erevan 1975).

8 0–0

Black has no real problems after 8 ♘b3 ♗d6 9 ♕d4 ♘f6 10 0–0 0–0 11 ♗xc6 bc 12 ♗f4 ♗xf4 13 ♕xf4 ♕b6 14 ♖fe1 c5 (Beliavsky–Vaganian, USSR Ch., Minsk 1979).

8 ... ♘e7
9 ♘b3 ♗d6

Weaker is 9 ... ♗b6, since 10 ♖e1 0–0 11 ♗g5 h6 12 ♗h4 g5 13 ♗g3 ♘f5 14 ♕d2 ♘xg3 15 hg leads to an advantage for White (Karpov–Vaganian, Budapest 1973).

10 ♖e1

In this position quite a few moves have been tried, but none of them achieve anything substantial for White; for example: 10 ♘bd4 0–0 11 ♗g5 f6 12 ♗e3 ♘e5 13 ♖e1 a6 14 ♗f1 ♔h8 15 h3 ♗d7 (Geller–Uhlmann, Amsterdam 1970); or 10 ♗d2 0–0 11 ♗c3 ♗g4 12 ♘bd4 ♗h5 13 ♖e1 ♗g6 14 ♘h4 ♕b6 15 a4 a6 16 ♘xg6 hg 17 ♘xc6 bc (Gufeld–Lputian, Moscow 1981).

10 ... 0–0
11 ♗g5

Equality also results after 11 ♗d3 h6 12 h3 ♘f5!? 13 c3 ♕f6 14 ♗e2 ♗e6 (stronger is 14 ... ♖d8!) 15 ♕d3 ♖fe8 (Renet–Uhlmann, Novi Sad Ol. 1990).

11 ... ♗g4
12 ♗e2 ♖e8
13 c3

Possible is 13 ♘fd4, cutting across Black's attempts to develop an initiative: 13 ... ♗xe2 14 ♕xe2 ♕d7 15 ♗xe7 ♖xe7 16 ♕f3 ♖ae8 (Tseshkovsky–Vaganian, USSR Ch., Vilnius 1980/81).

13 ... h6
14 ♗h4 ♕b6!? *(128)*

The start of most interesting complications. Black gives up his central pawn.

15 ♗xe7

A fundamental decision, since here too (as on his 13th move)

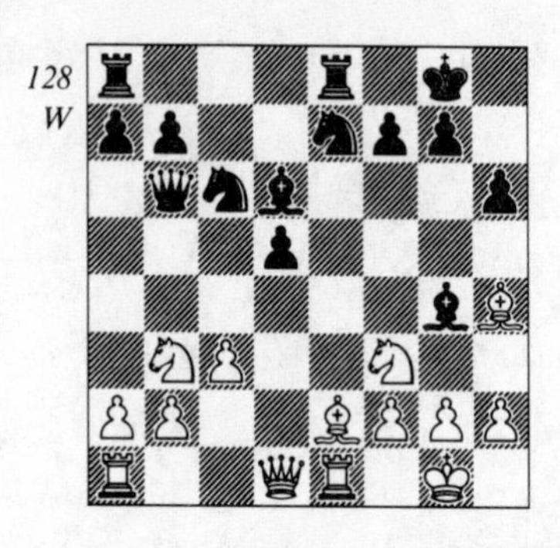
128
W

White could have defused the situation by playing 15 ♘fd4 ♗d7 16 ♗g3 ♗xg3 17 hg ♘g6 18 ♗f3, when after 18 ... ♖xe1+ 19 ♕xe1 ♘xd4 20 cd ♗c6 the position is roughly equal (L-Å. Schneider–E. Vladimirov, Gausdal 1990).

15 ... ♖xe7!

16 ♕xd5

If White declines to capture the pawn on d5 he does not obtain any significant advantage: 16 h3 ♗e6 17 ♘fd4 a5 18 ♘b5 ♗c5 19 ♕d2 a4 20 ♘3d4 ♗xd4 21 ♘xd4 ♘xd4 22 cd (Antunes–E. Vladimirov, Matalascañas 1990).

16 ... ♖ae8

17 ♕d2

It would not be good to play 17 ♕xd6, because of 17 ... ♗xf3 18 gf ♖xe2.

17 ... a5

18 h3 ♗g3

The tension mounts.

19 ♘bd4

An essential measure. It would have been bad to play 19 ♗d1? ♖xe1+ 20 ♘xe1 ♗xf2+!, when Black wins.

19 ... ♗xf3 *(129)*

It appears that Black has emerged triumphant. On the natural 20 ♗xf3 there follows 20 ... ♘xd4 21 cd ♕xb2! and the weakness of the back rank is decisive — White cannot play 22 ♖xe7 because of 22 ... ♕xa1+. But the improbable now happened ...

20 ♗f1!!

A truly fantastic move — it's difficult to believe one's eyes. The idea is profound: with a modest retreat of the bishop White vacates the e-file and defends the back rank.

129
W

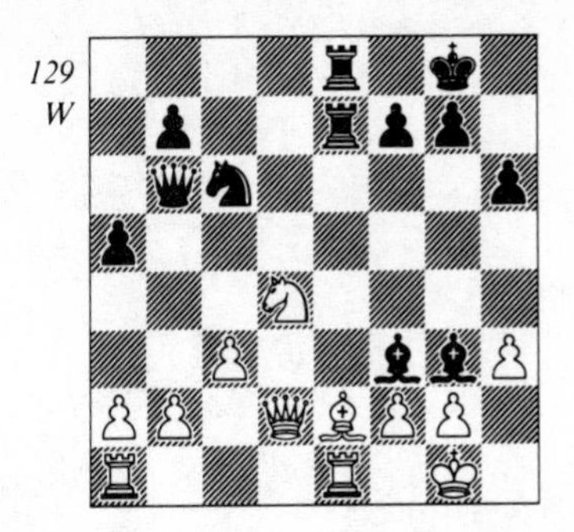

Now in the event of 20 ... ♖xe1 21 ♖xe1 ♖xe1 22 ♕xe1 ♘xd4 White has the variation 23 ♕e8+ ♔h7 24 ♗d3+ f5 25 cd, when the lost material is regained.

20 ... ♗xf2+
21 ♔xf2 ♘xd4
22 cd ♗d5
23 ♖xe7 ♖xe7
24 b3

After all this simplification Black's minimal advantage is purely symbolic.

24 ... ♖e4
25 ♖d1 ♕f6+
26 ♔g1 b6
27 ♗c4 ♕d6
28 ♕d3

Now a draw is inevitable.

28 ... g6
29 a4 ♔g7
30 ♗xd5 ♕xd5
31 ♕c4 ♕d6
32 ♕c3 ♕d5
33 ♕c4 ♕d6

Drawn.

A truly brilliant game!

Index of Variations

(Numbers refer to *page* numbers)

I Chigorin Variation/King's Indian Attack

1 e4 e6 2 ♕e2 *11*

2 d3 d5 3 ♘d2 ♘f6 4 ♘gf3 ♘c6 *92*
4 … b6 *40*

II Exchange Variation

1 e4 e6 2 d4 d5 3 ed *11*

III Advance Variation

1 e4 e6 2 d4 d5 3 e5 *13*

3 … c5 4 ♘f3 *165*
4 c3 ♕b6 *44*
4 … ♘c6 5 ♘f3 ♗d7 6 ♗e2 ♘ge7 *30*
5 … ♕b6 6 ♗d3 *77*
6 a3 *81*

IV Rubinstein Variation

1 e4 e6 2 d4 d5 3 ♘c3 de *15*

4 ♘xe4 ♘f6 *84*
4 … ♘d7 5 ♘f3 ♘gf6 6 ♘xf6+ ♘xf6 7 ♗d3 h6 *86*
7 … c5 *56*

V Classical Variation

1 e4 e6 2 d4 d5 3 ♘c3 ♘f6 *16, 55, 128, 153*

4 ♗g5 de 5 ♘xe4 ♗e7 6 ♗xf6 ♗xf6 7 ♘f3 ♘d7 *47*
7 … 0–0 *49*

4 … ♗b4 5 e5 h6 6 ♗d2 ♘fd7 59
6 … ♗xc3 7 bc ♘e4 8 ♕g4 g6 116
4 e5 ♘fd7 5 ♘ce2 119
5 f4 c5 6 c3 ♘c6 7 ♗e3 cd 100
7 … ♕b6 129

VI Winawer Variation

1 e4 e6 2 d4 d5 3 ♘c3 ♗b4 21, 30, 43, 115

4 ed 140
4 a3 88
4 e5 b6 133
4 … ♘e7 5 ♗d2 62
5 a3 ♗xc3+ 6 bxc3 b6 32
4 … c5 5 a3 ♗a5 6 b4 cxd4 7 ♕g4 ♘e7 8 ba dc 9 ♕xg7 ♖g8
10 ♕xh7 ♘d7 146
10 … ♘bc6 11 ♘f3 106
11 f4 69
5 … ♗xc3+ 6 bxc3 ♘e7 7 ♘f3 ♗d7 51
7 … b6 143
7 ♕g4 0–0 8 ♗d3 ♘bc6 23, 67
8 … f5 155
7 … ♕c7 8 ♕xg7 ♖g8
9 ♕xh7 cd 10 ♔d1 103

VII Tarrasch Variation

1 e4 e6 2 d4 d5 3 ♘d2

3 … a6 161
3 … ♘c6 4 c3 149
4 ♘gf3 de 123
4 … ♘f6 163
3 … ♘f6 4 e5 ♘fd7 5 f4 c5 6 c3 ♘c6 7 ♘df3 ♕a5 35
5 ♗d3 c5 6 c3 b6 158
6 … ♘c6 7 ♘e2 ♕b6 37
7 … cd 8 cd f6 9 exf6 ♘xf6
10 ♘f3 ♗d6 11 0–0 0–0 12 ♗f4 ♗xf4 13 ♘xf4 ♘e4 14 ♘h5 94
14 ♘e2 112
11 … ♕c7 12 h3 168
12 g3 96

12 ♘c3 *135*
3 … c5 4 ed ed 5 ♘gf3 ♘f6 *72*
5 … ♘c6 6 ♗b5 ♗d6 7 0–0 *109*
7 dc *170*